The Flight o

The Flight of the Crane

Harry Vine Norman
(1868–1900)

Elisabeth Green

EPWORTH PRESS

ISBN 0 7162 0498 3

First Published 1994
by Epworth Press
1 Central Buildings Westminster
London SW1H 9NR

Typeset by Regent Typesetting, London
Printed and bound in Finland by
Werner Söderström Oy

Contents

List of Illustrations

Harry in his College robe. Studio portrait taken in Salisbury, while he was training at the Infirmary.

Bishop Charles Scott with his staff and Chinese men and schoolboys. Harry is on the Bishop's left.

The rudimentary building at Lung Hua Tien which served both as school and church. The bell hangs from a propped-up stick.

The church at Tai Whang Chuang, built in a few weeks by local people.

Harry (left) and Charles Robinson in Chinese clothes.

Harry itinerating, with his donkey Faithful.

Harry's house at Yung Ching.

Harry's grave at Hsin-Min Chuang.

Acknowledgments

The author gratefully acknowledges the help of the following:

The churchwardens of Abbotsbury and Portesham parish, Ms Lovedy Cornish, Mrs Syntyche Davis, Ms Valerie Scriven, the Headmaster and Chaplain of Warminster School;

Portland Museum and the Royal Navy Museum, Portsmouth;

Canterbury Cathedral Archive Centre, Church of England Record Centre, Dorset County Record Office, National Maritime Museum Record Centre, Public Record Office, Wiltshire County Record Office;

The Bodleian Library, Dorchester County Reference Library, Warminster Town Reference Library, USPG Reference Library.

To my Mother

Introduction:

The Little Yellow Book

For as long as I can remember, a little book has been in the family, passed from person to person, and finally, about thirty years ago, it came to my mother, with a warning to keep it safe, as it was very precious. I have it in front of me now. Mottled and yellow, it is written by a local vicar from Powerstock in Dorset, a few miles from Portesham and Abbotsbury, where its hero, Harry, grew up. In flowery language it is titled: *A Dorset Captain in the Army of Christ*, and has some illustrations.

On a cold day in 1990 I sat down to thumb through its pages, and I soon became fascinated by the lad and later the man, Harry Vine Norman. Undeniably part of the interest lay in the fact that we were related, but he was also an interesting character in his own right.

My search to find out more about Harry has since taken me all over southern England. Initially I assumed very little would be left with which to tell the story of a very average and unspectacular missionary. At any time I could easily have given up, but the more I found, the more questions occurred to me.

My searches began at the Church of England Record Centre, where I almost abandoned my quest, as no records existed from one hundred years ago. The archives assistant suggested the Wiltshire County Record Office, which holds records from St Boniface College where Harry trained, and the United Society for the Propagation of the Gospel, under whose auspices Harry's mission operated. I spent days rifling through box files of papers, which – I might add – are anything but dull when you are on the trail of someone who is slowly but surely coming to life.

Over three years the evidence for Harry Norman came from the USPG files in London and Oxford, where I discovered his letters from China, untouched for a century, his Bishop's reports, and charming cameos of his life in China. I found his original application to join the mission and the references given him by his tutors and vicar. I even discovered a cousin whom I never knew I had, Harry's niece. From her came Harry's flimsy letters home to his parents and pictures sent back from the mission field. I am indebted to her for these.

Once on the hunt, it became almost an obsession, and filled both my thoughts and my weekends. As an example of incredible luck – or perhaps divine intervention – I chanced one day to be searching in Harry's parish church of Abbotsbury for a register of vicars there. In a corner, covered in the dust of years, stood an ancient photograph in sepia tints. It had been almost forgotten. By now no one knew who the young man in the gown was. I knew immediately – and Harry's photograph is now hanging in the nave. Much more exciting, though, were the newspaper cuttings glued roughly to the reverse of the frame. By these I gleaned evidence so vital to the end of his story – an eye-witness account which was recorded nowhere else, and I have looked in most places!

While this story includes imagined conversations, it is no work of fiction. Almost every sentence is based on fact – the weather, the reports, the events are all founded on records. Over the years I have come to know Harry and his colleagues. I hope I have gauged their characters correctly, and interpreted them in a manner of which they would approve.

· Harry, from my point of view, had the great good fortune to have joined the Church of England, which more than most institutions, kept extensive records. Had he entered most other professions, his story would certainly have been lost. My greatest asset has been the painstaking collation and listing of papers by Records Offices and the USPG. Add to that the love of his niece and his college, and I had treasures to find which added greatly to his story, way beyond what I had the right to expect. There is no space to recount the story of the search, but I commend the pastime as truly fascinating.

One of my last visits in my long search was to Canterbury, where Harry's brother missionary, Charles, was trained. Having completed my work, I turned, as almost every tourist does, to the cathedral. It was a beautiful day, and the sun shone through the windows. Becket's tomb underlined how Christianity had been tried and tested, and survived tribulations and efforts to stifle it. I carried on to the Lady Chapel, which had recently been redesigned as a martyr's chapel. There I lit candles for Harry and his friends in China, in the mother church of their faith. Their bodies and souls are elsewhere, but I can think of no more fitting resting place for their memories.

Almighty God, By your grace your martyrs shine as light in the darkness of our times; grant that we may be so encouraged by their example and strengthened by their prayers, that we too may bear witness boldly to Christ, who is the light of life, through Jesus Christ, our Lord.†

† Prayer for Saints and Martyrs of our time, Canterbury Cathedral

1

In Rural Dorset

Everything was grey – the half light of dawn, the fields misty with hoar frost, even the stone of the buildings. Only an occasional dog barking or horse shuffling and sneezing in its stable, broke the winter silence. Not much could disturb the quiet, for the year was 1868, and there were few machines around, no cars, no radios. In one house though, there seemed to be activity at that early hour. At Symes Cottage next to the dairy at the western extremity of the village of Portesham, there was a candle in the window, and despite the cold, the front door was ajar. Someone was expected.

Above the village, to the north, lay a high ridge, from which the sea was just visible to the south, stretching from Bridport to the west to Weymouth eastwards. Down in the village it was still cold and silent, the candle still burning in one window. The discerning eye could pick out a moving figure coming towards the village from the west. It was not, as could be expected, a man starting early for work on one of the farms, but a woman, clutching a basket. She was hurrying, bustling along purposefully. As she reached Symes Cottage she hesitated, her hand on the knocker, then thinking better of it, pushed the door open and entered.

Later that day, 10 February, the woman, Mrs Downton, left the cottage, her work completed. She had delivered Margaret, a local girl of twenty-one, of a fine healthy boy. As midwife, she looked on most of the village as her responsibility, and knew the families well. She walked the four miles to Abbotsbury without complaint, content in the knowledge of another job successfully concluded. Her only concern in the icy cold was that the baby would not catch a chill and perish, as so many did in their first few months, but he had lusty lungs and the family were strong by nature, she reflected.

Month followed month, and spring came to the village. The baby grew healthy. In the sunshine of spring, the village looked almost pretty, with thatched cottages surrounded by gardens full of bright flowers and evidence of future vegetables. But when it blew and rained, as it often did near the coast, the unmade lanes would fill with deep puddles, the hedgerows grew rampant before the hedgers and ditchers got to them, and life became less than pleasant. Baby Harry was kept indoors by Margaret most of the time, swaddled in layers of clothes, often in his cot by the fire in the one downstairs room.

Forced to work by sheer necessity, Margaret continued her part time work at home as best she could between feeding, washing and cooking. It was all very difficult, there was no source of water, save from the well in the street, so she left her mother to look after Harry, as she put the yoke over her neck, and trudged off many times a day down the lane, staggering back with two pailfuls of icy water. 'T'will fair shram you out there,' she howled as she collapsed into the settle after the umpteenth trip of the day, 'and 'tis all your fault,' she said to Harry, laughing and pointing a finger at him. And she was right, the nappies were there as evidence, round the fire, hanging in the washhouse, everywhere.

The chores done, she finally picked up her paid work, netmaking. Along the coast at Bridport were numerous net firms, established for hundreds of years, and all offering outwork to local women in their homes. Harry watched his mother, as her deft hands passed the thread over and under to create the knots. One by one the finished nets dropped into the basket by the cot, and Harry put out his hand to touch them. 'No,' his mother said sternly, while realizing he was far too young to understand. 'You'll spoil my work. These are to be collected tomorrow, so leave well alone,' and she gave him a rattle to play with instead. 'Tis about time we got the Devil out of you, and had you christened.' Harry only gurgled, in willing acceptance of the notion. He was duly christened that Easter, by the vicar, Mr Gorton, at St Peter's church in the village.

Harry's babyhood was the same as most in the village, mainly spent indoors, or in a cradle in the back yard. Sometimes he would be carried out by his mother, but there were no perambulators for ordinary folk – Dorset was a very poor county, and the roads, to make it worse, would have bumped and banged the first tooth out of his head. He watched the carters, the ragmen, and the sheepshearing gang, as they all travelled through, and waved to the carriage of the Lord of the Manor, Lord Ilchester, as he came to spend summer at Abbotsbury Castle, some four miles away along the coast. Occasionally the tallyman called, and his mother took the opportunity to buy some hardwearing but cheap material to make clothes for the ever-growing baby. Lengths of material would be held up beside him, and there followed long discussions debating the benefits of bought material over handed down clothes donated by a friend. 'I'll take that,' said Margaret, pointing to some blue material for a coat for him. 'Tis that or my new dress, so I know what will win in the end!' She scraped in her pocket for the payment. 'Twill never all go round' she muttered to herself. 'But we'll manage, we have so far!' and she grinned at the tallyman and shrugged. Her positive good humour was a gift which she had already passed on to her son, gaily blowing a bubble over her shoulder, as he watched the man jump up into the cart and trot off to his next call. They returned to the flagstoned room, and Harry was deposited back in his cot, while Margaret decided how to cut the little coat.

The summer was a busy time in the village, for as the weather allowed, the harvest had to be gathered in. Everyone helped. Apart from anything else, it was a valuable source of income to add to the meagre amounts the labourers earned. Just a few years previously the Tolpuddle Martyrs had paid the price for challenging the system, and the memory of all that, just ten miles away, was deeply ingrained. Given some extra work, everyone went to help, and Margaret and Harry went too, with all the family. Harry was happy enough, left at the edge of the field with the other babies and toddlers, while his mother helped to build the stooks of hay and separate the long straw for thatch, from the ears. It was backbreaking work from morning to night, in heat and dust. Occasionally there was a shout as a mouse or rat ran from the corn, but after a while there was little talking or singing, as energy was concentrated to the task in hand.

'He's getting a bonny lad,' said Florence, Margaret's friend, as she handed the squirming baby back to mother during the brief break for lunch.

'A bit too lively,' replied Margaret. 'He's walking now, and into everything. Yesterday he nearly reached the pan on the stove, before I got to 'en, and I've had to take 'en to the bootmaker for some stout little shoes for winter, but he hates them so. He's already grown out of all the things you lent me!'

Harry developed as any ordinary little boy of his day. His family were not wealthy. They thankfully had jobs – which was not universal. Advertisements in the local paper, the Dorset County Chronicle, suggested that healthy young men could buy a passage to Australia quite cheaply, and some did. With every bad harvest, every new bit of mechanization, every outbreak of disease, someone would be forced to look elsewhere for a better life. These were the last years of the supposed idyllic life-style in Dorset, before the traditional buttonmaking industry would be swept aside by northern factories, before the wheelwrights and blacksmiths would be overtaken by the car and the train.

Harry, of course, knew none of this. To him, life was sweet and easy. His memories were of sitting on Aunt Bessie's knee looking at books, which he loved. He began to learn letters, and then to recite numbers. Whenever they went to the village, he looked quite enviously at the older children as they lined up in the yard of the National School. 'One day you'll go there Harry,' said his mother, 'when you are old enough.'

'Go now' said Harry, eagerly pulling at Margaret's skirts.

'No Harry, when you are older,' and she comforted the little boy, whose lips quivered as he watched the children playing hopscotch and marbles.

The school had only just opened, and boasted thirty-four pupils so far. Margaret sighed, for attendance was neither compulsory nor free, and a few pence a week would be hard to find. But she was determined that he would go to school. Never would he suffer the indignities of so many and sign his name with a cross. Education would get him a trade, if she could possibly manage it. While it was no disgrace to be a labourer, it was no privilege either, with the annual worries of being hired or not. No, her son would go to school, and if he was apt, to be apprenticed to learn a skill. She often mused about what sort of man he would become, whether he would be tall and handsome, when he would marry and what family he would have. In fact, it was perhaps as well she could not see into the future, for the picture would not be one she could have guessed, nor would have wanted.

As he turned from baby to young child, Harry played in the little cottage, cosy if cramped, with one main room for daily life, a kitchen range and living area all heaped together. The smell of cooking was all pervasive, and pretty well continuous, a fire being common even in summer to heat water and food. Given the small windows, it easily became stuffy and smelly. To the rear was a lean-to, used as a utility and wash area for both clothes and bodies to be scrubbed as needed. Here Harry was brought, after a friendly game of 'catch me if you can', which he knew he would lose. Wedged between his mother's knees he would be scrubbed down in the way all little boys hate, darting back over the flagstones to the fire and a sniff of the cooking pot! He helped in the hindering way all small children do, with the shelling of peas and the making of pastry.

Most homes had small gardens or allotments nearby, so necessary to augment the otherwise meagre larders. 'Harry's' seeds were carefully tended as he impatiently willed them to grow. He quickly learned that a full stomach depended on hard work and good growing weather, for the family were all agricultural labourers and male physical labour for twelve hours a day, six days a week, was bound to brush off on to an impressionable child, keen to copy the adults.

He was used to the handsowing of wheat, scything of clover, thistles and corn, and ploughing all in due season.

A place he got to know well was the local church, where he was taken regularly, and where his grandparents, as well as his parents, worshipped. His mother pointed out the font where he was baptized, and the altar rail where his parents were married; but to a young child they meant little. Far more interesting was the restoration work going on at the time. Slightly frightened at the banging and crashing, he stole into the church to watch the men fitting new timbers, sawing, planing and chipping at replacement stone. The wood and the varnish smelled heady, and he longed to get his little fingers involved. He was more than once picked up and returned to an apologetic mother. Undoubtedly he had begun to notice the elements of church building. It was a time of restoration in a high proportion of country churches and he would see such work again many times before one day being in the position of himself not just restoring, but designing and building his own church.

Until the day, when, at the age of three, he was blessed with a brother Thomas, he necessarily spent a great deal of his time with adults. His grandparents looked after him proudly, and some of his aunts and uncles (Margaret's siblings) were still at home – some indeed were very little older than he was, as his mother was the eldest in a large Victorian family. It was quite safe for children to play in the lanes – in fact, given that the women were working indoors and the yards were full of washing, there was little option. The roads then were safe from molestation and vehicles – the occasional cart being the greatest danger that existed. If it was dry enough boys played marbles, bowled hoops, chased and climbed. When it was wet they got muddy, splashing in puddles and messily playing with snails and slugs.

One day, when being cleaned off for the umpteenth time, Margaret took him by the shoulders and said, 'Listen Harry. This little house won't take us all, with everyone growing up big and Thomas to add to it. Your Pa and I have decided we will move to a house of our own, where you can have your very own room to sleep in. Would you like that?'

Harry wasn't sure. He would miss his toys and friends.

'It's a place by the sea, Harry. There are fishes and boats, and places to paddle, and a school ever so close, and even a little garden.' That decided it – he smiled a huge grin and ran off to collect his best marbles and his wooden truck his Grandfather had made him!

A few days later his parents loaded all their possessions on to their cart, inevitably trunks would not hold it all, and pots and boxes were strapped on as securely as possible. Everyone was there to see them off. Margaret's parents, the brothers and sisters,

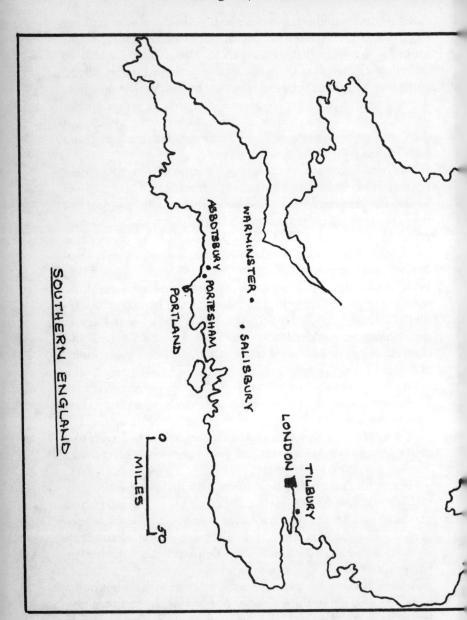

SOUTHERN ENGLAND

WARMINSTER •

ABBOTSBURY •
• PORTESHAM

PORTLAND

• SALISBURY

LONDON
• TILBURY

MILES
0
50

Aunt Bessie, and Florence, and even Mr Gorton wished them God speed as he watched them go. Harry, wedged between his parents excitedly gee-d up the horse, and father Jo manoeuvred the loaded cart along. But Margaret looked back and waved till she could see Portesham no more, then complained of something in her eye, and Jo put his arm round both her and the children, as he drove.

'Where are we going to, Father?' Harry was getting bored, and ached to be there, wherever it was.

'We're going to an island, further on from Weymouth, where the Queen has visited,' came the reply. ''Tis called Portland. They have great quarries where they dig for stone, and lots of soldiers there. We are going to live near the sea Harry, and you will be able to see huge ships, and trains, and wagons, for there's a prison there, and the men are driven through sometimes. You may even see the prisoners!'

Harry's eyes grew as big as saucers. 'Will I go to school? Can I see the prisoners, can I swim in the sea, can I, can I?'

'Yes, but one at a time,' laughed father Josiah. For Harry at least, the move was the best thing ever.

During the first few days and weeks of their life in Portland, Margaret busied herself with cleaning the rented cottage in the steep High Street, and trying to find a place for everything, before Harry and Jo got it all out again! They began to know the neighbours, and attended the local church on Sunday.

'We have a new family in our midst' the Vicar addressed the congregation. 'Mr Josiah Norman and his wife Margaret, baby Thomas and four-year-old son Harry, who we hope will attend our Sunday School. I hope you will take them to your hearts and make them welcome.'

In their way each did begin to fit into the community, Margaret with the women of the villages of Fortuneswell and Maidenwell on the hill, and Josiah with the increasing numbers of men finding work on the island. He was hoping to cash in on the development, by acting as carter for naval, military and prison needs. Directly above their house, above Fortuneswell village, was the neolithic mound turned into military barracks, known as the Verne Citadel, which generated apparently ceaseless to-ings and froings. The convict prison a mile or so south received official visitors, and the quarries required visits from city managers. A carter would always be busy carrying people and possessions round. In the first ten years of their life on the island, the Normans saw the island increase in size from nine to ten thousand. There was a better living to be made here than there was at Portesham.

Harry's view of the island was predictably different. The happy optimist made friends and investigated the school a few doors up the hill. He also began to reconnoitre the hill leading down to the sea – probably without his mother's permission! The sight of the huge Lyme Bay was awe inspiring. Small fishing boats, called lerrets, bobbed up and down, and occasionally large passenger and naval vessels could be seen. On a good day he could make out the pebble beach which acted as a causeway to the mainland.

'See, about there is Po'sham, and further Abbotsbury,' the fishermen told him, as he watched them unload their catch.

'I come from Po'sham,' Harry said. 'My grandparents and aunts live there. I could walk back to see them along that bank.'

'D'ye know how ye could tell when you'd be there?' he was asked. 'See, the size of these pebbles changes.' and the fisherman ran a mound of pebbles through his brawny fingers. 'The biggest are here, and by the time you get to Bridport over there, they're small as that.' The fisherman pointed to his smallest finger nail. 'Now when we land at night, we can tell just where we are by the pebbles. We're long headed, us Portlanders,' and he tapped his head.

Harry was impressed. These Portlanders were a different race from the Portesham people. Isolated, fiercely independent, with a certainty of their superiority. He was going to enjoy learning to be resourceful. He paddled in the rockpools, and knocked limpets off the rocks with pebbles, grazed his knees on slippery weed, and bruised his legs on the unstable rocks which lay about everywhere. There was plenty of danger about, translated by Harry into adventure, as he was too young to understand the powerful mastery of the sea. Being watchless, he often returned home late, to a distraught mother, and father with slipper twitching.

Whenever he was under oath not to go down to the sea alone

again, he travelled up, on to the hill above the village. From the top he could make out the village, the bay and in the distance, Weymouth. Directly below him the Royal Naval vessels were always in harbour – sailors were a common sight. He vowed he would become a sailor, able to sail to places far away, until he looked into the Citadel and saw the soldiers with gleaming uniforms and swords. The band would be the last straw – he would love to be a soldier! The gruesome little boy adored the sight of the convicts even better, watching them being moved through the streets, or working in the quarries in their broad arrowed rough clothes, flat caps and work boots, under the steely eye of the warders, armed with swords at the ready. Despite being told not to stare at them, it was too tempting. A warder had been killed by a prisoner, he was told, who had then been hung in Dorchester jail for his trouble. He was fascinated!

One of the most thrilling sights Harry remembered, shortly after they arrived, was the visit of an important man. 'He is the Prince of Wales, and will be King after our present good Queen,' his father told him. Standing with his parents at the edge of the road he saw the huge carriage roll past. Everyone cheered, and some had Union flags to wave. 'God save the Prince of Wales' he cried, along with the rest. He was sure the Prince had waved to him, but had no idea why he was there. In fact he had come to open the great breakwater, built by convict labour, and now containing a harbour large enough to house the entire fleet. 'And provide plenty of business!' thought his practical father, concerned at the recession in the stone trade, and the fear of reduced work from that quarter.

It was just as well that business was good, for six years later brother William arrived, and the family went on expanding to fill the house. Eventually the arrival of Josiah junior, then George and then Alfred would swamp poor Margaret. Her saving good fortune was the arrival of her sister Elizabeth and husband James from Portesham, together with – wonder of wonders – two daughters. That would even the balance a bit! It was possible to rent the house next door, and the women ensured the deal was completed, so Jo got his cart out to help the move. Girls were a bit of an embarrassment to Harry, but he kept his dignity and his distance for at least an hour, until he decided that they were actually quite good as playmates, even if they were both younger than he was!

It was at this point that Margaret stepped in to perfect a life of fun and adventure, and set Harry on the path which would lead him so far. He was now well over five, and the money could just be found to send him to school. She sat him down one afternoon and talked to him seriously.

'Harry, you are now of an age to go to school, and you shall go, after Easter, to the National School at the top of High Street. It is a large school, Harry, with many more children than at Portesham, but Mr Alcock will be your schoolmaster, and you will learn well from him.'

'Will I go every day, mother?'

'No, only weekdays' she smiled. 'It is an Anglican School, so is linked to St John's Church where you go to Sunday School. Look, here is a sheet which I have been given to tell us what you will learn.' Margaret produced the blue advertisement, printed when the school had opened some fifteen years previously, and still in use. She read: 'The aim of the school is to ground children well in branches of education which will be of most service to them as they advance in life.' Harry wrinkled his nose. It didn't sound much fun. 'Listen son,' she said, 'you will learn reading, spelling, writing, arithmetic, grammar, geography, and history. If you stay till you are older you will also learn book-keeping, geometry and algebra as well as navigation and astronomy. Pa says he wishes he had been able to learn like that! I want you to have a good education so you will be fit to take a trade, Harry. You could be a seaman, a craftsman or even work in an office.' The proud dreams showed on her face already. 'Would you like that?'

'Yes, mother' he said dutifully, not quite understanding all the words.

'You must work hard, for 'twill cost Pa pence each week to send you, and Thomas will want the same in a few years. Now the first thing is to make sure you can read some words before you go. I have promised Mr Alcock that you will be able to read simple words before you enter the school!'

So they sat down, and together spent happy hours over pencil and paper, Margaret forming letters and Harry guessing the words. The business of picking up written language was made interesting and even fun at his mother's knee. Long years later, he found the same thrill in learning Latin, Hebrew and Greek, but at five, he had more immediate needs. Mr Alcock would not have him in school unless he could read some words in his native tongue. 'Pa,' Harry said, as Josiah settled into his chair at the end of a hard day, 'I can read! Shall I show you?' Josiah raised his eyes aloft as the lad squeezed into the chair beside him. 'Go on then, son.' Apparently longsuffering, he thought that the child seemed quite apt and bright, as he listened to him recite the words he knew.

On a bright but windy spring morning after Easter in 1873, Harry was taken up the road, scrubbed and dressed in suitable clothes, to attend his first school. The boys' entrance looked forbidding, and most of the boys already going in were so much older than he was. 'Look, Harry, you can read the word carved up there' pointed Margaret, where 'Boys' was carved in stone over the archway. That first morning she took him in, but he soon got used to the routine by himself and enjoyed the independence of walking to school.

Once inside, the schoolroom was bewildering. Being one of the youngest, he sat at the front, on a bench with the other five-year-olds, with the older children ranged behind him. On the wall was a picture of an old lady, whom he recognized as Queen Victoria, and coloured maps, with red bits which he learned to know as Empire. Mr Alcock sat at a combined desk and chair at the front, and to Harry he was a little forbidding at first, especially when a boy misbehaved and the cane was brought out.

In the first year or two, Harry and the other younger children learned the usual number and language skills, some nature study and religious knowledge. In the school yard at playtime, he got to know other children and played traditional games. By the time he was eight, and of junior status, rather than infant, his brother Thomas was old enough to join him on the short journey up the hill to the little school, although pride dictated that Harry left Thomas at the door of the nursery class!

As he developed in school, he began to learn all kinds of

fascinating things. The maps on the wall took on a reality. Certainly his knowledge of the rest of the world was learned in terms of its relationship to Britain, the economic and political importance of other countries had value in so far as they affected Britain. So Harry learned of Africa and India, of both the new world and the old world of Europe. In all probability he learned little of the Far East, its customs, life-style, and way of looking at the world. Very possibly the Chinese were referred to briefly – if at all – as yellow savages, heathen who needed to be rescued from their ignorance by the dutiful British. It is far less likely that Harry would be taught that they had a proud and ancient culture, civilized before Britain ever knew itself as a nation. Much later, Harry learned at first hand that China, an enormous country, had a geography and a history which were both unique and un-appreciated by most Europeans. As he had an open and accepting attitude to foreign cultures, perhaps he did receive a relatively enlightened education from Mr Alcock.

Margaret was pleased with her son's progress. Whenever she asked how he was getting on, the replies were always positive. 'Mr Alcock says he is doing well, Jo' she said to her husband one night, after the children were safely in bed. 'His arithmetic is good, and he can measure and calculate well. Mr Alcock says he will start him on geometry and algebra soon.'

Jo grunted – he was not sure exactly what they entailed. 'Well, they're useful subjects anyway. Better to learn that than all the grammar and book reading he does. If he's going to stop on till he's fourteen, he's got to learn summat practical. He's got to earn his living, Marg.'

But Margaret was just proud of her son. Whatever it cost, she wanted him to learn everything Mr Alcock could teach him, even though the class was large and included children of all abilities. She had been told he was one of the brightest, and keenest, there. She still had her sights set on a trade for him ultimately.

Harry, meanwhile, thought little of the future. He was content to live for the present, streaking out of school, to beg a lift from his father when he delivered to the dockyard or the prison, or even better, the new railway station at the bottom of the hill. Helping to load trunks and crates, and holding the horse, he became quite useful, and Jo slipped him a farthing occasionally. Harry kept these with his other treasurers, a bone toothpick made by a convict, an ammonite he had found in a rock and a glass stopper found on the beach, which he had been reliably informed was from a pirate ship!

At heart, Harry was an activist, always keen to be up and doing, but able to apply himself to any homework needed, and ready to read any books he was lent. Given good weather he adored football, climbing, fivestones, marbles, swimming, anything practical suited him well; especially if it involved the cliffs and the beach nearby. He had little fear of danger, or if he did, he overcame it. He began to appreciate, though, the potential for disaster in everyday events.

One winter's Sunday, when Harry was nearly seven, the family were indoors, miserably watching the rain battering the windows and the wind howling down the High Street, when Uncle James from next door called from the scullery – his usual place of entry from the garden behind. 'Jo, Marg, have you heard the news, there's a ship ashore on the beach, will you come down to see?' Harry was desperate to go, and in the end Harry, Jo and James went, leaving the women behind. Standing on the beach, well back from the pounding waves which crashed up the shore, further than most expected, the three joined quite a crowd of local people. James discovered that the boat so perilously close, listing badly, was the *Marie Reine*. As Harry promised to stay put, held by an adult, his uncle and father went down the beach to see if they could help. With every breaker, the situation looked more desperate. The boat lurched ever nearer, and the crowd held its breath and silently prayed for the crew and rescuers. Fastened by a rope, the men swam out in the teeth of the gale, and mountainous seas, fighting the dragging undertow to reach the ship. The noise of the storm and cries from the terrified crew were all but deafening, while the crowd shouted encouragement as the first man was reached and held. Finally a rocket line was secured from the beach to the ship, and painfully slowly six crewmen hauled themselves, monkeylike, along the line to safety, clinging in icy weather, buffeted by the wind and battered by the waves. Suddenly one wave knocked a man from the line, and the crowd gasped. In vain the rescuers tried to reach him, but he was later washed ashore, dead. The rest of the crew, save two, were brought ashore by breeches buoy, and led up the beach to safety and blankets.

Harry watched, open mouthed, with the other children, frightened but unable to move. 'You must go home, this baint no place for a lad' said Jo, but Harry pleaded to stay, desperately wanting to see the men saved. There he remained, watching as at last only the Captain remained, traditionally staying with his ship. But he had sustained a broken arm in the storm, and ill-equipped to save himself, he drowned. So Harry first experienced the deep longing to help, to save. He saw the lengths to which people would go to save a life, even at the risk of their own. Later Harry did the same, but in order not just to save bodies, but to save souls.

Any island community faces such dramas from time to time, and Harry's parents, while trying to shield him from some of life's terrors, were aware that he had to find out for himself that life was difficult and dangerous. Harry never forgot his first experience of seeing death, but a greater and more devastating calamity occurred just two years later. By this time Harry was nine and a half. It was 11 September, an early autumn evening. Disregarded by most of the villagers, two ships were crossing off Portland Bill. One was the *Avalanche*, an emigrant ship bound for New Zealand with just under one hundred passengers and crew. The other was the *Forest*. Harry had been put to bed, and baby William had just been changed, when Jo was alerted by the sound of feet running down the High Street – not one person, but a number, hurrying down to the sea.

'What's up?' he called out, as someone passed.

'Two ships collided out there, there's people drowned,' called back the other as he ran on.

Immediately Jo put on his coat and called to Margaret that he was going.

'Take care, Jo' she said as she buttoned the collar and kissed him. The noise woke both children, and Harry begged to go, but it was not possible, on this occasion. Jo returned later, exhausted. 'There's no way we can do anything till morning, we have no searchlights. We just can't see what's to be done, but Marg, those poor souls, women and children too, there must be many lost.'

The next day it was obvious what had happened. Everyone went to look at the devastation. The *Forest* had had insufficient canvas to control her movement, and had rammed the *Avalanche* not once, but three times, at first disabling her, then holing her. The passengers, preparing for bed, had stood little chance. In all 108 were drowned, and some bodies were later removed from the sea. Only twelve were rescued. Driftwood came ashore for days, wreckage from the ships. Soon after, officials and salvagemen visited the area.

The whole island was shocked. Harry and the other children were kept away from the beach, and the only topic of conversation in the streets was the collision. 'Why?' Harry asked his mother. The sheer pointlessness and waste of it had stung him, even at his age. Many more pointless deaths would cross his path, but the scale of the *Avalanche* disaster was appalling. Two years later, the little family, with others, joined relatives of the dead at the consecration of a Memorial Church on the Island, the service being conducted by the Bishop of Salisbury. As far as they could, they supported the relatives, and mourned with them.

Slowly, thought Margaret, Harry was growing up. By the time he was fourteen, his education would be complete. Margaret and Jo often discussed what they would do with Harry when he left school. 'He can't come wi' me on the cart,' his father said. 'I don't make enough to pay him, and he would just take up space I could offer passengers, and anyway we would need a second cart and horse in the end and I can't afford it.'

'There's a lad locally been sent to Abbotsbury to be a wheelwright, Jo.' Margaret had heard of the boy and how well he was doing. 'He's nearly out of his time, and may be moving on. Perhaps Harry could learn a trade there and be close to Ma and Pa if he needs them. You have to admit we're getting cramped here.' By now the house was filled with the growing family, all boys!

William followed Thomas, then Josiah and baby George. Another was on the way, inevitably it would be another boy. Therefore it seemed a sensible idea, and Jo went off to discuss it with neighbours.

When it was put to Harry, he seemed quite interested. 'You would learn a proper trade, son,' his mother explained. 'It might cost us dear, but you could be apprenticed, and would have a skill to earn a living by. There would be other boys lodged in the village, and there seems to be plenty of work there, considering Lord Ilchester has farms there, and maintains a summer castle in the village. 'Tis only four miles from your grandparents, so you wouldn't be alone. Mr Alcock will write a letter on your behalf to say you are a good scholar. What do you think?'

'Yes, Ma, I would like it,' said the obedient son, who was willing to try it, but also a little nervous of his sudden propulsion into adult life.

He left school soon after his fourteenth birthday, and early that spring prepared to leave. Jo packed his bags on to the cart, and Margaret hugged him and straightened his clothes. 'Be a good boy, and do what you are told. Remember how you have been raised. Don't forget to visit Portesham.' He looked so young. As the cart trundled off down the hill, she and the smaller children waved until the cart turned the bend and was gone. Then she turned back to the house and gave herself up to thinking how to rearrange the house now Harry was gone. Somewhere deep in her heart she knew she had said goodbye to her son as a child. When she saw him again, he would be a young man.

As the horse plodded over the causeway, and through the villages towards Abbotsbury, both Jo and Harry were lost in their own thoughts. With both excitement and trepidation, Harry imagined his future, in lodgings in the village, perhaps returning at Christmas to his parents. He imagined a life of woodshavings and hot metal, farm wagons and coaches; possibly even a chance to start his own business eventually. What neither he, nor his parents could know was that he would make friendships and contacts in Abbotsbury which would entirely change his life, take him away from the village and the trade his mother had sought so hard for him, and launch him on a far more prestigious career. He would rise to academic heights greater than Mr Alcock would have guessed, travel further than any emigrants intended, and witness disaster and danger on a scale beyond that which he had so far experienced. But on that spring morning in 1882, Harry was destined for a village life as a wheelwright, and he set his sights on learning his practical skill.

That Sunday he said goodbye to his father, and decided that his best course of action was to walk round the village and get his bearings. His lodgings were adequate, and the couple welcoming, if a little strange to him. Before it got dark, he wandered out round the village, full of yellowstone thatched cottages. To the north lay the castle, imposing yet not quite part of the village. Pa had told him that Lord Ilchester came there in the summer from Melbury House near Yeovil. He had a dim recollection of a grand coach passing through Portesham when he was a small boy, and assumed that he must have seen Lord Ilchester. The castle was almost closed up for the winter, so he turned back through the village to the church and the lane to the sea. The ruins of a Benedictine Abbey still stood near the church. Close by was the Abbey duck pond, and an enormous barn, larger than any Harry had seen before, and which looked as old as the Abbey, though it was still used. Outside was a cart, obviously used for moving hay. Harry walked round it and felt the wheels and shafts, smooth from use, still brightly painted, despite its age. It would do no harm to get his eye in with the construction of a wheel.

'Arternoon,' called a voice behind him. He jumped. An elderly man appeared from the direction of the church, with a dog by his side. Harry touched his cap immediately. 'Hello Sir,' he said.

'You 'm not from here-abouts.'

'No, I'm from Portland. I've just come to start as an apprentice at the wheelwrights.'

'You're a young lad to be so far fro' home then, but there be other 'prentices for ye to get along with. I wish 'ee well.' And with that he was gone.

For some reason the kindness made Harry feel even more alone, and he walked on rather solemnly. The calls of the gulls made him realize he must be near the sea, and sure enough, within a few minutes he was on the beach, so familiar to him. To the left he could see Portland rising high at the end of the Chesil beach, the Citadel the highest point. 'Just below there,' he thought, 'there's Ma and Pa, Thomas, William and the babies. If I walked along the beach I could get home.' He picked up some pebbles.

The fisherman had been correct, the pebbles were smaller here. To the west must be Bridport, and even smaller pebbles. As long as he could get to the sea of an evening, life would not be too bad. He lightened his step as he returned to the lodgings to prepare for the next day – his first day as an apprentice.

The next morning Harry could scarcely eat his breakfast for nerves, but as his landlady fairly stood over him, he forced himself to the task, with half an eye on the large loudly ticking clock. Woe betide him if he were late on his first day. As the church clock struck 8, he walked into the wheelwrights in Rodden Row, in the centre of the village. Outside the pavement was significantly higher than the muddy road, and a ramp had been built to allow carts access up to the shop. Once across the threshold, the workshop was much darker, and Harry blinked, waiting to get acclimatized to the light.

'Morning, lad.' A man came forward, wiping his hands on his overall. 'You'll be young Norman from Portland then?'

'Yes, Sir.' Harry's mouth was dry and his voice came as a whisper and a squeak, as nervousness combined with the embarrassment of natural breaking into adult tones. 'Are you Mr Stoodley?'

'Nay – not me son, I'm Sam Mundy. Mr Stoodley's out the back. I'll take you through.' Sam smiled. At forty he was still young enough to imagine how the lad felt. As he introduced him to Mr Stoodley, he put his hand on Harry's shoulder. After all, he had children of his own.

Mr Stoodley was old, as far as Harry could judge. He was in fact sixty-eight, but his moustaches and white hair were all that were needed to label him in the boy's eyes. He seemed very stern at first, but increasingly Harry saw that he was simply businesslike. He knew his trade well, which inspired Harry's confidence. In fact he was both a carpenter and a wheelwright, and taught dual trades to any able lad. Arriving before the men, and leaving after them, he prepared in the evening the work which was to be done the next day, and negotiated the prices so skilfully, that Harry determined to emulate him. The more he looked at the craft of the wheelwright, the more he realized there was to learn, and the more he felt himself to be a passenger in the firm where everyone pulled their weight. At the end of his first week he was paid, but scarcely knew what he had contributed to earn it.

By now he had begun to know the other apprentices, both of Stoodley and of Charles Hayne, the wheelwright at the other end of the village. Henry Gill from Portland was no longer there, having finished his time and moved on. The remaining apprentices, Will Critchell and Fred Ford, both lived at home nearby, and were much older than Harry. Alfred Slade and his mother lodged with Mr Hayne. Father Slade, a gardener, existed, but apparently separately from his wife and son. Harry asked no questions, but sympathized with a situation which demanded that the Haynes, the father-in-law, two small sons, the Slades and another apprentice all crammed together in one cottage!

During the weeks that followed, Harry got used to the life of the wheelwrights shop, the banging and crashing and occasionally the whistle of contented men at work. Usually he was ankle deep in shavings, learning to plane or saw. The smell of wood hit him each morning, and left with him each night, together with the heady scents of resin, paint and varnish. The work benches were arranged in traditional fashion round the edge of the shop, leaving the central space for assembly. Tools were arranged on wall racks, axes, lathes, calipers, dividers, chisels and mallets. Harry stumbled over the names of each to begin with, forcing his mind to remember which implement did what.

Lesson one came from Sam Mundy. He took him to the yard at the back where the rims were fitted.

'Look at this wood, lad.' He pointed to long planks stacked in piles. 'D'ye know what its doing there?'

'Doing?' Harry was bemused.

'It's seasoning. There's no point trying to work new wood, it will only twist and crack. See the blocks put between the planks to let the air in – they let the weather dry the wood out and harden it. The numbers and letters are what Mr Stoodley put on when he chose the wood, so he could tell which seasoned first. See? No knotted wood. The grain has to run straight and true. Any disease and Mr Stoodley wouldn't take it. He's very particular – goes and selects the wood himself. He even studies the soil to judge the wood. He'll maybe take you sometime when he goes out.'

Harry frowned. There was a lot to the wood business that he hadn't realized. 'What's that for?' he asked, pointing to a pile of brushwood.

'We make besoms wi'that,' Sam explained. 'You don't waste the wood you can't season. What's left we sell as beanpoles or brushwood for the roads. There's a value in everything.'

As the season arrived for bean growing, Harry found out just how extensive was the need for beanpoles. He cut hundreds, and vowed never to eat another bean!

Later, Sam judged Harry ready for training in wheel making. Harry applauded the decision. He had sawed and planed, and tidied up long enough, in his own estimation!

'What's that wood?' Sam checked Harry's knowledge.

'Elm, Sir.'

'Good. Now elm we use for the nave. What is the nave?'

'The centre of the wheel, Sir.'

'Right. Now, you must measure the angles to judge the position of the spokes you are going to put in. Go and get the instruments.'

His first attempt was hopeless. The second was little better, but Sam seemed well pleased, even if he did laugh at it. Even Mr Stoodley grunted and called it 'a fair job for a lad'.

Next came the fixing of the sections of rim.

'Remember the name for these?' Sam quizzed Harry.

'Felloes?'

'Yes – made from?'

'Ash – because its more pliable.'

'Good. And the spokes?'

'Hard oak, Sir'

'Well done, lad. Now, I'll show you how to cut a felloe yourself, but you must choose the right pattern from the wall.'

Harry went to the wall where dozens of patterns hung in rows. For the life of him, Harry couldn't tell which pattern fitted which size of wheel, and it took a while to get the hang of it. He could eventually write home that he had constructed a wheel. Perhaps there was really less to the wheel making business than everyone had made out.

'I reckon I'm nearly trained already,' he confided to Will one evening. Will only laughed.

'You'm never trained, you fool! You mun learn the art o' metal heating and bending, painting and varnishing yet!' Harry was immediately deflated.

He had in fact scarcely learned the woodworking principles, for he had to acquire the skills of jointing – no glues or nails were used in wheelmaking. The spokes were never put in at 90° but at a slight angle to increase strength. Slowly the apprentice was gaining engineering skills too.

It just had to be a hot day when he began to learn about metal bending. The men stripped to the waist in the yard at the back. It was a team job to get a metal rim on, and everyone lent a hand. The furnace was burning fiercely by the time he got there, and the metal arcs were already being heated. Mr Stoodley was in charge of the fire, assessing the exact heat and length of time for the metal to expand. By now they were all perspiring freely and smuts were flying around the yard.

'Watch me,' ordered Sam, 'I'm going to lift out the strakes now,' and with huge tongs he lifted one of the metal arcs from the fire into the pit in which the wheel was lying. 'Too tight a fit and the metal will contract and break the wheel as it cools, and too loose, and it won't hold on,' he shouted above the noise of the men hammering the metal round the wheel. Finally the strakes were in place, supported until they cooled and bit into the wooden felloes.

The next wheel was the other half of the pair, and Harry took his share of the load this time. It was tougher, heavier and hotter work than he had thought, and by the end of the day he envied the older men the cooling relief of beer in the local inn. Mrs Stoodley gave him elderflower cordial, which had slaked his thirst but scarcely rewarded a man's work.

As days and months went by, Harry followed through the skills of the wheelwright. He painted the carts and picked out lettering and patterning on the sides as required. Each county and each wheelwright had particular specialities of design. Dorset was known for its particularly gay blue decoration on the carts, which with the curved shape of the body, gave them the appearance of ships at sea as they bounced along. Finally Harry learned the hundred and one skills of the general carpenter, for he not only learned to build the base of the carts and the shafts, but many other bits of equipment needed in any village – mangers, wooden parts for ploughs, yokes, ladders, seed drills, and even coffins. He could not know how useful all his skills would be to him in the future, but he would be able to bless Sam and Mr Stoodley for all they taught him.

Life was not all work, although a ten-hour day from 8 a.m. to 6 p.m. sometimes felt like it. Harry often stole away after work, to the sea, or up on the high hill overlooking the village, where he would walk through flocks of sheep to the very top, where there was a small chapel, and a magnificent view down into the village. After a hot day's work, he loved to feel the sea air on his face, and get some healthy exercise. He looked down to where he could pick out the workshop, his lodgings and the narrow roads. Out to sea, he could trace the Chesil Bank, the ancient swannery, and Portland in the distance.

Society in Abbotsbury was very different from Portland. Here there were no military or naval staff, no prisons or quarries. The apex of society was Lord Ilchester, when he arrived at the castle for the summer. With him came his retinue of companions, governesses, groom and cooks. The bailiff, gamekeeper and land agent were around most of the year. Somewhat below them in status came the school master and mistress, housekeeper, doctor, nurse, and collector of the poor rate. The vicar held an ambiguous position, as his salary was paid by the Earl, but his status was only a little below him.

Harry was, as an apprentice, in a fairly lowly position, but with the promise of becoming a tradesman with potential, just as his mother had wanted. As such he would ultimately rank alongside other skilled men, such as the thatcher, the tailor and the blacksmith. He was to be off the bottom rung, reserved for the likes of the labourers.

Each May brought the delights of Garland Day in Abbotsbury, and Harry was aware of something happening days in advance, as Sam's two little daughters danced around excitedly, running in from their home next to the wheelwrights to update everyone on their preparations.

'Get home chiel,' Sam bellowed, when Bessie or Minnie bothered him once too often.

'What's it all about?' questioned Harry.

'The young 'uns collect flowers from the fields and gardens and work them on frames for Garland Day. If I get asked once more to make a frame just a bit smaller or higher, I tell 'ee, I'll not be answerable.' Silence followed. 'Well, 'tis a sight, I must allow. We all stop to cheer them through, even the master.'

'What are they for, though?'

'There's no way of telling. It's been a tradition on 13 May, time out of mind. The garlands are all paraded to the shore. Tis a fine sight!'

Sure enough, on the day, the village was *en fête*. Harry was unsure whether to down tools and watch, or act like an adult and stay at work, until he heard Mr Stoodley at his shoulder. 'If I were thee, I'd get out front to see the procession before ye're too late. Anyways – the girls next door will expect to collect a farthing from a soft touch like you!' – this last with a smile. And he was right, Harry emptied his pockets of farthings for the children. The whole village seemed to be following the procession. He looked back at Mr Stoodley, who nodded and mouthed, 'Go on!' So Harry followed the crowd and watched the garlands taken to the beach, placed in mackerel boats and rowed out to deep water, there to be thrown into the sea, to appease the gods.

As the children raced back to the village, the adults, now numbering Harry among them, walked back in groups, chatting and laughing. Will and Fred caught Harry up, and they compared notes on their work until they reached the castle, where the Earl's servants had laid out a tea party for everyone. Games had been organized for the children, and the adults sat or stood in groups eating bread and cakes washed down with copious draughts of tea. Local shopkeepers had planned stalls for months, and were doing a roaring trade. 'Should have brought those bean poles and besoms!' Harry thought.

Eventually the party was called to order by a grand looking man sporting a waistcoat decorated with a half-hunter watch.

'Who's he?' Harry whispered to Will.

'Mr Hopson, Earl's agent,' whispered back Will.

'The Earl of Ilchester has graciously agreed to present all the children with a small gift, which he hopes will benefit them. Will all the children line up, boys to the left, and girls to the right.'

Harry watched as Lord and Lady Ilchester stepped forward, each with a servant carrying piles of presents. For the girls there was a length of cloth sufficient for an apron, and for the boys, a new pair of boots. Minnie and Bessie waved as they waited their turn, and bobbed a curtsey as they received their gifts, running back to mother with their prizes.

'Does this happen every year?' Harry asked Sam, who by this stage had appeared with Mr Stoodley and Mr Hayne. 'Yes, thank the Lord,' said Mr Hayne, with an eye on the gifts in his wife's hands, which would save a tidy sum. They all laughed. By the time they reached the village centre, the men felt the need to stop and talk, and Harry beat a tactful retreat, as they had wearied themselves outside the Ilchester Arms, and Harry would not be welcome there until he was of age.

Hard on the heels of Garland Day in 1883, after Harry had been in the village some fifteen months, an even more memorable day dawned. Sam had been talking to the agent, and to the vicar, and both had told him that the Duke and Duchess of Edinburgh were to visit the village. Mark Hopson was like a cat on hot bricks, as he had to receive them in the absence of the Earl and Countess. It was another excuse to stop work, and the children were scrubbed to a shine, Bessie and Minnie with their hair brushed a hundred times to make it curl. The coaches were to come from Portesham. 'Well I never,' Harry said to no one in particular, 'They'll pass Grandma and Grandfer's place, and afore that will land at Portland. P'haps Ma and Pa will see them disembark from *HMS Hercules*.'

The wait seemed endless at the side of the road. The children held streamers and handkerchiefs, hopping from foot to foot in the midday heat. Eventually someone heard a clatter of hooves, and two carriages came into view, carrying the Duke of Connaught, Mr Hopson, and the Duke and Duchess. Waving graciously they trundled through the village, passing Harry with feet to spare. The carriages turned and stopped outside the Ilchester Arms exactly at 1.30 p.m., the guests alighting for a light lunch. After an interminable time, during which there were many comments concerning the food that was being consumed in the Ilchester, the party reappeared, and were shown round the village. Harry had never seen people as important before, he thought, though he had a vague memory that as a four-year-old he had seen an important man in Portland, and Pa had pointed him out to him. He thought contentedly that life in Abbotsbury was not as dull and mundane as he had imagined.

Apart from such occasions of community interest, life went on as usual in the village. Harry went with Mr Stoodley to choose trees for felling, and began to feel at last that he was pulling his weight in the carpentry shop. Every week he tried new skills, and gained confidence. He was also growing up, and began to take responsibility for locking the workshop, speaking to customers about orders, or going on important errands for his master.

Nevertheless, each November he tried to get home to Portland for the traditional fair in the village of Chiswell, at the entrance to the Island. As he walked in the door, Margaret dropped whatever she was doing and hurried to the passage to meet him. 'How you've grown,' was her usual first comment. 'Almost as tall as Pa already. Your trade must be suiting you! Let me look at you. Are your lodgings still good, son? Are you happy there?' The barrage of questions was ceaseless, until Harry, laughing, calmed and reassured her.

Brothers seemed to be a growing breed. A new little brother, Albert, had taken up residence in the cot, by the time Harry had been away a year. The three under-fives, Josiah, George and now Albert, made the house a noisy and overcrowded place. Harry was quite relieved to take the two older boys, Tom, now twelve and William, six to the fair. The mechanical organ churned out songs and marches and happy shouts and laughter added to the mayhem. Harry spent up all his spare cash on rides and sticky sweets and trinkets for his brothers, waiting for them amid the smells of gaslamps and boiling sugar. Occasionally he saw an old friend from school, and they compared notes on their work. Eventually he dragged the boys home, all happily tired.

Pa was home from work by the time they got back, and sat in front of the fire with his boots off curling his toes in front of the flames.

'Welcome son,' he called. 'Come and sit down, and tell me how life is going on in Abbotsbury.' By now Harry had been away eighteen months, but Pa never tired of hearing how he was progressing.

'Same as ever, Pa. We had a to-do a couple of months ago. Did you hear about the storm which damaged the swannery back along?'

Pa nodded.

'Well, a ship, the *Christiana*, foundered off the beach, and the men went down to see what could be done. But it was too late and two men were lost. We had to get two coffins made up in the yard. It was a bad do, Pa.'

Josiah shook his head. 'A bad do, to be sure. But you know as well as most what the sea can be like. 'Tis a hard master, lad.' They sat in silence watching the flames, until Margaret reappeared, having put the excited children to bed.

'Your Ma and I have been thinking,' Josiah continued. 'You're coming up sixteen soon, and tis about time ye were thinking o' confirmation, lad. You are regular to church I hope?'

'Yes Pa, of course I am. I've been helping with the boys in Sunday School all year!'

'Good. Well, ye must talk to vicar about the classes, and arrange it for y'self, as we can't do't for 'e.'

As it happened, when he returned to Abbotsbury Harry made no immediate moves to organize his confirmation. The old vicar, Mr Penny, was leaving and it was not until a few days after Harry's sixteenth birthday that the new man came. The parishioners were a bit uneasy. Mrs Stoodley openly worried. 'What'll we do wi' a man from Cambridge? We're not used to educated ways, and Mr Penny's been here these thirty years. He's been good enough for us.' As it turned out the new vicar, Mr Fairbairn, was a likeable man, with a son only a little younger than Harry. He and his family moved into the Manor House that spring. (The Vicarage, confusingly, housed Will Hawkins, the surgeon and public vaccinator!)

30

A year after, Harry was confirmed, in March 1885, when he was just seventeen. He helped regularly in the church, and had found a niche for himself looking after the boys section of the Sunday School. Fairbairn was pleased to have some help round the place, and encouraged Harry.

'Young Norman' – Fairbairn called Harry in his usual form of address. 'What do you think of these plans?' Harry looked at the enormous architectural plans of the church which Mr Fairbairn had laid across the pews. 'The old box pews here will go,' he pointed, 'and we will have open benches. The north gallery will go, making more light, and the stone floor will have tiles, and the organ and choir will go from the west end behind us, to the chancel.'

''Twill be a big change for some folks,' said Harry.

'But if it will improve the worshipping, Harry, then it's worth the effort and cost. The Bishop has allowed us to hold services in the schoolroom till the building is finished. Next month, you wait, you won't know the place!'

Too true! The crashing and whistling of the builders over the next months was most un-churchlike. Piles of stone and wood littered the churchyard, and villagers mumbled as they squeezed into the tiny schoolroom. Girls complained that weddings were not 'right' in a school, and older residents hated change of any sort. Mr Stoodley was asked on more than one occasion for pieces of wood and equipment that the builders needed. Generally the village was quite put out.

At last the day came when it was complete, and to mark the occasion, Mr Fairbairn had been in touch with Salisbury. Word went round that the Bishop himself would visit and on Sunday 7 March 1886, the whole village seemed to attend the church, or be standing outside. Harry found the only space left was not in his usual pew, but behind a pillar to the side. By craning his neck he could just see the pulpit. Still more people piled in, and he offered to stand, but mercifully there were enough seats for all who wanted them. To the sound of a fanfare from the newly-moved organ, the procession started. It began at the Manor House, and the aisle of the church was the final stretch. First came the choir, then Mr Fairbairn, Mr Purvis his curate, and finally the Bishop in his splendid robes. It was a fine service; singing in full voice with gusto, Harry and the rest entered into the celebrations fully. After the Bishop's sermon, a new jewelled brass altar cross was dedicated by the Bishop, in honour of Mr Fairbairn's mother. As the Bishop processed out, Harry remembered the scene, almost exactly a year before, when the Bishop had confirmed him there. The evenings of preparation with Mr Purvis, the learning of his catechism, seemed so long ago. He looked down at his inscribed Prayer Book, given him that day, with fond memories.

At this point the story could finish. The rest could have been easily imagined. Harry would complete his apprenticeship, eventually marry and raise a family, become a master wheelwright, watch his sons go off to World War 1, settle into old age. But none of this predictable future was to be like that. The next fourteen years were to unfold because of what happened one night late that year.

Harry was almost eighteen, still a youth, but enough of a man to act as companion to the vicar occasionally on his travels. It had been a gloomy day, and the rest of the week stretched ahead dully. 'Harry' – the vicar's voice called across Rodden Row to Harry as he walked to work. He crossed the road. 'Morning sir,' he replied with his usual cheerful grin.

'Harry, would you like to come to one of the missionary meetings I told you of? There's one in Weymouth tonight. I've promised to be there, but it's a long miserable journey alone. What do you say?'

'That'd be grand,' Harry replied eagerly. 'What time, for I must arrange my tea to suit.'

It was a bit of a scramble, as he had to leave the workshop, change and eat in a few minutes, but he did it willingly for the sake of an interesting evening out. On the journey they discussed and debated in a way which delighted them both. Finally the bright lights of the Weymouth Gospel Hall shone out on the cold dark evening.

Harry was amazed. The hall was full, there must be a hundred people there. Two or three clergymen were talking at the front, and Mr Fairbairn joined them. Harry waited at the side, feeling self-conscious and alone. Presently they brought him forward, and he was introduced to the speaker, an ex-missionary. The time had come, and the clergy were to take their places on the platform, so Harry returned to the anonymity of the hall, finding a seat at the back.

The service was brief, but lively. Led by the pianist, they sang rousing hymns almost from memory, and prayed earnest prayers for the saving of souls. The speaker was on his feet for almost an hour, telling tables of the wonderful change in the lives of heathen men and women on hearing the gospel. Harry had not realized that such savage lives existed, completely without the moral ethics of Christianity. How could people be so different? What a joy to see them healed and saved! Roused from his thoughts, he heard the preacher say, 'We need so many more to go, to work for the saving of lost souls in distant lands. We appeal for funds, and for men to go.'

Before he realized what he was doing, he had jumped up, raised his arms aloft to gain attention, and with a clear voice, eager and certain, called out, 'I have nothing but myself to offer. I offer myself.'

The congregation murmured, and a few turned to see who it was. At the front Mr Fairbairn sat stunned.

'Well done young man, come forward,' said the speaker.

Harry was propelled forward. His legs felt like jelly, but oddly he was not nervous. Some inner conviction had taken hold of him. He was absolutely sure that he had done the right thing. Nothing would dissuade him.

As they returned home along the black lanes in the pony and trap, neither said much. Finally the vicar broke the silence. 'Why did you do it, lad? You can't throw in your apprenticeship now?'

'I can, and I will,' was all he said.

'There's more to it than the work you are doing in the Sunday School. Harry, look, the man meant men with more education than you have. They have to learn theology and Hebrew and suchlike. You haven't the funds to do it. You are serving God wonderfully with the boys in Sunday School.'

'It's not enough. Somehow I must find the money. Why can't I learn? If God wants me to go he will find a way.'

'But, Harry . . . '

'No "buts". I'm to go. I know I am. I don't know how, but I must. You say we must follow God's will.'

The vicar sighed. The fervour of youth! Harry would forget it as soon as he got back home.

But Harry did not forget it. He bothered Mr Fairbairn regularly, and even asked to borrow his theology books. As time went on, it became increasingly obvious that the idea was no passing dream. Fairbairn watched Harry as he busied himself around the church, now taking an adult role in the parish. Although zealous, he had kept his head, and continued working hard at the wheelwright's. He was a sensible, practical, intelligent lad, diligent and popular. He was also obviously frustrated and miserable with no answer to his problem. There was only one way out and Fairbairn took it.

On returning a book at the Manor the following week, Fairbairn welcomed Harry with unusual vigour. 'Come in Harry, I want to talk to you.' Before he knew it, Harry was in his study, seated amongst the piles of books and papers.

'Harry, I've been talking to Mr Sanctuary, who works for the Earl. Now, don't get excited, but he has spoken for me to the Earl, and I don't know why, but it seems he may be prepared to sponsor you to train for missionary work. Now hold fast lad,' – this as Harry's eyes lit up and his mind raced. 'The Earl may be wealthy, but he already pays my salary, and many besides. Even he won't throw good money away, but it is being discussed. There is a College I know well at Warminster which combines practical trades and theological training, but it would mean considerable work Harry – years. Do you realize what that would mean?'

'Yes, and I will do it well. I don't mean to fail you.'

'I'm sure you don't, but you must realize you will be failing Mr Stoodley and Sam. You may not be released from your training. They have trained you until you are useful, and now you are asking to go. Mr Stoodley is no longer young, and needs help in the workshop. And Harry – this is important. You are not yet of age – your parents must be consulted.'

Harry had forgotten Ma and Pa in the excitement. His first tiny doubt crept in. Whatever would they say?

'You must talk to them about it, Harry. There is nothing definite yet – nothing.'

What turmoil invaded Harry's mind then. Did God really want him to cause this upheaval and upset people? Did he have the ability to learn Hebrew, Greek, theology? How could he be sure? But he was, he knew it. He had never been more certain of anything. There were the doors opening for him at least, he had to recognize them.

His parents were not so sure. The news came as a bombshell. Whatever had he been getting up to in Abbotsbury, being led into crazy ideas with dreams above his station?

'But Father, 'tis not others but me. I want this, I have been called, no one put the "idea in my head".'

''Tis Father now is it – now you're thinking o'grand things. I mind when it used to be "Pa".'

'No Father – Pa. 'Tis not to be grand, but to do the work of God.' Harry pleaded. 'I don't know how I will do it no more than you do, but you can't stop me following the call.'

So it went on. Margaret sat quietly listening. Eventually when the arguing stopped, she said, so quiet that they scarcely heard her, 'Josiah, the lad must go. 'Tis not what we hoped for him, but he is to be helped, so others must think him able. Perhaps 'twould be wrong to stop him, even though he will go so far away. He must go with our blessing.'

It was decided. Secretly both Margaret and Josiah were delighted, once they were over the full shock of it. Margaret set about fitting him out with the clothes he would need for a College, determined that his humble background would not disgrace him. Proudly the parents told the neighbours. 'He will be the first sponsored student from Dorset,' they said to one and all, 'sponsored by Lord Ilchester himself, to go to a College to train to become a priest.' The news impressed everyone.

Harry meanwhile left Mr Stoodley and Sam, with a lump in his throat and so many claps on the back that he felt bruised. Sam made a small wooden cross for him to put on his dressing table or window at College, to remember them by. Mrs Mundy and the girls said goodbye with armfuls of kisses, and the boys at the Sunday School cheered him the last day. The whole congregation promised to pray for him, and Mr Purvis was quite overcome. Finally, Harry said goodbye to Mr Fairbairn, standing outside the church on the last Sunday he was at Abbotsbury.

'Thank you for everything, sir. You've started me off, and I mean to reach my goal. 'Twill be a hard road, but 'twas ever thus for a Christian.'

Fairbairn touched his shoulder. 'Take care, young Norman. You take our love and prayers with you. Write to us when you have time. Oh – and tell the College that Mr Sanctuary is sending the money they need for the first term. God Bless.' Harry nodded, finally lost for a word. He turned and walked up the lane for the last time. Harry, the fourteen-year-old boy who had entered the village to learn a trade, left it as a nineteen-year-old young man beginning a professional career, and a long long journey into world history.

2

From Warminster to Peking

By the time he reached Warminster, Harry was a mass of conflicting emotions. He was excited, but also wary, not so much from uncertainty as from insecurity and lack of experience. For a start, he had never been on a train over any distance, never even been out of his home county. Clutching his holdall, he felt conspicuous and very alone, as he stood on Warminster station, while everyone jostled round him, all apparently knowing exactly where to go. Following the crowd, he found himself relieved of his ticket, and was propelled out on to the street.

'Excuse me.' He cornered a porter who had just deposited baggage by a pony and trap. 'I am looking for St Boniface Missionary Training College.'

The porter looked at him carefully, eyeing the young man up and down. 'Mission House – down road into town, turn right, then right again into Church Street. Ask in town, lad, everyone knows it.' And with that the porter was gone on another errand.

Scarcely noticing that he was obviously still taken to be a boy rather than a man, Harry set off down the road, with a determined look in his eye, and a nervous stomach. His sandwiches for the journey, so carefully prepared, remained half-eaten, in his bag. He was still amazed that he had come from Dorset in four hours, even acknowledging he had had to change at Westbury.

Suddenly he was brought back from his musings by a shout of 'mind yerself then' as a large cart of coal narrowly missed him, as it turned into the yard next to the coal office. Harry began to look around. There was a public weighbridge, and further on a large Post Office. He made a mental note for future needs. Here the road came to a junction, so he turned right as he had been told.

What a town! The wide street hummed with life. There were shops of every description, butchers, drapers, ironmongers, banks, more shops than Portland and Abbotsbury put together! The displays in the shop windows and on the pavements were enticing, but he knew they would not be for him for the next three years at least. He dodged perambulators, delivery boys and numerous dogs as he made his way through the town. Finally, he saw the sign for Church Street on the right.

It was immediately obvious where he should head. For, on the left was an enormous building, larger than anything else in the street. He looked up at it – four storeys high, in Victorian brick, crowned with turrets and high chimneys. It looked forbidding, as there was no door evident at the front. It seemed the way in was at the side, so Harry walked down the driveway, until he reached the rear of the building. The area behind the College was land-scaped with glorious lawns and herbaceous borders and behind this again were playing fields and a kitchen garden. It was all very grand, and he could scarcely believe it would be his home.

'Hello there!' A cheery soul came up, and before he realized, had taken his hand firmly and shaken it. 'New man, then? Welcome! Which one are you?'

'Harry Norman, sir.'

'Oh, the Dorset man – good, good!' This was followed by a hearty pat on the back.

'I'm on my way down to the Minster, but you will find someone to help you. Main entrance is there.' And with that he was gone, hurrying down the drive, leaving Harry a few feet short of the main door.

As he walked to it, he could see inscribed in stone above the entrance, 'God forbid that I should glory, save in the cross of our Lord, Jesus Christ'. 'Galatians 6,' thought Harry automatically. He remembered from way back looking at the inscription over another door on another first day. 'You can read that Harry,' he could hear his mother saying. Suddenly his confidence left him, and he wondered what he, a nineteen-year-old semi-trained wheelwright, was doing out of his depth in a place like this. Not for the first or last time, he steeled himself, remembering the Mission Hall in Weymouth, Mr Fairbairn, Lord Ilchester and the rest, adjusted his tie, cleared his throat and rang the bell.

Within the first few hours, Harry realized that he was among the youngest there. No one was allowed to train until they were eighteen. Most, like him, were from fairly modest backgrounds, but by no means all local. They had come from nearly anywhere in Britain. Some regional accents were quite unclear to him. Eventually he was shown to his room. Unpacking did not take long, and he put his Bible and Confirmation Prayer Book by his bed, and carefully unwrapped Sam's little cross, and put it on the window sill. Out of the window, high up, he could just see the top of a large church – evidently the Minster.

The new students were asked to gather to meet the College staff. Harry nervously glanced at the rest, as they did him, with shy smiles and stilted conversations about journeys and background. Eventually they sat down, and the staff, resplendent in gowns, went to the front of the room.

'Good afternoon, gentlemen,' said the first man, of mature years, and very imposing. 'I am Sir James Philipps, and I am the Warden of the College. I should like to welcome every one of you as new students. Your time here is very precious, and it is hoped each of you will achieve the examination preliminary to Holy Orders. The training is demanding, but with diligence and application, you may all achieve your aim.'

Sir James began to pace to and fro, sticking his thumbs in the breast of his gown, in the teacher's mode. 'Let me tell you something of the College. As vicar in charge of the Minster of St Denys, down the road, I was able, some twenty-seven years ago, to purchase this building, with the help of public donation from the good people of the area, and a gift from the diocese of Salisbury. It was then called the Mission House – most people in the town still call it so. Since then we have added an orphanage opposite, and I hope to start a College to train women for the mission field as well. I shall see you all later, as I conduct some of the theological teaching. At present, I am afraid, you will find that the parish church of St Denys – the Minster – is in confusion – as we are in the throes of restoration.'

'Not again!' thought Harry. He remembered well the noise, dust and rubble of structural overhauls in Abbotsbury.

The next speaker was the Subwarden, Sidney Boulter, who Harry recognized as the man who had welcomed him so heartily in the garden. Boulter beamed at the assembled group, catching Harry's eye. He began to speak of the practicalities of the future life in College. Harry warmed to him immediately. He was a definite man, sure of what he wanted. 'Sometimes,' he said, 'I am accused of being dogmatic. But you must learn to get to the heart of the issue when talking to people. Talk to them, not at them. My maxim is "Do little preaching, but much teaching". Think about it – you will find it works!'

Finally, the new Principal was introduced. John Welsh had joined St Boniface about a year previously. Numbers in the tiny College had dwindled to just seven – below the twelve needed for viability. During Harry's three years, he would see the complement rise to thirty, and the College buzz with overcrowded activity. 'I have plans that could see the numbers rise to fifty' said Welsh enthusiastically, while the new entrants listened, faintly incredulous. This man had big ideas for the little College. Welsh's dream was realized, but Harry would never see it, for the heyday of the College was fifteen or twenty years away.

The new students soon settled down to a strict regime of study the like of which few had experienced before. The days were filled with Hebrew, Latin and Greek, mathematics and English (literature for some reason!) and the rudiments of theology. Whenever their brains were overloaded, they had training in practical skills – gardening, printing, bookbinding and carpentry. Harry was, naturally, quite at home in the joinery shop, already having plenty of experience with wood. The printing workshop was a new area for him to master, with machinery, inks and metal blocks, which challenged and fascinated him. He would return from an afternoon in the workshop, covered in ink, but clutching printed evidence of his new skill – this could be a useful thing to know about!

One afternoon, dirty and tired, when he was returning to the main house to clean up before supper, and the mountain of Latin homework he had to do, he heard someone call his name. It was Mr Boulter, the Subwarden, and Harry hurried across the lawn to join him.

'Norman, just the man. I've been looking for you. I need your help.'

'Me sir? How?'

'You seem to know a fair bit of carpentry from your Abbotsbury days, and I was wondering whether you would become superintendent of the joinery workshop? You could help to teach the other men. They might appreciate your help, being a similar age. You would also be responsible for the shop – the tools and supplies – that sort of thing. What do you say?'

'Well – I could. But could I do it with my other studies?'

'It is almost expected,' replied Boulter. 'Most men take on some extra responsibility in a workshop, in the chapel or the house. Think of it as a service to our little community. It would be good training.'

There was little option, but in fact for Harry it was an enjoyable chore which he took on willingly. The small wooden hut had benches round the walls, enough space for at least ten men to work. It was larger than the wheelwright's shop back home, but similar in many respects. The smells, the tools and the noises took him back to his early days at Abbotsbury, and he began painstakingly to teach his fellow students as he had been taught, by experience and continual practice.

Harry was, in fact, in his element, and had to curtail his enthusiasms. Nevertheless, he could not resist the chance to design and build something himself. He spoke frequently to the Subwarden about the needs of the workshop, and one day made a suggestion. 'Perhaps we could help the men by making something of practical use for the College, not just useless exercises.'

'Such as?' Boulter knew Harry's propensity for good ideas.

'We need a sports pavilion. There is nowhere to change, rest or keep the equipment on the sports field. Look, I've done these drawings.' He pulled sheets of paper from his pocket, detailed drawings to scale, with rough estimates of costings. 'Twould not be hard, and the cost is as low as I can get it. How say you, sir?'

Boulter scratched his head and smiled. He liked the boy, he liked him very much. He was honest, open and above all, positive. However, his ideas were not always matched by concerns of financial viability. 'Hold on, hold on.' He made damping down signs with his hands. 'You move too fast. We have no money for this, Harry. It's a good idea, but – your studies must come first. Leave it with me. I'll do what I can.'

Time passed and Harry continued doing well at his studies. After five and a half days spent each week in study, there was little enough time left to think of his plans for the pavilion. Sundays were probably the busiest day of the week, for apart from attending services in the Minster, each student was sent off to a local parish to help with pastoral work. Each dashed in a different direction on those busy days, meeting, exhausted on Sunday evening, before starting the round again on Monday.

It was to be weeks before Harry heard about the pavilion. In fact it was the day of Mr Boulter's great announcement. At the end of chapel that morning, before lectures began, the news was given out that Mr Boulter was engaged to be married. A cheer went up. The men knew, inevitably, of the links between Mr Boulter and Mary, the daughter of the Headmaster of the town Grammar School. They liked Boulter, and were genuinely pleased for him. As they filed out, shaking his hand and murmuring congratulations, Harry was on duty collecting hymn books. The rest had gone.

'Thank you for your help, Harry,' said Boulter.

'A pleasure,' grinned Harry as usual. 'Sir, may I add my congratulations? 'Tis a fine piece of news.'

'Thank you again. I am indeed a fortunate man. Next year I am to leave for parish work, so we will set up a home of our own, Mary and I. We are likely to go to Dorchester, so we may meet you away from College. Would you like that?'

'Oh yes, but I need to be allocated to a parish at weekends and some vacations.'

'You could come to us, if we are in Dorchester,' suggested Boulter. 'I expect there would be room in the vicarage.'

'If you are going, sir' ventured Harry, 'will you be able to inquire about the Pavilion beforehand?'

'I almost forgot.' Boulter slapped his forehead. 'Welsh has agreed. I cannot think why, for we have no finance for it – but go ahead, go ahead man,' and with that, he was off, leaving a very happy student clutching the pile of hymn books.

Whatever spare time Harry had was spent on the pavilion. To

an extent he was helped by the others, but some of the more complex tasks fell to him. The ground had to be prepared, and a firm base laid, before any evidence of a building showed itself. It was a small affair, with a felt roof, but it stood, and was useful, for almost a hundred years. Mr Welsh often came to inspect Harry's handiwork as it rose, for he was himself a keen foot-baller, and turned out regularly for a game with the students despite the difference in their ages.

'Coming on well', he commented, as he walked round it and patted the timbers. 'I hope it'll be ready for the new term, as numbers will be up again. We will make good use of it.'

''Twill, I hope. But it needs a coat or two of paint and some varnish.' Harry stood up rubbing an aching back. 'It's a small room, but will last well, and 'tis something I can do for College, which has done so much for me. Wi' my examination over I may have to leave the completion to others, and I must think o' what I do next, sir.'

'Come to see me later, in my study,' Welsh said. 'We have some ideas for your future, but you will want a few years in a parish in England before deciding whether to serve at home or abroad. I will discuss it with you this evening.'

As Harry watched Mr Welsh stride back to his study across the playing field, he could not avoid thinking that he had actually already made up his mind about what he wanted, and was convinced, as he had been years earlier, that he was meant to serve abroad. The sooner he could get there, the better he would like it. Never mind about 'a few years in a parish in England'. As he put his tools away and prepared for his duties waiting at table that night, he wondered whether he would be able to convince Mr Welsh.

That evening he knocked on the door of the Principal's study with some trepidation.

'Come in Norman.' It was to be a formal discussion, he could tell. 'Sit down.' Welsh shuffled some papers. 'Now, your future.' He looked directly into Harry's eyes. 'You know it depends on your examination results, I expect. I can tell you now that you have passed, second class. In three years that is quite some feat — well done.'

43

Harry blushed, and felt very relieved. Welsh continued. 'I can tell the Earl's agent that his assessment of you has been proved correct, and his investment of £30 a year has borne good fruit. Now – have you thought of your future?'

'Yes, and I would like to go abroad. I am sure I am meant for the Empire somewhere, not just for work at home.' Harry hesitated. 'And as soon as possible, for there is no advantage in waiting.'

'You're not trained yet, young man.' Welsh looked serious. 'If you mean to go abroad, and that may not be the service God intends, you must have some real experience in parishes, not just your Sundays here. We have some ideas, Norman. Welsh sat down and bent forward. 'We would like you to stay on a term or two more – now wait' – as Harry mouthed a 'but', 'we need your help in the workshop still, and what's more we want you to be senior student. You will be invaluable to the new men. You're still only twenty-two, you are very young. When the winter's over, we will try to arrange for you to get some medical training, perhaps in a hospital in London, before you embark wherever you are needed.'

Silence followed. Harry was bitterly disappointed at what he considered to be unnecessary delay. Welsh continued. 'It won't be too bad. Time will go fast. Mr Boulter has written to me, asking if you can help him in Dorchester at weekends and vacations, so you will be well used, and it's ideally situated so close to your parent's place. Now, think of it as an advantage. Some men don't get the chance to have extra training. You know, half of our men never even reach Holy Orders. This way you will improve your chances and be more employable. Anyway there's always the pavilion to finish.' Welsh raised his eyebrows meaningfully.

Harry managed a rueful smile. 'I must own I didn't think o' staying on, but if I must, I will. I'm glad I haven't let Mr Fairbairn down. I can write and say I have passed.'

'Good man. Accept your position, and use it well. Off you go, now. I can hear the bell for Compline.' And the interview was at an end.

Harry stayed at College until the spring of the next year, 1891. He travelled as often as he could to Dorchester, to the village of

Fordington, an ancient and poor parish to the east of the town. Sidney and Mary welcomed him, and gave him jobs in the parish as needed. He visited the elderly and sick, helped in the Sunday School, and accompanied Sidney on his long trudging walks round the village. He actually learned a lot there, the problems and disappointments of the reality of parish work, and the demands to be made on a parish priest. He admitted Welsh had probably been right to make him wait! The wise, experienced man knew Harry's worth could be doubled by giving him a good grounding before he left Britain.

In the spring, Welsh wrote to numerous London hospitals, to try to obtain a training place for Harry, but with no success. He had to admit defeat, and looked a little closer to home. So many hospitals in the west country were no more than cottage hospitals, unused to the types of surgery and care Harry would need to know. In desperation, he wrote to Salisbury Infirmary, which he knew about from his trips to the cathedral town. Eventually a reply came from Dr Coates, who had put his application to the General Management Committee. It had been accepted. Could Mr Norman start as soon as possible?

'Pack your bags, Norman – you're off to Salisbury at the weekend,' was his greeting to Harry that morning. At that exact moment, Harry was hurrying to the workshop, to set up exercises for first year students.

'Salisbury? So soon? I can't go – I have the students, the pavilion.'

'No matter. Someone else will have to take it on. I have had enough trouble getting the position, so we cannot afford to turn it aside,' Welsh replied.

'Well, if 'tis God's will, I will go gladly' Harry said, his mind racing over all the ends he had to tie before he could leave with a clear conscience.

Somehow, over the three years he had acquired an amazing amount of luggage, books, notes, an extra suit, more tools, an academic gown. In the end he bought a second-hand suitcase which he filled with ease, and staggered to the main door with suitcase and holdall. It seemed a mixture of no time at all, and a very distant day, when he had first entered that front door. Then he had been nothing but a country apprentice. Now, with luck, he was within months of travelling abroad, and his admission to the priesthood. He felt no different, but John Welsh saw the change in him. As he wished Harry 'God speed' on the steps, he was certain that he was looking at a potential missionary, and a fine young man.

'Let me know how you get on.' His request was in earnest. 'Anyway, we will see you again, for you must return to sort out your applications when the time comes. We will miss your cheery face, Harry. The workshop must fall to another, I hope they will keep it as well as you did. Come now, let me help you with the bags – I have taken the liberty of bringing the trap round – you can't heave that all the way to the station!'

And so Harry left St Boniface. He smiled as, on reaching the station, he saw the same porter he remembered from his first day, still loading and unloading vehicles. 'Dear old Warminster' he thought, as the train pulled away.

Salisbury was entirely a different experience. The city, the first he had ever visited, was huge and sophisticated. Harry wandered the streets in naive amazement. The shops, a theatre, and dominating all, literally, the cathedral, with its gigantic spire and splendid setting, all spoke to him of a wider world. There seemed to be churches everywhere, of all denominations, all calling to the people of the town. It was very confusing. That evening he was quite glad to scurry back to the little room which had been allocated to him, and prepare himself for the first day of hospital life.

Nothing, in fact, could prepare him. He had no idea of large hospitals, and swallowed hard when he saw the enormous brick building.

'General Infirmary, supported by Voluntary Subscriptions 1767' he read. He crossed the street, and looked at the hospital more closely through the railings. People were being set down by the front door, and occasionally a gift was brought, some meat or vegetables. The hospital took what it could get! He walked to the front door and enquired for the chaplain at the little lodge window. As he waited, the undeniable hospital smells met his nostrils; the smell of disease, of carbolic, and horribly of cooking cabbage, wafted along the corridors.

'Come this way please,' he was beckoned.

At the end of the corridor, up stairs, along another corridor, past nurses seemingly calm, past the entrance to a ward and the sound of men groaning, trays, trolleys, a girl scrubbing the floor. Finally he was ushered into Mr Woodall's tiny office.

The man he met was neat, precise and quiet. He was a listener, he had to be, considering the job he had. 'Norman? Good to meet you. I trust you are well settled in. Come and sit down.'

Harry sat nervously on the edge of a hard chair. 'Good day sir. Thank you. I am perfectly settled, but from what I have seen so far, I have a great deal to learn here.'

'Hm! That's true, you will learn a lot, both about life, and death. Have you experienced death ever, Norman?'

'No, sir.'

'Sadly that is a great part of our work.' Woodall surveyed the floor morosely, shaking his head. 'There is Russian influenza about at present, and the wards are full to overflowing. I have also just heard one nurse has contracted typhoid, so we have plenty of trouble on our hands. The staff are working desperately to stop contagion spreading, but its a battle. Come, let's waste no time, and I'll show you round.'

Woodall jumped up, rather taking Harry by surprise, and they set off on a whistlestop tour, Woodall pointing out theatre, sluices, Matron's office, dispensary, chapel, like bullets out of a gun, as they hurried past.

'You will be learning some surgery here, so you must be kitted out with overalls and mask. People either love theatre or hate it. I hope you are not prone to fainting. Accident Ward is where you will do most of the work, but there are seven others besides, and you will help in all of them. There are only about two dozen nurses and nine of those are probationers, so any extra pair of hands, even yours, will be useful. Just beware Matron. I do.' – and he winked!

'Some days you will be with me, doing ward services and chapel duty – not to mention running the Nurses Fellowship – but I would like you also to help me in the local Church of England

Sunday School along the road. I am teaching religion there a little, and the youngsters need some handling. We will settle on a routine for you in due course.'

By the end of the morning Harry was physically exhausted by Woodall's breakneck pace, and his head was spinning. This was going to be some six months, if he ever survived it – but at least it was useful and different. He was determined to reap the benefit of it.

He was more accurate than he had dared suspect, and by the end of the first week he collapsed in a heap, wondering how he would ever cope. Anatomy, physiology, surgery, pharmaceutics, there was so much of it. Secretly he wondered how he would cope with the blood and stench, the trauma of death, and the anguish of pain. Mercifully he did, and his stamina increased with the weeks as he learned the basics of anaesthetics, surgery, first aid and diagnosis. He worked for nothing but his keep, – but that was no hardship, for he had not been paid for years! The nurses earned only £25 – £30 a year, about the same as the cost of keeping him at Warminster. The poor laundresses, porters, cooks and maids commanded only half that!

One way and another Harry worked almost full-time in the hospital. If he were not under orders from the doctors or matron, Mr Woodall wanted him to do something. He just had to get back to Warminster, or write to find out whether he would be likely to get a reference for missionary work at the end of six months. Secretly he feared that he would be required to spend time in a local parish first, but he wrote to Mr Welsh nevertheless.

About a week later he received the reply, and rushed to the chaplain's office, as soon as he had a moment.

'Sir, I have had a letter from the College, to say they will put my name forward to the Society for the Propagation of the Gospel in foreign parts. If all goes well, I shall leave for somewhere just a few weeks after I complete here. I can't believe it – 'Tis better than I'd hoped.'

'That's good news, Norman. You have worked hard for it – do you know where you will go? Eh?'

'They say they may look at China,' said Harry, running his eye down the letter. 'Yes – possibly China. But there's nothing definite yet. Oh, 'tis wonderful news!' Harry was off on to clouds of reveries, until the reality of it all occurred to him. He would need to write a formal application, collect references, and organise some finance for his passage. Apart from anything else, he needed to check precisely where China was. He had assumed he would go to some place within the Empire, China had never entered his head.

By the end of August, Mr Welsh back at the College had requested an application form from London. The whole business seemed to be back to front, for the Bishop in China had already been approached and was in theory prepared to accept Harry. Welsh immediately wrote to Harry, enclosing the form, which looked all too disappointingly brief. Welsh had told him to remember to include himself and Sir James Philipps among his referees. Harry agonized over the others. Perhaps Mr Woodall, and Mr Fairbairn – also dear Mr Boulter, would vouch for him? He went along to ask Mr Woodall's advice.

'I would be delighted to propose you, Norman,' said Woodall immediately. 'I rather assumed you would ask. You know I think very well of you. Just sorry to lose you so soon. I suspect the Nurses Fellowship will be too – you know the membership has risen significantly recently – I don't know what you've done with them!' He looked at Harry questioningly, but Harry knew there was no need to explain himself.

'I shall miss you too,' he replied, 'though I didn't think I would be saying that a few months back! Do you think I can approach Boulter and Fairbairn now for references?'

'You must. They have been significant in your training.' Woodall was adamant.

'Right. I will contact them straight away. I have had a photograph done in the studio, in my gown, and have had copies taken off, and I meant to send them one each anyway. 'Tis not a bad likeness. Mother is pleased as punch with hers, and has it framed in the parlour! I only hope Mr Fairbairn can recognize me after this time.'

That evening Harry wrote to Boulter and Fairbairn in Dorset, to get their permission to be given as referees, and enclosed copies of his graduation portrait. He then turned his mind to the actual application form, which looked deceptively simple. There was very little opportunity in such a limited space to create any sort of impression. Name, date of birth, baptism, confirmation and education – no problems there. Equally easy was it to state he was single, healthy, unencumbered by debt, but equally not in receipt of a private income. Harry stopped at that point.

'What considerations have led you to offer your services to the church in foreign parts?' Somehow the question was simple, but at the same time terribly difficult to answer. Whatever form of words he thought of, sounded wrong – too obsequious or too pompous. He racked his brains, and finally opted for the direct approach. A practical man, he gave a simple answer. He dipped his pen in the ink and wrote, 'Love for mission work'. It was a relief to get it down on paper. Everything looked neat and correct so far. All that remained was to put the names of his referees, and the form that he had longed to write could at last be posted.

By the end of the week all was complete. His six months were finished at Salisbury, and nomadically he packed his bags yet again. Farewells were becoming commonplace, to the school-boys, the doctors, nurses, even some patients. The staff available gathered to say goodbye, and one young nurse was pushed forward with a parcel for him. They had all clubbed together out of their meagre earnings to help kit him out for China. Lost for words, for once, Harry blushed and mumbled his thanks, and promised to remember them. He left the Infirmary with happy memories and gratitude to the chaplain and staff.

There was nothing left for it but to travel back to Portland to await developments. There was nowhere else to go. His homes in Abbotsbury, Warminster and now Salisbury, had gone. The by now worldly young man slipped back on to the island of his childhood once more, up the hill and in through the back door of his childhood home, for what was to be the last time, if he only knew it. For the next few short weeks he would return to boyish life with no responsibilities.

The headquarters of the SPG in late September was scarcely conducive to hard work. Many staff had been on vacation, and were only just returning to work at anything like full speed. After a heavier lunch than normal, the Secretary, Mr Sketchley, looked with resignation at the pile of papers on his desk, placed there days, if not weeks ago. The pleas for money could be put aside – begging letters were not his forte – when would these missionaries learn that the Society was not made of money! Perhaps he could manage a little light reading, an application or two just fitted the bill. He picked up the papers with regard to an H. V. Norman, from Warminster. The references were all there, and had been waiting for some time. He thumbed through them:-

From Sir James Philipps, well known to the Society, his usual terse comment: 'He has the qualities required, piety, zeal, discretion, aptness to teach, a cheerful temper and active bodily habits!' That seemed all right. In addition he had written, 'I have a very high opinion of him. I think he will make an excellent missionary.' Good news indeed. Sketchley sifted through the papers. Apparently this one was earmarked for North China, under Bishop Scott.

He was about to investigate further, when the Chairman of the Society entered the room.

'Afternoon, Sketchley, anything I should know of?'

'Not really, Thornton. Just another application come in. It looks quite promising. The references are good as far as I have gone. A man apparently already allocated to Charles Scott.'

'Trust Charles,' replied the Chairman. 'Constantly bothering me for more men, or if not men, he's after money. Another young man will pacify him for a while.'

He sat down in the leather armchair, as if for the afternoon, stretched out his legs and crossed his arms, 'Read me the references for the chap.'

'Right. This one is Harry Vine Norman. Interesting situation – carpenter I think, a tradesman. Been sponsored by the Ilchester Estate, so someone thinks highly of him. Already got his prelim., and apparently Philipps thinks well of him.'

'Hm!' Thornton acknowledged the merit, agreeably impressed.

Sketchley continued to read silently, then, 'Here's a reference from a parish priest in Dorset: "From what I know of Mr Harry

51

Norman, and his career at College, I believe the Church of England will have a very earnest and single hearted worker" – seems all right as well.'

Another silence followed, interspersed with a few chuckles and tuttings.

'Well?' Thornton could contain himself no longer. 'What's so funny now?'

'Sidney Boulter – the ex-Subwarden at St Boniface. Written his reference on the chap, from holiday at Nailsea – listen to this – "May I ask you to enter my name for a continental summer chaplaincy for next June (1892) if you think well: I should prefer Switzerland or a German-speaking country if possible." Darned cheek.'

Thornton snorted. 'Did he manage to say anything about this Norman, then?'

'Yes, shall I read it?' As there was no answer, Sketchley read on, 'As I have known H. V. Norman well during the greater part of the time he was at St Boniface I am glad to answer your questions. He spent his Sundays with me during his vacations, and I have occasionally looked over his papers among others sent me from St Boniface. I have a high opinion of his character. In simplicity, truth, self-restraint and perseverance, I believe him to be really in earnest in his desire to be a missionary. His conduct has always struck me as being very satisfactory – without pretending to be a gentleman, he has such natural refinement and tact as to make him a pleasant social companion and to qualify him for any society.

He has never, so far as I could see, fallen into the silly mistake of so many students, and formed undesirable acquaintance or ties with persons of the other sex.'

'Thank God for that,' came the comment from the chair.

'Hear, hear! One thing less to worry about. Shall I go on?'

'Please do; forgive me, Sketchley.'

'His abilities are somewhat remarkable. His knowledge of Greek, Latin and Hebrew is far more sound than his English would lead me to expect.' 'Dorset dialect, I expect,' commented Sketchley. He then continued, '... and his theological work is good. Indeed for a carpenter's apprentice – and he is a good carpenter – to pass the exam "Preliminary to Holy Orders" in the 2nd class, within about three years, speaks for itself.

I think him, and I speak as the late Subwarden of a Missionary College, eminently qualified to make a good missionary. He helped me in my work in a populous poor parish, and I found him always ready to take up and do, to the best of his power, whatever piece of work I gave him. In teaching rough lads or reading to old women, he equally gained their interest and affection. I feel that he is pious, zealous, sober and discreet, and apt to teach, while I have found him to be of cheerful temper, and have been witness to his active bodily habits, his power of physical labour as a carpenter, and of making long walks.

I know of no reason against such an appointment being offered him: I know him to be poor, but I believe him to be not ashamed of it, and to pay his way. He is still, I believe, unmarried, and he has never given me any reason to think him engaged. I may add that he was the first student supported by our Dorset Missionary Studentship Association, and that I think all the members are satisfied and encouraged by him.'

'Good reference.' Thornton shuffled in his chair. 'Scott will be pleased with a practical builder. Any more references, or is that it?'

'Just one, from the Chaplain at Salisbury Infirmary. Norman seems to have done some medical training there. Darned small handwriting.' He peered closely at the neat hand and read slowly, bending to the light.

'I beg to say that I have been intimately acquainted with him for five months, during which time he has been a medical student in the Infirmary where I am Chaplain. I have formed the highest opinion of his character and conduct generally, and have every reason to believe what I have twice heard from different sources, that he is one of the best men sent out from Warminster. As he has helped a great deal, both in my ward and Chapel Services, and has also catechized for me on Sunday afternoon in a large school of which I am Chaplain, I am able to testify as to his abilities and aptness to teach, and there is nothing in your questions which I cannot most conscientiously answer in his favour.'

'Can't be bettered!' Thornton slapped the chair arm. 'Arrange for him to see me sometime. Where are we – end of September – well sometime shortly in October. Can you arrange it, Sketchley?'

'Certainly, I will write to him.' Sketchley sounded efficient, and rustled the papers, knocking them into shape with his hand. But significantly, the papers went back on to the pile from whence they came.

Harry, meanwhile waited in Portland. He had saved very little money, and urgently needed every penny to buy his equipment for China. He knew he could not afford to sit around idly. Neither his family, nor Bishop Scott could afford that. He helped where he could, enjoying family life, his little (and by now not so little) brothers. He fished, he helped Pa on the cart, he helped round the house. There was little opportunity for contemplation. There was always enough time to watch for the postman, just in case.

One morning a letter did come for him, and he cut it open, eagerly. ''Tis from Leeds, from Bishop Scott's brother who does all his arranging in England. It can't be, but he says I'm to sail on 15 October.' He looked in horror at his mother. 'Mother, 'tis only eleven days away, and I have no money for the passage, nor have I been interviewed by the SPG. Why have they not called for me – whatever are they thinking of?'

'Perhaps you should write to them again, son,' suggested Margaret.

'Course I should!' Harry raised his voice in anger, not at his mother, but at the wretched Society. 'Sorry mother, 'tis me, I'm all strung up wi' waiting. 'Tis too bad they keep a man hanging on like this. How can I plan when I don't know if I can take the sailing? 'Tis all very well for those who sit in an office and go nowhere.'

Harry sat down to compose himself, his head in his hands. Margaret put her hand on his shoulder to steady him. ''Twill work out for the best, son,' she said quietly. 'They know what they're doing, be sure. Now calm down and write to the men in London.'

After a few grunts and comments under his breath, Harry controlled himself sufficiently and wrote, 'Dear Sir, Have I to be examined by the SPG? If so, I have heard nothing from you about it. I filled up a form, as you remember. I have to sail on 15th, and I am anxious as I have not heard anything about Cannings Fund, to which I applied for passage money. I do not know whether it will be paid from Cannings Fund or the SPG. If you could tell me what to do, I should be grateful. Cambridge Local Exam – I have passed twice (Second class). Yours sincerely, H. V. Norman.'

It was abrupt and almost a scribbled shorthand, but the post would not wait. Harry fairly ran up the hill to catch the postman. Too bad that the submissive student mask had slipped, to expose the fury of urgency met by a brick wall. There was nothing else to be done but to try to move the hierarchy that had his future in its hand.

The letter was sufficient to evince a reply, but it was simply a stalling action, saying nothing. Harry threw it in the ashcan and out came the pen again,

'Thank you for your letter of information. I have had, as yet, no letter asking me to come to London. Must sail on 15th. Passage taken – sailing on P. & O. boat *(Ballaarat)*. Can you arrange for one member of Board to see me on *Tuesday 13th*. I have just heard from Cannings Fund, grant given by them amounts to £35. According to Canon Scott (Bishop Scott's Commissary) I need nearly £80. Will SPG help toward this? If you can arrange for Tuesday October 13th, it will be a cause of great delight to me, as I have to go to Leeds on day previous, and coming back I can call and see SPG Board. I am, dear Sir, Yours sincerely, H. V. Norman.'

His mother read it. 'A bit angry in tone, Harry. You may not do yourself good by so speaking. What is all this about Leeds anyway? I thought you were here till the 15th?'

'I have to see Bishop Scott's brother in Leeds, mother. He needs to have the papers filled in, and to tell me of the arrangements for when I reach China. I can't afford to visit Leeds and then go to London separately. I shall go next weekend, depending when they say.'

Margaret was deflated, robbed of her last few days with her whole family together until she knew not when. 'Oh Harry, I shall miss you so, and so far away, and so soon, so soon.'

'Don't fret mother.' Harry hugged his mother. 'Before you

know where you are I shall be back on furlough, with lots of tales to tell. There might even be a bedroom free for me by then.' And they laughed, though silence followed.

Back in London, something finally stirred at the SPG. As it chanced on the same day that Harry wrote his second letter, Wednesday 7th, Mr Thornton picked up his pen to reply to a note from Sketchley.

'My dear Sketchley, I shall be very pleased to "interview" Mr Norman. On Friday I shall be home between 10 and 11. I am engaged at 11, but I shall be back by 12, and remain till 1.30. On Saturday I expect to be home all the morning. I am afraid I could not arrange for an afternoon visit. On Monday I shall most likely be in from 10.30 to 1. Very sincerely yours.'

When Harry received the news, he was at once relieved and disappointed. He had to be in Leeds on the Monday, and if he had to see Mr Thornton on the Saturday, he would have to leave Portland on the Friday, via London and Leeds for embarkation the following Thursday. Another letter followed. Finally the interview was arranged for Tuesday. The effort in just organizing dates had been phenomenal. To make matters worse, the family had been buzzing round him, asking questions, suggesting final visits to numerous friends and relatives, including his grand-parents in Portesham. He was even being measured for gloves and socks by his ever practical aunt!

What he wanted was just what he was not to get – time on his own to prepare and contemplate. The day before he was due to leave, he escaped the house and walked alone out to the cliffs, to sit on the rocks and watch the breakers roll in. Memories overwhelmed him, the *Avalanche*, the fishermen, the children's games on the beach. He looked out to sea, across the bay, where he could almost make out Abbotsbury. He could hear Mr Stoodley and Sam as if they stood right by him, could almost smell the wood. How on earth had he got from there to where he was now bound, if not by God's plan? His friends from school were in trades locally, some even married. Life was mapped out ahead of them, clear and straight.

'Oh God, have I done right?' He scarcely knew if he spoke or thought it. 'How can I know if you want me so far away? All I know is carpentry, so many people can do that. Won't I be as useful here, at home?'

There was no reply, but in the cold wind of evening he saw Mr Fairbairn, Boulter, Welsh and Chaplain Woodall, and he knew that they had perhaps more confidence than he had. If he was meant to go, he would get there, he thought. With that he said a mental farewell to the beach and hurried home for his last evening with the family.

Inevitably the cart was called into service next morning. Nothing could stop father from seeing Harry off in style. He only had to be taken to the bottom of the hill, where Portland's railway station awaited them. The whole family went, mother and father with Harry on the cart, and the boys running and whooping alongside. The luggage had to be seen to be believed, as the cases were unloaded on to the platform.

'Mother, I must carry that all to Leeds and back.' Harry laughed, as he saw umpteen cases and bags. 'I can't take it all. Whatever have you got in there?'

''Tis your fault for having so many books to go. There's only a few extras,' shrugged Margaret. 'Some food for the journey and warm things for winter. You will need all you can carry if it is as cold as they say out there.'

'Send us a letter, send us a letter with a China stamp,' called the youngest, Albert, jumping up and down.

'And some Chinese writing, so I can show 'em in school.' This was George, already fascinated by the Greek letters Harry had shown him, and determined that he would show off in class.

Pa cursed the boys lightheartedly as he eventually handed up the luggage to Harry in the carriage.

The train was ready, and the guard impatient to close the doors by now. Harry jumped down to say goodbye.

'Bye mother, dear. Take care. I'll remember to write I promise, probably before I even leave port.'

Margaret couldn't speak, but buried her face in her son's chest and held him tight. 'Oh Harry,' she mouthed, through her tears.

'Bye father.' Josiah just nodded and waved him into the train. 'Thanks for ... for ... being the best Pa I could have had!'

There was no time for reply, for with a lurch the train started, and a puff of steam snorted up from the wheels, for a second obscuring Harry from the family on the platform. When they saw him again, he was a silent waving figure, receding through the smoke, getting ever smaller, as he was taken from them.

The next few days went past in a whirl. The mere sight of a mainline station in London was strangeness enough, but it was compounded by the trauma of trying to cross the metropolis and link with a connection to Leeds, encumbered by what Harry had come to realize was his total worldly goods. He thought, standing on the platform, waiting for the Leeds train, that he was like a creature in limbo. He had given up his trade, his security, his home for something he had never seen, and even worse, he was totally dependent on others to get him there.

At least one of those others managed very quickly to put his mind at rest. John Scott, the older brother of his future Bishop, Charles Scott, was a master of practical common sense. He arranged for Harry to stay overnight in Leeds, and gave him a mound of information. A man after his own heart, he had had the same problems as Harry, trying to inject some urgency into the SPG.

'I know,' he rejoined, after Harry had told him the hair-raising details of his problems. 'Look, this is what I wrote to Mr Tucker, who manages the finances in London. They are as slow with me as you, if it consoles you at all.'

Harry read the letter. 'H. V. Norman of Warminster is sailing next week for China. Cannings Fund have voted him £35 towards passage. As he has passed SPG for one of their staff in North China, will SPG grant him anything towards passage? Fare to Shanghai £50. Subsequent fare to Peking about £20 perhaps – rather up, but they always hand over anything they do not spend to the Bishop, who restores it to the fund or Society. I am yours faithfully, John Scott.'

'Don't worry,' said Scott, 'It's quite simple – no money, no missionary. They'll pay up, they have to, and they know it. They are just as close with money as they can be. It's always the same. Charles is driven to distraction by them. He is always begging for money, they have no idea of what the problems of missionaries are.'

'You think so? 'Tis Monday now, I only have till Thursday.' Harry had less faith than John Scott.

'You wait' – Scott was confident. 'The interview will be a formality. Charles is expecting you – few men would argue with that!'

He was right, the interview was a formality, even though his discussion with the Chairman put the fear of the Almighty into Harry. In fact, in the end he left Leeds, and saw Mr Thornton on the Tuesday. He waited outside his room afterwards, wondering if he had said the right things, and how on earth he could face the people at home if, at this eleventh hour, he was to be rejected. Eventually the double doors opened, and Thornton reappeared.

'Congratulations are in order, Norman. I see no reason why you should not be recommended, and have written accordingly to Scott in Leeds. Now you sail on Thursday, so we have organized your passage, and you should collect your tickets from the P. and O. Office. They are all fully paid, thanks to Cannings Fund in part.'

So John Scott had been right. The SPG in the end had paid what they knew they had to.

'This will cover your fare from Shanghai.' Thornton pressed a wallet of twenty sovereigns into Harry's hand. 'Whatever you don't need, you give to the Bishop on your arrival. And here's your letter of authority. Good Luck, and God be with you.'

Suddenly Thornton seemed to be gone. Having waited so long for everything to be finalized, at last it was, and Harry was left feeling slightly helpless. The sovereigns felt comfortingly real and practical, while reality felt increasingly like a fairy story. He looked down at the letter, the only proof he had that it was all truly happening.

The Board of Governors, appointed in accordance with the 19th byelaw of the Society, have inquired into the fitness and sufficiency of Mr Harry Vine Norman of Boniface Mission House, Warminster, for a missionary appointment; and they have agreed this day to recommend that Mr Norman be accepted by the Society for employment in missionary work in the diocese of North China.

Signed: R. Thornton (Chairman)
Dated: 13th October 1891

Staring made it no more real, but Harry couldn't help it. Something inside him did a double somersault for joy, and he left the building with a wide smile and a jaunty step, immune to the need to find lodging in the strange capital for two nights before he sailed.

By the time Thursday dawned, Harry had come down to earth with a bump. Utterly alone in London, he had taken himself on his one and only tour of the capital of the Empire, but while acknowledging its grandeur, he was not overly impressed by some of what he saw. The sheer size, noise and anonymous bustle contrasted with everything he knew and held dear. The very rich seemed to pass the very poor, no contact or regard between the two. He ended up almost looking forward to the intimacy and comparative peace of the boat.

Early on Thursday, he heaved his baggage on to the dockside in the Port of London. Nervously he felt in his jacket for the bundle of letters that he had been given, and the money from the SPG – more cash than he had ever before handled. It was all still safely there – he knew London to be a dangerous place, full of thieves and pickpockets. As he watched, trying to avoid porters, sailors and passengers, people were making tearful farewells, kissing and waving. Most of the vessels were travelling long distances, and he was not the only one to say goodbye to dear old England for years, before he could return.

Before he needed to ask, he saw SS *Ballaarat* for himself. That first sight amazed him. The *Avalanche* had been the largest passenger vessel he had ever known, but this far exceeded her. Built some nine years previously, he knew she had been described as 'remarkably good looking' – she was certainly that. She and her sister ship the SS *Parramatta* were built to take goods and emigrants to Australia, and she seemed to be loading both with some speed. Harry gazed at her twin tall funnels amidships, with sails fore and aft. Below, he could hear the stokers, as they prepared the engines in readiness for her to slip her moorings.

Having gone through the paper formalities, Harry set foot on the gangplank at last. He looked back. 'However many years will it be before I set foot back in England,' he wondered. 'It may be as many as ten years, and the family will have grown up. I shall be over thirty by then, and 'twill probably be the twentieth century!' He shook off the thoughts and turned back to the gangplank, and the rickety walk to his home for the next six weeks.

He settled himself in his cabin, along with the other 47 second-class passengers, and 160 enjoying first-class privileges. Cramped it certainly was, but no worse than it had been at home in later years. He would have to keep his belongings tidy and in neat order. His Bible and Prayer Book were put in his locker, and some of his clothes unpacked. He wondered how long it would be before he would be searching for his summer weight clothes again, as they travelled south.

Back on deck, he watched the loading in process. Crated manufactured goods were piled on the quay, and eventually lowered into the hold, to the shouts of dock workers and crew. Everything seemed at last to be stowed, and Harry removed his gaze to the families still on *terra firma* watching and waving. The gangplanks were being taken away, and the funnels began to belch black smoke, as the stokers powered the engines. Suddenly he felt slightly dizzy, as if everything had moved sideways. He held on to the rail, then suddenly realized that he was all right, the land had moved sideways in front of his very eyes. They were moving! Feeling a fool, he waved to the crowd below, though they had no idea who he was. It was an automatic reaction, a farewell to England.

The Royal Albert Dock and the Port of London slipped away into the autumn mist as, escorted by tugs, the *Ballaarat* headed out for the sea at Gravesend. Rather as an anticlimax there she stopped, while more passengers embarked, but only briefly, then finally out to sea, and away from land, and into chilly greyness.

Harry went round the ship, trying to find his way about, and investigate the public rooms and general layout, and after luncheon, he was back on deck again, just in case he was missing anything. One sailor was just finishing an obligatory swabbing down of the deck, as Harry picked his way past.

'Mind yer feet, Sir' he called, as Harry danced through the wet.

'Sea sickness will get to most of the passengers, begging yer pardon,' and he touched his cap.

Harry smiled and swallowed hard. He had felt perfectly all right until that point.

He looked back at the sailor, and on an impulse returned to him. 'Where would we be now, do you think?'

The sailor shrugged. 'Hard to tell. Sure to be past Pompey and the Isle of Wight – may be Bournemouth or Portland – but we're well out o' sight o' land.' Harry sighed, and concentrated his eyes on the skyline, but there was nothing.

'Ever been afloat 'afore?' The old salt eyed Harry with the jaundiced eye of one handling a novice who is going to ask a thousand questions.

'Only an odd fishing boat,' replied Harry. 'I have certainly never seen a ship like this. Cabins with their own iron bedsteads, and the dining saloon! The carvings and decorations are like a country house! I am told there will be performances given in the music room of an evening. 'Tis very grand.'

'Aye!' The sailor wrung out his cloth and slapped it in the bucket. 'She's got all the trimmings for sure. They've got refrigerated lockers below, and food can be kep' froze till wanted – not many ships have that. Mind you, they're a crafty lot at the Admiralty – she fits the needs of war too, so she can be turned into support in time of battle! If we get trouble, her'll be stripped of her finery as quick as that and pressed into service.' He picked up the bucket.

'Let's hope that will never be, please God,' said Harry. A cold chill came over him as he thought of the beautiful ship in the middle of battle, ready to take survivors or the injured to safety. Fatefully, he had no idea how prophetic the sailor's words were to be, and how *Ballaarat* would reappear in the story later. On a more mundane level, he would neither be aware of the wholesale asset stripping of her fine Italianate carvings that would go on when she finally came to the end of her life, and how it was said that pieces were painstakingly removed bit by bit, to adorn the homes of the P. and O. Directors!

As he walked on, he reached the purser's office, where letters were left for posting at the next port – he vowed to keep a regular consignment of letters to Warminster and Portland. There was a map showing their journey. The purser showed him their route – Gibraltar, Malta, Brindisi, Port Said, Aden and by mid-November, Columbo. When they eventually reached Australia, they were destined for places which meant little to him – Albany, Adelaide, Melbourne and finally Sydney. He had heard tell of the Tolpuddle Martyrs trip to Australia, but this was somewhat different!

As day succeeded day, friendships were struck up. Some people starting out for a new life in Australia were eager to find out all they could about conditions. Others were intent on business or government positions in the Empire. Very few were missionaries, but here and there they showed themselves, returning from furlough or sick leave. In vain Harry looked for a man returning to China. They seemed to be going everywhere else, but not a soul to China. Nevertheless, even if he could not get much advance knowledge of China, he could use his time profitably. The chaplain was delighted to have any help offered, and a young priest in training was a useful addition to the staff running services on board!

Harry was only too delighted to help, and Sunday evening service in the saloon became a regular feature of the voyage. For more secular entertainment there were games laid on, books to borrow from the small library, and ample opportunity to watch the myriads of strange goings on whenever they reached ports.

Harry sat one day on the deck, in as much shade as he could get, to write back home to his parents. 'Aden, Arabia' he wrote at the top, either to help his family, who may have been slightly at a loss as to where exactly Aden was, or to provide himself with a point of identity in an ever-moving world. How on earth could he explain the vastness of the ocean, the strange places he had seen from the ship, the perspective he was gradually developing of a greater world than Dorset? This was his third letter home, and the first that had required some explanation of a truly alien culture.

'Dear Father and Mother' – So far, so good. How could he get them to understand? 'A few more lines. Of course, you got my second letter from Brindisi in Italy. I posted it last Sunday, and you got it, I hope, a few days after. Brindisi is a very curious and dirty place, the people appear to be the same. We left that port about 1 or 2 o'clock on Monday morning. It was indeed a miserable Sunday there, everyone busy packing, and getting things ready to be off again. After we left Brindisi, we saw little save a few small islands, until we got to Port Said on the following Wednesday. There we saw some very curious sights. I did not go on shore, for we did not get into port before 12 o'clock midnight, and we left again the same night at 4 o'clock.'

He stopped and thought about that night, when, not being able to sleep for the heat and sounds of the crew, he had got up, and armed with a deck blanket, watched the dockside workers, listened to the strange eastern language, the gesticulations, the eastern smells and noises. Back to work, he bent to his letter again. 'The natives were very curious. Never did I hear such a noise as these people made. They were as thick as bees, and more like a lot of noisy rooks than human beings. You may imagine what they were like, when I tell you that in two hours they put 200 tons of coal on board of our boat! I remained on deck all night watching them, and other things. They are a savage lot of people!'

As he had hung over the guard rail, draped in his blanket, he wondered if the Chinese would be like these Arabs. There was consolation in watching the English crew from time to time, refreshingly familiar in their behaviour. But he knew from that first time he encountered men of other races, that he could not rely on trying to drum their habits out of them, to turn them into perfect English gentlemen. He was always genuinely fascinated by other cultures, and both mature and modern enough to respect them, while offering what he felt would help them.

There was only the one sheet of paper, and he had to write closely. 'After we left Port Said, we came at once into the Suez Canal. This canal is only wide enough for one steamer to pass through, except at what are called the Stations, where a steamer waits for another to pass. The canal is about 70 miles long. It took us over 30 hours to get through, for we are only allowed to go at 4 miles an hour through it. It is a curious place, quite a desert – on one side is Africa, and on the other Asia. When we got out of the canal, we came into the Red Sea. We saw a lot of mountains here.

It is the hottest part of the voyage, and a lot of the passengers are ill with the heat and the sea. Last night it was a bit rough. Until then, for a week past the sea has been like glass. I seem to stand the heat and sea fine. I enjoy myself awfully. Of course, the hot weather makes one feel very limp. My head is often like a wet rag dipped in water. The perspiration drops off my face in small streams. I have never seen anything like it before. Many of the ship's crew are ill with work and heat.

We have a great many amusements, but chiefly a kind of cricket to keep ourselves alive. I took the English church service on board here last night. It was fearfully hot in the saloon. The ship too was beginning to roll. But still we had a very nice service and a fair congregation.

We shall get to Ceylon next Monday or Tuesday. You will, God willing, get my next letter from there. I expect that it will be some time in coming.

Goodbye. Hoping all are quite well. With kindest love to all – Harry.'

He read through the tightly packed lines – it did not do his voyage justice, but it gave some impression of shipboard life. 'I enjoy myself awfully' – yes, that just about summed it up. Never one to let an opportunity slip by, Harry had denied himself the indulgences of heatstroke or *mal de mer*. 'Thank goodness,' he thought, 'I am a healthy mortal not laid up with every turn of the weather! The cricket and quoits are at least exercise, and I keep my brain going by writing the homilies for evensong. At least I have a captive congregation here!'

Apart from an occasional spat of bad weather, day followed day with unending similarity. The ubiquitous blue of sea and sky became monotonous. How much they all yearned for the sight of land! No one became seriously ill, no one died. The voyage ground on and on, until finally Sydney was reached in early December.

As they neared the harbour, the last 6 weeks of limbo fell away, and everyone gathered private thoughts about their next destination. Harry repacked his cases, and turned his mind to the sovereigns on loan from the SPG, and the need to find a ticket office, where he could negotiate the purchase of an onward ticket to Shanghai. One thing was for sure – no boat to China would be as glamorous as this. He would be back to bunk beds, shared cabins and salted down food. He looked round with regret as he left *Ballaarat*, the last links with European civilization, before setting sail in whatever vessel was about, towards China. It had been a convenient half-way house – not England, but nowhere else either. Sydney docks brought him back to reality with a jolt.

The advantage of his onward journey was that he was mixing no longer with emigrant families, looking for a new and better life, but with single men and women, travelling for their work. A few wives of business people were to be seen, for the most part looking lonely and dazed, as they followed obediently to a country which meant less usually to them than to their husbands. Eagerly he sought out anyone going to China, Shanghai if necessary, or perhaps Peking. 'You wait', he was told. 'Third-class devil you'll be called, and possibly spat at. They've no time for Europeans. You have to watch out for them all the time. Don't trust them.' It sounded dreadful, and this and dire warnings of atrocious weather made Harry begin to wonder what he had done.

He experienced one of the most disoriented Christmasses of his life, aboard the working boat, in the middle of yet another ocean. He offered himself as server to the priest conducting communion, and sang carols, and ate a strange Christmas meal. But there were no cards, no presents, few games and almost no decorations. The air of unreality had to give way to serious preparation. Ask most people nowadays what they know of China – its geography, climate and economy, far less its customs and language – and information would be scanty. Harry had only the sketchiest idea of what to expect, and learned what he could second-hand from anyone he could find.

His arrival in Shanghai, he reflected afterwards, might as well have been in Bombay for all he knew of it. ''Tis much larger than I thought,' he observed to a tea importer, with whom he had struck up an acquaintance, as they both watched Shanghai draw closer. 'I've never seen or spoken to a Chinaman, they look so strange with their pigtails and huge jackets. What's that?' He pointed to a rickshaw.

'You'll get used to it all,' his friend replied. 'Just keep them at arm's length, or you will be in trouble. You can't trust them that much,' and he measured an inch between thumb and forefinger.

Harry reflected that that was scarcely the attitude of a Christian man, and certainly not a missionary, and determined to see the good in these strange yellow people. 'I shall need their help in travelling to Peking,' he observed.

'God help you then – beg your pardon, but they will fleece you if they can. Keep the upper hand with them, and give them half of what they ask for! Well, I must be off – the tea trade calls. Good luck, Norman.'

'Goodbye.' Harry watched his erstwhile friend disappear along the companionway, and picked up his bags.

He was, by now, heartily sick of living out of suitcases, and of travelling. One last journey confronted him, and he had no idea how he was to make it. No trains existed between Shanghai and Peking, so he imagined a boat or a cart journey. Thankfully he was to be met by a local missionary in the town and guided, but without any Chinese, he felt extremely vulnerable. The huge grain ships, steam tenders and bobbing sampans caught his attention, until, 'Norman? Are you Norman?' He turned and finally met an English face on top of a clerical collar. Relief swept through him.

'Yes, thank goodness. I thought I should stand here alone forever!'

The next few days were a confusion. He stayed in a relatively Western house in Shanghai, but attended by Chinese boy servants. He was introduced to the intricacies of chopsticks, basic Chinese words for 'yes' 'no' and the like. His precious sovereigns were changed into cash – coins with square central holes, threaded on a string. He also managed to get letters home, to his parents, and to Warminster. At last he was told of his journey, and warned about extra socks and gloves – it was extraordinarily cold.

'We had hoped to send you by river, but it is quite iced over, the road is your best bet, but wearisome and uncomfortable. You will have one of the men for company.'

The man, in the event, turned out to be a taciturn middle-aged

Chinese, who spoke more to the donkey than to Harry, and pointed to what he spoke of until Harry guessed his meaning. The journey did not promise to be fulfilling. Nevertheless, Harry decided that as it would take a matter of weeks, and cover apparently, 700 miles, he had better make the best of it. In the event, they travelled by 'boats, donkey and barrows' as Harry put it, and Harry suspected that the tea importer was right, and he was being overcharged. They jolted along at an interminably slow pace – Pa would have got his cart going a sight faster than this! The nights were scarcely any more comfortable, in miserable wayside inns, with a simple rice meal and a high hard bed to lie on. At times Harry wondered if he would ever be warm again, his whole being concentrated on getting his circulation going!

Slowly, however, he got his Chinese companion to say a few words, and he began to learn numbers, and a few nouns to pass the time. After a few days it was evident that the man understood more English than he had admitted at first, and Harry learned of his wife and children, and found out that he was a Christian. He could haltingly say the Lord's Prayer in English, which they rehearsed a dozen times a day for practice, in return for Harry's lesson in Chinese. Sadly, at Nanking, the man could go no further, and handed Harry on to another, until they reached Suchow. At Tsinan, the last leg of the journey began, and Harry wondered if he would ever, ever get there. He had left home in October, and it would be March before he reached Peking. He was already a year older, having had an uncelebrated birthday en route on the road! Now he was twenty-four, and had all but fulfilled his dream, which had started, it seemed so long ago now, that evening in Weymouth Gospel Hall.

As they eventually rattled into Peking, Harry felt that the long months of delay since October were finally at an end. He would soon be at the Mission and able to prepare for ordination. He would meet his new Bishop – he had letters for him from his brother, John – and all the men already experienced in service in China. Excitement welled up in him as they jogged through one of the ancient gates of the city and along the narrow streets. The place was enormous! It took ages to pick a way through the streets, and the smells and sights were mystifyingly new.

Although the Chinese men were everywhere, pushing rickshaws and carrying palanquins, women and children swarmed about too, mainly round the outdoor markets on the streets, where stallholders squabbled over the oddest merchandise. But there were also Europeans, soldiers, men in morning dress, business men, Western ladies. As they reached the Western centre where the legations were, the Europeans were almost in the majority in some streets.

The cart stopped, and the carter pointed to a building opposite, saying something in Chinese and indicating he should get down. Was this it? Evidently he would go no further, as his bags were already half off the cart! Cramped, Harry lowered himself down, and stretched his legs. He felt extremely out of place in his Western suit, and taller than the average Chinese. Jostled and watched suspiciously, he made his way across the street, following his baggage. Grateful at last to have reached his destination, he pulled the bell rope. Somewhere in the depths of the building he could hear the bell ringing. Eventually the door opened, and he met a smiling, bowing Chinese boy. 'Welcome, welcome, Sir,' he kept repeating. This sounded hopeful.

'I am Mr Norman, from Warminster in England.'

'We expect you.' The lad bowed again. 'Come.' So Harry started his life as a missionary.

Intermission:

China

Harry had finally arrived in Peking, the capital of an enormous country, with a civilization and culture which predated those of Britain, and most of Europe. The perception of China to Westerners was intrinsically of a heathen, somewhat savage place, whose only hope was to be westernized as fast and as far as possible. The assumption of European superiority was only to be matched by Chinese assumption of theirs. The cultures did not live happily together.

In fact the Chinese had known organized major religion some 500 years BC. Confucius had lived and preached at that time and his tenets of propriety, ceremonial and the way of righteousness were embedded in the Chinese way of life by the time Christianity began to spread. In addition, the teachings of the Buddha also spread to China. He taught that sufferings in this life stemmed from human desires, which could be overcome by living an ethical life, and following an eight-fold path to Nirvana.

A number of the beliefs of Confucius and the Buddha were common to Christianity, but others were not. When Christianity arrived in China, it was generally regarded as superfluous. The religions they already had were sufficient, they thought, but the convert-seeking Christians had other ideas.

As early as the sixteenth century, the Portuguese Jesuits and Spanish Franciscan monks had landed in Goa and then reached the mainland of China. The trail had been blazed – as was so often the case – by the merchants eager for trade, rushing to acquire spices which till then had been almost the monopoly of the Arabs. Quickly the stories trickled back to Europe of large numbers of heathen, who worshipped multiple gods, and had no conception of salvation. Horrified, the church ploughed money into sending staff, and the search for souls was on.

To begin with it was mainly the Catholic Church which responded to the challenge, sending principally monks and lay brothers. The Jesuits, ever practical, had the sense to adapt to oriental ways, and dressed, ate and adopted the customs of the Chinese. As a result by 1700 it is estimated that there were roughly 300,000 Chinese converts. The unbelieving Chinese took them on suffrance, but did at least accept them.

The Chinese could see that there might be something to be gained from the Europeans, and allowed them to stay. In neighbouring Japan, most Christian missionaries were expelled, tortured or killed. The Chinese absorbed what they could from the foreigners, especially the Western education which the Jesuits offered. Mathematics and science interested them, but Western culture and language did not. There was little social mixing, and therefore precious little understanding the one of the other.

So far things had progressed, if slowly. But the development of missionary activity was ruined by a squabble which broke out between the Jesuits and the Dominicans. The practical Jesuits were quite prepared to say that they had come to fulfil the teachings of Confucius – ancestor worship was accepted as an act of filial piety. The Dominicans argued the toss, claiming that ancestor worship was nothing more nor less than idolatry. The whole row simmered, bubbled and boiled, until it reached the ears of the Pope, who sided with the Dominicans. The Chinese naturally objected to the hard line, and implication that their religion was denigrated.

The position of the Catholic Church in China suffered as a consequence. The Jesuits were furious. They had managed to agree points in common with the Confucians – a historical religion, a central character on whom to concentrate attention. Even the common belief in life after death was worth working on. The Chinese believed that the status of the dead was in fact dependent on the lives and behaviour of the surviving relations, but no matter, the concept of an afterlife was a start. The Jesuits battled away when faced with offerings at graves, and visits by Confucians to talk to and appease long-dead forebears. They did what they could, but progress was slow, particularly following the rows conducted only too openly between the Catholic brotherhoods.

It was to be the arrival of the Protestants at the beginning of the nineteenth century, free from orders from the Vatican, which provided the impetus for the next surge in activity, which brought the SPG to China. According to the official historian of the Anglicans in China, a Dr Morison, while working in the British Museum, found a single document in Chinese. It was part of a New Testament, and from it he set about an understanding of the language. Very few Europeans, let alone British, had any experience of written or spoken Chinese at that time, and he laboured at his language studies in near isolation. Finally he managed to persuade the London Missionary Society to send him to China, and in 1807 he set off on the long and dangerous journey, one of the first non-Catholic missionaries to set foot in China. Seven years later he had translated and published the whole of the New Testament in Chinese. As his skills improved he worked faster, and four years later he had published the Old Testament. Four years later he had published a Chinese dictionary in English. He accomplished a great deal, but by the time he died in 1834, there were still only four Protestant missionaries in the whole of China. In the next fifty years, the missionary 'business' would really take off, bringing thirty-seven Protestant societies alone to the country. By the time Harry arrived they were thick on the ground, representing societies from Germany and America in particular.

One reason for the great increase in activity was the religious zeal at the time. Victorians were deeply concerned for the plight, as they saw it, of the heathen dying in ignorance of salvation. In the same way Harry had been attracted to work abroad, many other men and woman were offering themselves for training to work in all parts of the non-Western world.

The other reason for European presence in China was the insatiable desire for trade in the fashionable commodity of the day, tea. The East India Company in particular were desperate for quantities of tea for home consumption. The British government supported and encouraged them – after all the tea tax accounted for 10% of government revenue! To a lesser extent silk and porcelain were imported, but it was tea which was to be China's undoing in the end. Unwittingly, she became part of the golden triangle set up by the East India Company. Tea left China for Britain, manufactured goods travelled from Britain to the Indian subcontinent, and fatefully opium was the crop callously exported from India to China. Theoretically, trade with China had to be conducted through Canton, and the East India Company was far more interested in supporting local traders in illicit deals across the North China border. So, like Pilate, they washed their hands of all responsibility, denying their involvement. But involved they were. Both the Company and the Indian farmers had a vested interest in continuance of the traffic.

For those who had eyes to see it, the Chinese were the losers in the arrangement. They had not asked to be swamped with opium, and discovered too late that their young breadwinners were turned at best into useless idle layabouts. At worst they would die. Occasionally missionaries spoke out – no one else did, the traders dare not ruin what was the backbone of their success. One missionary, A.E. Moule, who was, as it happened also from Dorset, later spoke up at a missionary conference in 1877. 'Our sale of opium is worse than their smoking,' he thundered. 'It makes it hard to be moral about its use.' He was right. Over the previous hundred years, the import of opium had risen from 200 chests, to 80,000 chests a year, providing someone with an income over the period of approximately £200,000,000.

But even decades earlier the effects of opium were obvious.

The opium dens were full, so full that it would be smoked openly on the streets. Addicts were accused of immorality, frequenting dens for purposes of prostitution. If, as a result of their habit, they ended up by committing suicide, they were accused of that as a crime too, bringing disgrace on the whole family, which by now was practically destitute. Anti-opium societies understandably sprang up around Peking – mainly just south of the city, and were often a cover for anti-Western activity. The Chinese authorities prosecuted both dealers and users, and demanded surrender of opium consignments.

Eventually the whole business flared into combat, and in 1839 the opium wars between China and Britain began. Surprisingly the merchants and missionaries were not ejected. China was soundly beaten, and humiliated in the treaty which followed. The merchants or 'traders in death', as they were called, did extremely well out of the treaty, and the missionaries caught the benefits of their good fortune. Until the war, all trade had, theoretically, to be conducted through Canton. That had meant that consulates, courts and right of abode for families had been severely restricted, awkwardly at the southern tip of China, miles from Peking and Shanghai. After the war, more treaty ports were agreed, opening up whole new trade areas, ripe for the picking. The missionaries rode on the wave of freedom, being allowed to travel in the Chinese hinterland, buy land and erect buildings as required. It opened up opportunities for development in their work.

It was easy to understand the hatred with which the Chinese viewed the Europeans. They had been weakened by enormous indemnities which had been exacted, and could do little. Eventually they embarked on a period of self-strengthening, encouraging students to learn in Western schools, which operated mainly in the treaty ports under the auspices of the missionary societies. By the mid 1870s there were 347 such schools, with some 6000 pupils. Western teachers were engaged in the Chinese medical, mining and military academies. In the middle, the missionaries were, on the one hand branded as being involved with the hated traders, and on the other courted as potential assistants in Chinese strengthening.

It was an ambivalent position to be in. Tolerated at best, they were accepted in good times, but easily became a scapegoat when times were hard.

Unaware of, or unconcerned by these portents, the USPG arrived on the scene in China as late as 1863, following behind the trail-blazing Church Missionary Society, and London Missionary Society, which had sent out Dr Morison. The first USPG man was Dr Stewart, who arrived in Peking on 28 April 1863, thirty years before Harry. He was welcomed and sheltered by members of the Church Missionary Society, who lent him a room from where he worked. He inevitably worked in the Medical Mission – chillingly described as 'not entirely unconnected with opium' – as well as the orphanage in which Chinese boys (no girls at this stage) were being taught English.

That autumn Francis Michell, fresh from Oxford and St Augustine's Training College in Canterbury, came out to join him as a new deacon. It all looked promising until it was realized in London that Dr Stewart had embarked on what was considered to be a spending spree. Without permission from the USPG, he had purchased both a hospital and a house. Frantic letters were exchanged, and Stewart was recalled to London in the embarrassing flurry which followed. Michell was sent back to Shanghai, and thence to Calcutta, where he saw out his missionary days. The USPG retreated, its feathers ruffled, and it was to be a full ten years before it dipped its toe in Chinese waters again. This time it sent two men together, with strict instructions concerning spending. One of the two was Charles Perry Scott, Harry's mentor and father figure.

3

A New Land and a New Language

It appeared to Harry, as he stood, surrounded by his baggage in the hallway of the mission, that not a soul was about. Finally he heard the shuffle of indoor slippers, and the Chinese boy returned, still smiling. 'Come, Mr Norris this way' and he beckoned Harry down a corridor lined with Chinese prints, and sepia photographs of groups of Chinese and English, staring back at him from their place on the wall. He turned into the sitting room, complete with fire and easy chairs, totally Western, a refuge from the East.

'Hello. Frank Norris.' A young man leapt up from his chair and shook Harry's hand warmly. 'Come in. Lu, fetch some tea for Mr Norman and me will you?' The boy disappeared.

'You must be exhausted,' he continued. 'It's a dreadful journey up from Shanghai at the best of times, and it's certainly not that at present. They say the rivers are solid to a depth of feet down river.'

'I'm afraid so,' Harry replied. 'Still, I saw a great deal of the country and picked up some words of the language. I'm glad to be here at last though. It has been five months wasted almost.'

'Let me take your coat,' said Norris. 'Come over by the fire and sit down. I'm afraid everyone else is out at present teaching or on duty at the legation. The Bishop will be sorry to have missed you, but is due back later on. I've been struggling with the accounts, and failing miserably.' He smiled, and his bright eyes danced, his ruddy cheeks glowed in the firelight, and altogether Harry decided he was an approachable, warm human being.

'That reminds me.' Harry fished in his pocket, and retrieved what was left of the sovereigns, now in Chinese cash, in the little bag. 'I have to return what I did not need to spend on the journey. Mr Thornton gave me sufficient, so there has been some to spare.'

76

'Oh! Well done, Norman.' Frank fell on the coins. 'We need all we can get. You wouldn't believe the hand-to-mouth existence we lead. This will come in handy for books or medicines.'

At this point the tea arrived, less strange by now to Harry, in low bowls, with a pungent Eastern scent, and not a hint of milk. It tasted surprisingly good. The conversation turned to the journey, and what was going on in England. Frank was obviously keen to hear any news he could. At last Harry left Frank to his accounts and, with the help of the young servant boy, heaved his cases to his room – tiny, but at last home. He unpacked clothes he had not seen for months, shook them out, and laid them in the flat drawer. He found homes for his books and his photographs of his parents, his wooden cross, even his childhood ammonite treasure. He had always kept this in his pocket, and it appeared from the depths of a case. He held it for a moment, thinking of Portland and the fishermen, the smells and sound of the sea. He had certainly had his fill of the sea recently, but knew he would miss it here so deep inland.

He opened the shutters wider, and looked down on the compound below. The servant boy was sweeping up, and beyond the low wall he could see a group of children playing in what seemed to be a school yard. The design of the building was strange, the roofs were bent up at the edges into comical curls, the roof tiles like waves at sea. Low walls round each house were fretted in patterns, and here and there people squatted in doorways, taking in the watery sunshine. Below him, to the right, he could see the street, with rickshaws and carts wending their way between the pedestrians. Everyone seemed to be making a noise, the men gesticulated to each other and mouthed the same incomprehensible babble as the carter. Groups of women laughed and called to children, who in their turn ran about the wheels of carts, yelling and creating chaos. Dogs and chickens seemed to meander at will amongst the traffic. It all reminded him of the scenes in port at Brindisi and Aden, where he had looked down like this on the goings on in the docks, as the locals went their strange way about their business. Now he had the chance to get out and become part of it. He turned back into the room and took off his walking shoes to stretch his feet. He sat in his chair to test it out, found it comfortable, and determined to write home to tell his family of his safe arrival. But the journey and the strangeness of it all had been more than he had realized, and the next he knew it was an hour later, and the servant boy Lu was asking him to 'Come, English tea time with Bishop please.'

Harry stood up with a start, overcoming a sudden cramp. He flattened his hair with his hand and checked his suit and shoes for dust. Fumbling over the laces, he prepared as quickly as he could to meet his new master, and hurried downstairs after the boy.

At the bottom of the stairs a young man was taking off his overcoat. He looked up as Harry came into view, and passed his coat to the boy. 'Thank you, Lu.' He waited for Harry to join him. 'You must be the new man at last. You are sorely needed. We've been rushed off our feet here this winter. I have just got in from a day in the school. I need some tea. Come on, I expect the Bishop is back by now.'

Back to the sitting room they went, now laid out with tea cups and some odd looking biscuits and patties on plates. 'I've found the new man and brought him in for tea.' 'Well done, Thompson,' came the reply from someone with his back to Harry, bending over Frank's work, correcting something. He turned, and Harry met his Bishop.

Charles Scott was, to Harry, middle aged. At forty-four, he had the look of an older man, with long side-whiskers and a face weathered by many years in China. Right from their first meeting they had an affinity for each other, even though Charles was from Hull via Cambridge, and Harry was from Dorset, via nowhere in particular. As well as being Bishop and trainee priest to each other, their relationship was to develop into that of father and son, tinged with mutual respect.

Over tea Harry discovered that Frank Norris and Walter Thompson had only been in China a year or two themselves and were still deeply involved in their Chinese studies. Frank had also been at Cambridge, but Walter had trained in Canterbury, in a college very similar to St Boniface. Both were trained priests and simply had their language skills to achieve.

'You must meet Geoffrey on his return' said Walter, in mid-biscuit. 'He was at Canterbury directly after me, and will be priested about the time you are deaconed, I expect.'

'I don't know yet when that is to be.' Harry was rather embarrassed in the presence of his Bishop, who would obviously have the final say.

'Let the poor man settle.' The Bishop waved Walter back in a joking way. 'Chap's not been here five minutes and you're at him already. I know the pair of you couldn't wait to get him here, but I get the right to strike first. Norman – finish up your tea and come and meet Frances, my wife. She should be home, as long as no one has called for her. She is a trained doctor, you know – always in demand!' and he grimaced, raising his eyes skywards.

The first day in the mission house continued in similar manner. Frances was delightful, lending a welcome gentle tone so needed in a house full of men. Charles and Frances shared a small apartment since having married a year previously, and Harry was immediately invited for a meal. As Frances bustled round organizing the house servants while the meal was being prepared, Harry passed over letters and reports from John Scott to his brother. By the end of the evening, Harry's mind was a whirl of new experiences, and he still had not set foot outside the building.

By the next morning, he was quite refreshed, and almost bounded down the stairs. Frank was breakfasting, the others having finished. 'House prayers in about twenty minutes,' he said seriously to Harry, who helped himself to tea and some strange rolls. 'Did you sleep well?'

'Yes, fine, thanks. I'm just relieved to have a proper bed at last.'

'Those roadside inns are notorious,' agreed Frank. 'Bed bugs, lice, they have them all. Vile places, but they have to be borne. After prayers you can come to the school with me if you like, then I'm due at the legation to take communion for the diplomatic wives.'

It seemed a simple enough expedition, but to Harry, out on the streets of Peking for the first time, it was a revelation.

The school next door was reasonably familiar, since rows of boys behaved the same the world over. He could only beam at them and say 'Good day' in Chinese. He longed to be able to communicate with them, frustrated by his handicap. Frank seemed to be able to jabber away to them with ease.

'I would love to teach here, Frank.' He spoke from the heart.

'No doubt you will, when you have mastered Chinese.'

'How many boys do you have here?' Harry weighed up the need.

'It varies.' Frank totted them up 'About eighteen or twenty boys normally. We also have a girls school, with slightly fewer numbers. Here we have an industrial department – the boys are taught either carpentry or Chinese wood type cutting and printing. For the past two years we have been turning out trained boys, who can earn their own livings.'

'But remember, the priority is to get you deaconed, and useful. Then you have to go through what Walter and I did, and start learning Chinese, which isn't easy, believe me. Only then could you cope here,' and he nodded towards the rows of black heads intent over their slates.

'It's awful, I feel dumb, deaf and stupid with them.'

'Then you have your first lesson in Chinese this afternoon,' replied Frank, happy in the role of language teacher for a change. 'Next stop the legation, where the language problems are fewer thank goodness,' and he ushered Harry out of the school and on to the busy street.

As they walked through the mercantile quarter, Harry's senses were assaulted by smells and sounds quite unfamiliar. He questioned Frank endlessly about the strange products on the stalls, sweet potatoes, black figs, innumerable types of tea, strange fish with dull malevolent eyes. Spices filled his nostrils, and his eyes automatically strayed to the stalls cooking foods – boiling dumplings, steaming and ready to be covered in sticky jam, honey or nut confections. Tobacco, different from English types, wafted about, and just occasionally, another odd indefinable smell, which he had come to recognize as opium.

'If you won't take your eyes off those stalls, you'll get lost.' Frank pulled his arm.

'Sorry – there's just so much to take in.' Harry was already

80

half-watching some serious haggling at a stall when, realizing the need to avoid a rickshaw, he pulled himself together and set off after Frank.

'How do you find your way around these narrow alleys, with everything in Chinese?' Harry was impressed.

'You learn the directions. One of the first Chinese lessons will be in place names anyway. You can always find the legations, as they're near the centre where the Imperial Palace is. There, what do you think?'

They had come out of a lane and were suddenly facing a square the other side of which was a high wall, with a guard. 'That's the entrance to the Palace, where the Empress lives. It's said she has thousands of servants behind those walls. Eunuchs, hundreds of them. We can't enter, nor can the Chinese, there is access to the forbidden city for only the privileged few. She rarely comes out. Weird set up we say, but there you are.'

As they walked nearer the legations, the numbers of Europeans in morning dress, or at least Western suits, increased. Harry could almost have been in London for a few seconds. The legation was a sanctuary of Britishness, and Harry saw possibilities.

'They're not too keen on us here,' Frank whispered. 'Take us on sufferance because of chapel duties, but missionaries are the underdogs here as everywhere else. We're not here to make money, you see.' In the chapel, a small group of English women had gathered for communion, and Frank prepared for the service while Harry sat in the main body of the church. Throughout the service his thoughts strayed, and he imagined himself here in a few months, finally dedicating himself to the ministry. It was a small, almost insignificant place, not in the slightest like Salisbury, where, had he been in England, he would have been deaconed. But that did not matter, the act was the thing, not the place.

He waited for Frank at the back of the chapel. Frank eventually emerged and hurried over. 'Sorry to keep you waiting. Well, what do you think of it?'

'Very much like home. A haven of Englishness!'

Frank laughed. 'All too true. You wait till you see the Chinese church.'

81

'A Chinese church too?' Harry had not considered that two distinct places of worship existed.

'Yes,' said Frank, 'in the Chinese quarter. I'll show you later. We say Mattins and Evensong daily there, only on Sundays here. I expect we see fifteen or twenty at each native service though, and the church membership is close on two hundred. We progress slowly. Now, come on, we must progress fast if we are to get back in time for lunch!'

On the way back to the mission house, Frank had to tear Harry away from stalls and shops all over again. Eventually he gave in, and invited Harry to try to buy some tea, handing him some coins. 'Keep the coins – called cash – on a string. See, they all have a central square hole in the brass, so it's quite safe. Usually 25 equal a penny, but in the provinces it can vary – you have to haggle, they expect it!' Harry got into a dreadful muddle. He pointed to the wrong things, and upset the stallholder, until Frank stepped in, amused, to sort it out. Thankfully, Harry retreated with his wretched purchase, mumbling the need for language lessons as soon as possible!

That afternoon he sat down to learn, he thought, some Chinese. 'You do realize there are 50,000 characters don't you,' teased Frank. 'Honestly, it's no good until you have mastered at least 1,000, and 4,000 are needed to read the Bible.' Harry quavered. 'Try speaking words first, it's easier,' and they went through numbers and easy sentences. He practised all the time, while shaving, lying in bed late at night, even before services. He wore his new friends down with questions about the Chinese for this and that, but privately they commented on his diligence.

A few days later the Bishop found Harry poring over a Chinese primer and sat down. 'You've done well Norman, but you mustn't overdo the studying, you'll strain your eyes. It's about time we turned you into a Chinese, you'll stand out like a sore thumb otherwise.'

Harry frowned. 'But we all wear Western dress.'

'We do here, but not out in the villages,' and Scott pointed over his shoulder. 'Frances has got you some garb, so you must try it for length.'

That evening Harry paraded in the sitting room in an

enormous quilted jacket and baggy trousers tied at the ankles. Everyone fell about laughing, as he walked pompously up and down, almost tripping up as he want. 'Come here,' Frances spluttered, her mouth full of pins, trying to make alterations in his ridiculous attire. He waited, fidgeting. ''Tis too bad! I can't be seen in calico stockings and wooden clogs.'

'You wait – try on this.' The long overgarment was wrestled over his head.

'What on earth's this?' said Harry, muffled inside it all.

'A pongee – sign of status,' said Frank. 'It will help when you travel south. Now try the skull cap. And a black satin cap was wedged on his head.

If only his parents could see him now! He felt such a sight in it all, the long sleeves had to be constantly pushed up before he could do anything. Picking up his skirts, he padded into the hall to find a mirror, to the amusement of the servants and English alike. He needed a photographic studio to provide proof at home that he was now a true Chinese.

As day followed day, Harry settled down to a routine. After morning house prayers, he would work at his Chinese, then later visit the legation or the school if he were needed at either. Later, when the Bishop returned, he would sit with him, discussing his preparatory studies for his deaconing. The Bishop was determined this would be as soon as Palm Sunday – just a few weeks ahead – 10 April. Harry was horrified, and begged to be allowed a little longer to prepare. But no, Palm Sunday it was to be. Evening after evening Harry studied the theology he needed, battling against time, for although he had been theoretically prepared, his mind had grown rusty, a whole year without study. The Bishop quizzed him occasionally, assuring him that he was 'checking up on Warminster, not Norman'.

In the late evening both often sat by the fire in the Bishop's study, while Frances busied herself elsewhere.

'Were you deaconed out here too?' Harry asked Charles, on an impulse.

'Heavens, no. There was no Bishop out here then to do it. No, I was deaconed and priested in London, and three years a curate at St Peter's, Eaton Square, before I came out.'

'Go on,' Harry urged him. 'How did you come to be here?'

'Do you really want to know?' Charles looked back at Harry, a smile escaping from one side of his mouth. 'All right then. My vicar, Wilkinson, had proposed to both Archbishops that we should have a United day of Intercession throughout the country to raise funds and workers for the mission field. As the curate at St Peter's, I was very much involved in the arrangements, taking care of the speakers, organizing services and so on. Quite simply, I heard the speakers and was convinced I was called. I don't think Wilkinson quite expected me to resign, it was a bit close to home,' he chuckled. 'Anyway, I wrote to him, properly. I remember, it was just before Christmas, and my family were as amazed as yours must have been. I was about the same age as you, twenty-five. Anyway, that's how it came about.' He looked distantly into his tea, and took a sip.

'In the spring I began to prepare myself along with another man, Miles Greenwood. You'll meet Miles soon I hope. He's currently in Chefoo, on the coast, but hopes to come up to Peking for Easter, God willing. Miles is some, let me see, nine years older than me – Lancashire stock, but had the good taste to have been up at Cambridge too, so we had plenty in common. Anyway, I digress. We had a parishioner at St Peter's, Dudley Smith, good man. He was equally moved by the appeal, and donated £500 for five years – imagine that – on condition that it was used to open up missionary work in China. So there it was – we came to China. Actually, Smith has been a lifesaver for us. He also provided a £10,000 endowment to finance the bishopric, so we have developed almost entirely thanks to him.'

'Did they just send you as a curate, with no training?' Harry was getting interested by now, and bent forward in his chair, warming his hands, before the fire lost its heat. 'Gracious no,' Charles replied. 'We went to Guy's for some pretty grue-some medical training, and learned some basic Chinese. The advantages of London living.' The Bishop wagged his finger wisely. 'We actually set sail, appropriately, on St Peter's Day – that was eighteen years ago now.'

The silence that followed was full of thoughts, Charles with his memories, Harry considering that then, he had been a Portland

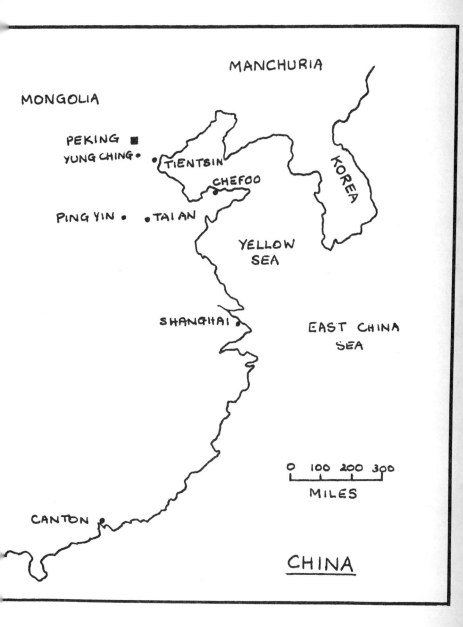

child in the first days of his schooling. At this point Frances came into the room, and sat, tired by the day, at her husband's side.

'Nothing to talk about, you two?'

'On the contrary, my dear.' Charles put his arm round her. 'I'm telling Norman about how Miles and I came to China.'

'Oh,' Frances replied knowingly, and smiled at Harry. The story she had heard many, many times.

Charles continued, 'I was just thinking, we were lucky to arrive in Shanghai in the autumn – best time of year really – and we got to Chefoo on 3 October 1874. I'll never forget it. It was a beautiful town then, Harry, with a good temperate climate – it attracted large numbers of Europeans. Hudson Taylor always said "Once visit Chefoo, and you will never be satisfied with England again." We called it the "Brighton of China!" We spent the whole winter there, Miles and I, at the home of dear old Dr Nevins – a Presbyterian Minister. He was a good friend to us – taught us Mandarin Chinese, or tried to, poor chap. He'd worked with Hudson Taylor you know. I suppose we had a base there on and off for almost two years.

You have it easy now, you know. In those days when we travelled inland, most of the Chinese had never seen a white man. When we started – before I became fluent, I just had to submit with a good grace while they pulled my whiskers, my buttons, coat and boots, and wanted to know my age and "honourable name". As a rule they were very friendly, but on one or two occasions, while preaching at fairs, we were pushed and jostled and had a few stones thrown at us from behind. Anyway, we survived. In that first year I accompanied Nevins on his quarterly tour of eight walled cities, you never saw a more dilapidated, ugly and dirty collection of places. We just preached and handed out tracts as best we could.'

'I suppose you had no church, and just went from town to town then,' Harry almost thought aloud.

'It wasn't that easy.' This time Frances interposed. 'Tell him about the famine, my dear.'

'Hold on. I was just going to.' The Bishop playfully gagged his wife, and she feigned cowering submission.

'As I have been reminded …' They all laughed. 'The next year the winter was terrible. Far worse than this year. You know, they guess between 9–13 million people died in China, Harry. We couldn't win. We gave out famine relief and were accused of buying converts with rice. "Rice Christians", they were called.'

'Didn't you think of giving up?'

'No,' Charles snorted. 'Nor will you. No, we fitted up old warehouses in Chefoo – dreadful place it was, but we had a church, and one of us worked in Chefoo, while the other itinerated the villages with the mule. It was a lonely business, but we soon learned to dress in Chinese style – the garb you laughed at has its value in the countryside, believe me. We got on specially well in Tai-an and Ping-yin, we have contacts there still. We decided to give up on the rice running, as people thought we were buying souls, so the SPG got us 2 oz bars of silver to take to the officials in each locality. The poor mule wasn't very pleased on a round trip of up to 1,000 miles, but the thing worked, and food was bought using silver. I used to take a young Chinese lad on those trips, and thank God we were never robbed. Anyway, enough of me.' He slapped his knee. 'It's all changed now.'

'What happened to Miles?' Harry was not content with a story half told.

'Miles, dear man, is in Chefoo still, with other workers, particularly William Groves, who has been with him eleven years now. They are doing sterling work in the hospital there. It has support from European residents, and the local magistrate, otherwise it couldn't continue. You know, Harry, Miles is so dedicated. I doubt I would be such an example. We haven't been able to pay him recently. He just goes on, no pay, nothing, month in, month out.'

'I didn't realize we had workers elsewhere.'

The Bishop was quick to reply. 'Dear chap, we do! You have just missed Henry, Henry Brereton, who has just left for Tientsin on the coast. Now he's another old stager! Transferred from the CMS some twelve years ago. I've just had a letter from him, he's building a parsonage and a churchroom there I hope. We have a loan for the building of £1,000 – repayable at £100 a year interest free. I suspect Dudley Smith again, but can't be sure. Now, where was I? Yes, down in Tai-an, where I used to be, we have Henry

Brown, and Frank Sprent, and young Geoffrey Iliff is there for a while, but is due back for Palm Sunday for his priesting with you.'

At this point both realized they had strayed from Harry's training for his ordination! The hour was late, and the fire burned down. Charles removed his arm from behind Frances' sleepy head, and they all decided to give in, and begin again tomorrow.

Harry began to see where he fitted in to the pattern of things. Planning was essential, and progress was slow. Letters took days, parcels longer. Visits to other missionaries were attempted with care, routes and provisions had to be thought out in detail before leaving Peking. If there were other societies operating in the area, relationships had to be fostered with diplomacy, each providing practical and psychological support for the other. Vast areas still remained untouched by any mission. There was so much still to do.

Shortly before Palm Sunday, Geoffrey Iliff appeared in the mission house, straight – if not fresh – from Tai-an, with messages from Henry and Frank, and eager to complete his ordination. He was a young, rather serious man, who looked, Harry thought, as if he were permanently frowning. First impressions were wrong. He was simply full of thousands of ideas, bubbling over with questions and projects. 'We're a strange lot here,' he admitted. 'We don't let the grass grow under our feet. In the year I've been here, there have been so many changes. I came out on the same boat as Mrs Scott you know! Here,' he beckoned Harry to come closer, with a roguish gleam in his eye, 'the Bishop is quite mad you know – or at least, that's what London think! He gets away with almost anything. By the end of last year, with me, Thompson and Norris on the staff, he was overspent by £500! He had to "dispose of" – shall I say – some property, but he's still after a doctor and money to build a hospital, a larger girls' school and a retreat outside Peking for us! Apparently Henry Brereton – in Tientsin – has asked for another £500, as the land he wanted for a church and parsonage is under seven feet of water. Honestly, I don't know how he does it!'

'I wonder how he could justify having me, then,' Harry mused.

'That's another instance,' Geoffrey was in full swing by now. 'It's almost funny, but you have to hand it to him. He's a constant beggar for us, the SPG have no idea what the needs are. We've come almost to expect he can work miracles with their finances. Anyway, you're here, and so am I. Are you looking forward to Sunday?'

'I can't wait. It's been such a long struggle. I can't believe I'm there yet. I only wish I were being priested like you. Still I will be able to take proper part in services at last, and I'll get my robes!'

Harry's dream was realized. He and Geoffrey stood together that Sunday in the legation chapel, to be ordained by Charles Scott. Frances, Frank and Walter watched delighted, together with other missionaries and some legation families. 'At last,' Harry thought, 'I am now on my way in my work.'

It was about this time that the Bishop decided it was almost time Harry received his honourable name. 'I have one, we all do. It's a Chinese custom. They simply can't understand it if we don't have one, so we do,' said Charles. 'You'll feel a bit foolish, but it will grow on you. I have decided you are to have the name Meng Heling. Now, come on, as part of your language training, can you work it out?'

Harry concentrated in vain. 'Not quite. Ling means something like – age – the other parts mean nothing so far.'

'Never mind. Meng is a corruption from Mencius or Meng-Tzu, an ancient and important philosopher to the Chinese. He signifies a crane, which symbolizes longevity and association with God. So together, it means wisdom, long life and closeness to God. Will that do?'

'Sounds perfect to me, except that I have to remember it, and write it now.' Harry practised writing his honourable name that evening to the amusement of the others, who bowed in mock homage. Nevertheless, Harry was pleased with his title, and wondered how he could explain it in letters home.

By the end of the year Harry had become part of the team in Peking. He kept busy at his studies, and also helped in chapel and school duties. In his report to London in the early days of 1893 the Bishop wrote that Harry's language ability was improving fast. Predictably, he also had to report that Harry could not be kept away from the school, and wrote, 'Norman is getting to know the boys, and has been able to lead them in making the little

(Chinese) church beautiful for Christmas, and in getting up some carols with accompaniment on the handbells.' Handbells were not Harry's natural strength, but he had enough musical ear to sing. The boys made a strange noise, singing Western tunes in a foreign language, but it was enough to entice parents to the church, which was, in part, its aim.

The Bishop continued his report. It was generally positive. After his ordination, Geoffrey Iliff had returned to Tai-an where Henry Brown was, and they had just reported 30 new confirmations. However – it was also reported that the Catholics had been trying to obtain a house in the town, and a petition of 800 Chinese signatures was sent to oppose it! Harry's co-worker, Frank Sprent, had left for furlough after eight years without a break. Frank Norris had just gone fifty miles south of Peking to Yung Ching, and had found it necessary to enlarge the meeting room! Even Charles' dear friend Miles in Chefoo had reported that the two boys from Peking School, who had been sent to him, had been helping him in his little hospital, and he was considering sending them on to the fast developing Tai-An area. However, between them they had seen over 1700 people, mainly outpatients.

In Peking, a native deacon, Chang, was helping in the dispensary, and a female doctor, Alice Marston, had been working with the sick women and children for three years, helped occasionally now by Frances. Eleven girls had been enrolled in the new girls' school, and lay female workers were helping there too. What hope there was when all seemed to be going so well!

The only problem, it seemed, was Henry Brereton, working in Tientsin. He had been in China for many years. Charles had acquired him when he took over the workers from the CMS. He pondered Henry's problems. Firstly, there was the building problem, the land offered had been a quagmire! No matter, money for buildings was a relatively simple problem to overcome. Charles knew Henry was even more worried about his family. At twelve and ten, his two boys ought to be educated in England, and accommodation had to be found for them in a boarding school, and with a clergy family in the holidays. Henry's wife and little daughter had both recently contracted typhoid fever, and all four needed money to get to England. Not long after, news reached Peking that the little girl had also caught diphtheria, and died. Such were the costs, when missionaries tried to maintain family life. Thankfully, the Bishop's staff generally were neither married, nor responsible for families back home.

By February, Harry had reached his twenty-fifth birthday, remembered by Frances, and celebrated in style with gifts and food. Harry was delighted and embarrassed at the same time. 'It certainly is an improvement on my birthday last year,' he beamed. It almost coincided with the Chinese New Year, so was twice as festive.

'You must see this,' said Walter, as they craned their necks out of the window to watch the New Year celebrations.

Downstairs the pair flew, and out on to the street. 'It's a time for fresh beginnings, and an opportunity to settle debts. The people all go to visit their relatives – their *dead* relatives,' Walter shouted above the din. As they reached one of the Chinese cemeteries, Harry could see little groups round graves, decorating the areas and talking to the dead person.

'What a shame, surely.' Harry shook his head. 'If only they realized they can't influence the dead by their actions in this life. What a terrible burden to carry.'

'Ancestors are all-important here,' replied Walter. 'When they build the railways, the engineers are terrified that they'll accidentally dig up someone's ancestor and incur their wrath. The fuss, if they do, is dreadful. The British engineers, I know, are plagued continually. Come, it's cold, let's get back to happier celebrations. The New Year festivities are spectacular.'

Back in the streets near the centre of the city, the whole world seemed to be out for a good time. Firecrackers popped and banged everywhere, and red paper decorations fluttered happily from doors and windows. Before Harry realized it, Walter had bought two hot jam dumplings from a stall. Harry could only think, 'shades of Portland Fair, but noisier', and he munched happily as they walked.

Apart from occasional opportunities such as New Year, the serious business of operating a mission station had to go on. The

staff could devote themselves single-mindedly to the work, and
Harry pursued his training for the priesthood. Daily, he was also
able to converse and write more easily in Chinese. This he did
with relish, always keen to develop links and build up relationships. So many of the Europeans, especially from the business
fraternity, disdained the Chinese, and the missionaries contact
was generally frowned on by Westerners.

Harry hated what he saw of the treatment meted out by some
of his countrymen to the Chinese. Having by now been in China a
year, he realized that the next batch of graduates would be
leaving St Boniface, and he wrote to them frequently, both to
keep in touch, and to encourage them to help in his work. In an
open letter to the College magazine he wrote:- 'There is, I believe
– but why I do not know – something odious in hearing the name
of a Chinaman – at least to many people it is so – and his look,
almost repulsive. This is anything but truth. To me it seems that
there is, hidden beneath the coat of a Chinaman, a quality of
benevolence something more than human, it is not far from
divine. A little influence, a little conviction, and then Christianity,
and that spark would be enkindled, and shine out with a zeal
almost unparallelled.' That got his message across. He thought of
the people he had come to know, the children in the school and
their parents, the servants in the house, the hospital assistant.
They were all good people, and just as worthy of salvation as any
Englishman. They were also interesting, and their style of life
fascinated him. He knew most about the ordinary people, but he
had heard that the nobility were not beyond the touch of
Christian love. If only the evidence of success were more obvious.
He sighed and thought, then continued. 'So far we can see little
Christian influence reaching upper class life in China, it is chiefly
among the poor – but we have strong hopes and a lively faith. The
Emperor himself is not against us, only those who bear rule under
him, keep him back. Our Queen has presented him with *The Life
of the Prince Consort* which he is having translated into Chinese,
and he is also making a study of English.'

'Writing home?' Frank had come into the sitting room without
Harry noticing, he had been so concentrating on his letter.

'Not at present. I'm trying to explain to the students at St

Boniface what it's like out here. I promised the college principal I would keep in touch, to give them an idea of what the work is like. It's a problem to know where to start.'

'Tell them about the need for money.' Frank's answer was automatic, having wrestled that afternoon with the accounts, yet again. 'However well meaning, they have no idea in England that there is no organization like the Church of England to cover every debt. Tell them the projects we discussed, it might be helpful,' and Frank smiled ruefully.

Harry grunted assent and scribbled on. 'Our mission here is not very large, but there is good scope for future work; outside the town there are villages innumerable, and in these, lying very still and almost unapparent, are all our hopes and joys for future work. We are poor. Will not someone help us largely? I want money to start a dispensary. I want money to provide for the maintenance of several boys who cannot keep themselves. We want money for our work in general. Who will help us? £50 would be of great service.'

The arrow flew from the page, straight to its mark at St Boniface, where John Welsh read it with a mixture of pride and happiness that Norman had so obviously settled himself well in China. He smiled wryly as he remembered the £8 still outstanding on the cost of the pavilion Harry had pestered them to let him build. How typical of the chap to be trying yet again to get projects to turn into reality. He really was incorrigible. Welsh knew that somehow, whether from St Boniface or elsewhere, Harry would get his money, and his naive letter would succeed. He could never stay in the realms of doctrine for long, life to him was the realization of ideas in practical concrete terms.

Welsh was right. Harry soon rejoiced in the provision of some finance – and he got his dispensary, but not in Peking.

The winter that year was no better than the previous one had been in China. As Harry wrote his letters home, he and the others huddled round the fire, and dashed up to their rooms at night as fast as possible. Peking was perhaps warmer than the villages, but nevertheless it was reported by Frank – for whom coldness meant money spent on fuel – that it was minus 15 outside.

'Now I know why the Chinese wear these great baggy clothes,

Harry mumbled, sitting wrapped in as many layers as he dared put on without looking ridiculous. 'Do you think it blasphemous to pray for spring?'

'I would hand you my stipend to buy fuel, if I hadn't given it already.' Walter was dejected. 'I wonder if the SPG sit with no fires, and hand their salaries to the Secretary.'

'At least we earn £30 a quarter,' Frank interposed, 'Geoffrey and myself. It gives us some leeway. You have nothing to spare on £25, especially if you only take spending money from that. The one I feel sorry for is Miles Greenwood — imagine having no salary at all for years. If it helps, I know the Bishop is touched by anything we give, and I certainly can balance the books better. I saw his last report home — he said something about not being able to have a more dedicated, single-minded and capable staff of clergy to work with, so he does appreciate us, even if we are cold! Let's throw caution to the wind and use another log!'

They survived the winter, spring came, and the world thawed out. The blossom burst on the trees, and the warm sun returned. As with nature, the humans expanded with the warmth, people crept out of a kind of hibernation, and Peking came alive again. It was getting perilously close to Harry's ordination.

His studies nearly complete, Harry had to devote himself to taking his full share in the work of the mission for the first time. He took services in the legation still with help, and was considered able to visit outlying stations accompanied only by a local man or boy. To his delight, he helped in the little boys school next door, in the hospital with Dr Marston, and in the dispensary with a Chinese deacon, Mr Chang.

One day, with the dispensary finally closed, Chang had gone home to his large family, and Harry and Alice were clearing up.

'How do you find working in the hospital, Harry?' asked Alice. 'You seem to have the stomach for it.'

'Well, I'm glad I had some training at Salisbury, for sure. I'm at least used to basic problems, even if some of these tropical diseases are new to me. The opium is the worst problem. I can't come to terms with what it does to people — and there's no cure.'

Alice agreed. 'And it's principally our own fault in importing the wretched stuff. It should be a crime, not a source of wealth. It

makes me angry. Families like Chang's are broken apart by it.'
She was angry now. Then her mood changed. 'By the way – have
you noticed anything strange with Chang lately?'

'No, should I?'

'I don't know. The Bishop was asking some very odd questions
about him this morning. He might ask you too. I just thought you
might like to be prepared.'

'He's a good worker.' Harry jumped to his defence. 'An
eloquent preacher and a very useful, all round man. Whatever can
be the matter?'

That question echoed the same evening after dinner, as Harry
and Charles worked together.

'I can't go into details, Norman,' the Bishop said. 'Suffice it to
say that there have been problems you haven't known of, for the
past three years. Now there's a charge of serious misconduct
against him, and I can't ignore it.'

'I can't believe it,' Harry exploded. His mind raced through the
possibilities – opium, family problems, weakness of morals,
dishonesty. 'He's a deacon, after all.'

'That is no protection, sadly.' The Bishop looked down, worn
and worried. 'There have been too many facts brought to me to
deny it, but yet I cannot prove it. It's the worst situation to be in. It
was my idea to train Chang in the first place, my first experiment
in handing over real responsibility to Chinese. I must admit, I
dread the ordeal of talking to him tomorrow. Even his own
people refuse to support him. How can I insist he is a good
example?'

The next day the dread interview took place. Inevitably everyone knew it was going on, and muted whisperings relayed what
little anyone had picked up – a raised voice, Chang's face as he
left. Bishop Scott looked pale as he emerged from his study. 'I
can't believe he did it – his previous excellent character ought to
outweigh against suspicious circumstances. I counsel forgive-
ness.'

It was tantalizing. Everyone knew something was wrong, no
one knew what. The Chinese lost confidence in Chang and his
influence with them, once so important, was diminished. Poor
Chang was seriously affected by it, and his health began to fail.

Disease was abroad in Peking, and within a few weeks in May, four of the congregation died, including Chang, who died the very day Harry was ordained. He had been sent out of the city to Chefoo, to Miles Greenwood, and died peacefully there among friends. He left a widow and five children. It was to be some time before the experiment with native deacons was tried again. Meanwhile the Bishop kept his counsel and did not reveal in his reports the details of Chang's supposed misdemeanour.

The date was set for Harry's ordination, Trinity Sunday, 28 May. It was a traditional ordination date for priests around the world, yet Harry could scarcely believe it was coming. It was the culmination of so much. Was it really only six years ago that he was a carpenter in Abbotsbury, visiting the Weymouth Mission Hall? Was it really only last year that he had been deaconed, fresh from England and useless? Gone were student days, England, his family, and lifestyle. Surely it was too early.

He questioned the Bishop. 'May I not wait a while. I am longing to finish my ordination, but do you think I am ready?'

'When I say you are ready, you are ready, Norman. Believe me, I have seen enough men. You're ready without doubt. There's a new young man due out from England any day and I need you to see him through his deaconing, as Geoffrey did for you last year. Anyway, the sooner you are useful, the sooner you can attend to the dying, take communion, and confirmation classes as the others do. Oh yes, I have plans to keep you busy!'

'Who is coming out, Sir?'

'A young man who glories in the name of William Tertius Pigrum by all accounts. My brother John says he is very young, but with handling, will do. At least he is eager. I thought you would like to see him along?'

'Fine,' Harry replied, delighted in the opportunity to get his teeth into a project, and even more pleased that he would no longer be the most recent recruit.

Young Pigrum duly turned up and Harry was responsible for some of his training. He sat him down and showed him the rudiments of Chinese and theology with infinite patience, but Pigrum was slow, and needed to be reminded about quite simple matters. Harry reported Pigrum's speed – or lack of it – but the

Bishop encouraged him to persevere regardless. Consequently, on Trinity Sunday, Harry had to steer his young protégé through the mysteries of his ordination. The two stood where Harry had stood a year before, in the legation chapel, and Harry finally took his vows, which he kept to the end of his life. That day he became a priest, and a new life began.

One of the factors which bound Bill Pigrum and Harry was the fact that they were both old St Bonifacians. They exchanged reminiscences into the evenings. Harry was particularly pleased to hear that the carpentry shop was well used. Bill had done his best there as elsewhere, and was a little in awe of an ex-superintendent of the shop, who was also his mentor. 'We must write back to tell them of our ordinations.' Harry was not above issuing directions to young Bill, who in truth was only a little younger, but whose maturity differed by about ten years.

'I'll tell them of the service if you like,' he agreed.

Harry had previous letters to reply to, so was happy for Bill to busy himself with the details. He had written a long letter to his parents and grandparents as well, so had no great desire to repeat the description.

'Fine. I'll keep off that then. I'll tell them a little of the work we do' – and he started another letter to Welsh. 'News from Warminster is always gladly welcomed. It helps us to remember the dear old "alma mater", as well as shows that we are not forgotten by those whom we left behind, where we, for a short time, spent some happy years ... For myself, as far as I know, I have finished with examinations in Chinese, so on that score I feel happy ... Three days after my ordination, it fell to me to administer the Blessed Sacrament to a dying Chinese Christian; so for the first time I used my portable altar (others had used it before.) The Chinese were quite delighted with it, and for my own part, I found it very convenient.'

They wrote on, and their letters were duly published in the college magazine. Harry continued to pump what Chinese he could into Bill. All told they were together for just three months before the Bishop, shortly after their ordination, dropped the bombshell.

'You're to stay in Peking, Harry, and Bill is to go south to Tai-an to work with Frank Sprent. You've done a good job so far on what is, candidly, indifferent material, but you can't be a full-time tutor while I have work for you here.'

Harry was dejected. It was just like St Boniface all over again, when he had to stay for an extra six months. He kicked himself for not having learned that what he wanted was unimportant. The needs of the mission, and above that, God's will, weighed much more than his individual wishes. Nevertheless, he was just a little jealous of Pigrum.

He watched as Bill was bundled back into the cart which so recently had brought him to Peking, only to return south along the same long route, now in the heat of summer. He had become a deacon, and had only the scantiest smattering of Chinese. He had admitted to Harry that he was dreadfully concerned about the long journey – the sub-deacon who was to travel with him had less English than he had Chinese. Poor Bill looked utterly lost and bewildered atop the cart. Harry handed up his personal bag. 'Good luck,' he almost whispered. 'God be with you. You will like Frank Sprent – he's another Bonifacian, and very experienced – a far better teacher for you than I. You will soon come to feel at home in the celestial land.'

Bill smiled in reply, a weak but brave smile. Harry felt him quiver, and knew he was afraid and out of his depth. 'I wonder whether he can stay the course?' he asked of no one in particular, as he watched the cart trundle off.

Weeks later, Harry could report to Warminster that 'after what had been an irksome journey, travelling for 14 days, he (Bill) got to his destination in safety, being none the worse for his rough and uncomfortable experiences'. What he did not report was that things were going less than smoothly for young Pigrum. He owed him that much in loyalty.

Things were not going as well as Harry had hoped for himself either. He had imagined flocks of Chinese attending services, but the going was rough. Added to that was Walter's strange behaviour. His moods swung from light bonhomie to surly bad temper. He became secretive, and behind his back comments were made. At last the fateful word was out – drink!

'It can't be!' Harry was aghast. 'How on earth can a young priest take to drink? Other things should be sustaining him!'

'I know,' Charles replied. 'Believe me, none is more saddened than I, but you can smell it on his breath. Last night Frances actually watched him weaving his way across the yard. He was absolutely sunk in drink. I grant he seems all right by morning, he hides it well, but drink has got him. I have no option but to send him home before it becomes any more obvious. I'll need to keep an eye on him, Norman. If he's too far gone, for goodness sake keep him indoors. We'll have to think up some excuse and ship him home. He is not strong, but his weakness is not my prime concern.' He shook his head sadly. 'A clear instance of a man given to drink!'

Walter bluffed it out to the last. He left, apparently a sick man. They kept the charade going for everyone's sake, not least the local Chinese. A letter finally reached Peking from Walter, en route home, still claiming illness. 'My throat is seriously affected,' he wrote

Charles guffawed. 'I bet it is. Affected by the lack of alcohol until they reach port, no doubt. That's a fine tale, and not without an ounce of truth – almost amusing, eh?' But they all knew it was far from funny.

Further bad news saddened the year. Charles' old friend, who had looked after him and Miles, Dr Nevins, died of a heart attack. He had been in China longer than any of them, and his loss was hard to bear.

To add to it, Charles himself began to show signs of ill health – scarcely surprising after such difficult months. He and Frances were forced home on furlough, and Harry began to look around nervously. Bill, Chang, Walter and now Charles, all gone from Peking. He was going to be busy, not only to keep the mission going, but to restore confidence in their work.

Some people renew their vigour and are positively encouraged in adversity. Harry was one of these. However busy he was, there was always something more to do, some greater goal to attain. Nor did Harry forget to write home to England, however late the hour. In the late evening he was quite often seen scribbling away another letter home or to St Boniface. One evening he determined to write yet again to his old college, as the servant boy Lu stood at the door of the sitting room.

'What is it, Lu?' he said.

'Mr Norman sir, you want me now?'

'No – you get to bed now, it's late.' He looked at the clock. 'I shouldn't be up either. I'm due at the legation in the morning. Off you go, I shan't be long.'

It was all well intentioned, but he knew he would be up another hour if he was to get his letter written. He stretched and began. 'Our Christians are gradually increasing in numbers. A few catechumens (native lay students) have lately come forward. The number of our school boys is also increasing. These are only the sons of Christian parents. (i.e. not new converts). After the hot weather is over, I am going to open a school for heathen boys. It has been done before, but proved a failure. I hope that it will not be so again. These boys will only be taught Chinese classics at first; after, I want to impress upon them if possible, the truths of Christianity. By this means, I hope to gain access to the homes of the boys, and so get on familiar terms with their parents.' Harry fell to thinking about his plans – it was a well-used ploy, often tried and generally successful. The Chinese always approached education from a traditional, classical standpoint. Trying to entice them to school to study strange subjects would have proved fruitless. The poorer people were just beginning to appreciate the value of education – Harry had heard the Chinese had a higher level of literacy than the British! Anyway, he was only following the good Jesuit precept; education was the key to the mind! He began thinking of all the parents he would meet, and homes to which he could gain access. A certain amount of guile and craft were essential in the making of a successful missionary!

Nothing remained equable for long, though. His thoughts turned to the hardships in the little school in one of the villages he had visited. The weather was always unsuitable. If it was not too hot or too cold, it was too wet or too dry. In another letter, written late on another evening, he wrote: 'Now we are in the midst of our most inconvenient weather – the rainy season. This year we have been flooded, and our loss is considerable. For two days the water was knee deep in my room, but our church suffered most, where the water was up to my waist. We saved what we could, and then set about helping the sufferers. The little bread and potatoes that I had, I shared with the schoolboys, and then, after seeking a comparatively dry spot, I began to administer quinine and brandy in small doses, for many of our Christians were shivering with wet and cold, and there was fear lest fever should be caught from the poisonous germs in the water washed into our compound. We had many scares during the progress of the flood, which in the hand of an artist, would have made excellent illustrations.'

No way, he thought, had the missionary college trained him for all that. At least he had the duty to tell present students what they might realistically expect of missionary life. Now he thanked God, too, for his training in Salisbury. He had cursed the delay at the time, but Welsh was a wise man, who had made sure he was armed with another precious skill. Unaccustomed to Western treatments, the Chinese considered Harry's medicines to be magical, and took his abilities very seriously. He perhaps understated the value of sharing privations with the people. It simply did not occur to him to do anything else.

By the end of 1894, Harry could reflect that he must now be an experienced missionary. He had worked in the school in Peking, and also ventured out to the villages on a number of occasions. He had greeted yet another new face in the mission station, this time a young man with more potential than poor Pigrum – Henry Mathews, bringing welcome news from Warminster with him. He had been sent off to help tired and sick Henry Brereton in the now complete and consecrated church room in Tientsin, and was due back in Peking. Geoffrey Iliff was also back as the senior man in the Bishop's absence, and Frank Norris was mainly absent itinerating around the countless villages south of Peking. He seemed to be particularly busy and had recently completed a new school room in Yung Ching town.

By now, Harry and Geoffrey were firm friends, having each other's company to the exclusion of most others in Peking. 'I wonder what 1895 holds in store,' Harry inquired of the fire, distantly.

101

'I'm not sure.' Geoffrey's answer alerted Harry, for it sounded more than unsure, it was apprehensive.

'You worried about something? Tell me, if I can help.' Harry was concerned.

'It's nothing. It's just that I was at the legation, and they were talking there about trouble from the Japanese. I've also just received a letter from the Bishop in Chefoo. I wish he were here, not wintering on the coast, even though I realize he is safer there. Apparently Lord Rosebery has alerted him to attacks reported recently on missionaries. I knew we had heard of them, but if word has reached London, they might be more extensive than we realized. Our men in the south could be in trouble. The war, and fear of the Japanese army reaching Peking, hang over the mission like a cloud.'

'I know,' Harry admitted. 'I heard today there are gunboats at Tientsin to protect the Europeans. Poor Brereton, eh – just completed his church room there, I hope it remains intact while he is away from it.'

'Honestly!' Geoffrey was exasperated. 'If things weren't hard enough anyway, without the Japanese causing trouble. Any problems, and the Chinese look for someone to blame, and it always seems to be us. Look at this pathetic report the Bishop has just sent through to London.' He read: ' "Many Chinese soldiers are coming in, who have escaped the fighting at Port Arthur, some of them wounded – but not severely, for only those slightly wounded could possibly stand the journey overland in this bitter cold ... They express themselves very grateful for the care and attention bestowed upon them at the mission hospitals." The poor Chinese are helpless, watching everyone pick up bits of their land, they are nothing but a subjugated race now – how can they be expected to like us. Their wretched government's no better – see he says it here.' He prodded the letter. ' "They are a most governable people. The mercantile and agricultural part of the nation have many valuable and sterling qualities, but everything is choked and marred by the want of an ordinary, upright and capable government." How often have I said that – either no action, or not enough. Now the Japanese are snapping at them, and they haven't enough strength to fight back. No wonder there's trouble.'

'It's the winter, too.' Harry, ever practical, thought of the details. 'It's even colder this winter than last. No food, no movement. We're all shivering from either cold or fear – or both. Come the spring, surely things will improve. Now the Marines have been called up to Peking, the Japanese will surely release their grip.'

'I just hope you're right.' Geoffrey looked worried. 'It looks like Brereton is due to be invalided out, and may have left for Hong Kong by now. That means we will be in charge of young Mathews – there's a challenge for you! I can see you gossiping like a couple of old women about Warminster.'

Harry was right, and the spring did ease matters. The rivers unfroze and the Japanese threat also melted away. With the Bishop and Frances in Chefoo, and Brereton by now on the way home to a year's convalescence in Bournemouth, closer to his boys, Peking was in the hands of Geoffrey and Harry, with Frank appearing when he could, saddle-sore from itinerating in the villages fifty miles south round Yung Ching. Young Henry Mathews stumbled through his Chinese lessons much as Harry had, and Harry could see a reflection of himself from what seemed so long ago – it was, in fact, only three years. By now, in addition to the lady workers, the mission boasted two Chinese readers, a catechist and a schoolmaster. Perhaps at last the work could prosper.

It was with the greatest pleasure that Harry took his share of training Mathews. He seemed to have a keen mind, and took to Chinese well. It was not long before Harry dared to take him into the school, to help. 'You can't study all the time without putting it into practice,' Harry insisted, and Henry gladly put his pen down and stretched his cramped hand.

'Fine with me. I'm seeing double, I think! I'd love to do anything else just now,' he replied eagerly.

'Right. I'm off to the school to teach them some English and geography. You can help with that, with little Chinese. It'll be a good break.'

Harry had a pile of books and rolled maps ready, and the two let themselves out of the back door of the mission, to walk across to the school. But they got no further, for hurtling round the corner came one of the schoolboys, far too keen on looking back, to make sure he had not been seen, to look where he was going. They collided, and the books and maps flew in every direction. Before he knew what had happened, Harry had, literally, collared him.

'Come here, you young varmint,' he bellowed, as the lad stopped, nearly suspended by his collar, his eyes popping out of his head with surprise. 'Well, well! It had to be Wang! Where are you going this time?'

No reply. Wang had the sense not to offer an excuse.

'This,' Harry nodded at Wang, 'is one of our little problems. Due to leave school and return to the family farm soon. Not done a stroke of work, he's either a dunce or idle, but I suspect the latter. Wang, you can't go on like this.'

'I don't want the farm. I now have been to school.'

'No one is ever too good to earn a living by good honest work, Wang. You do not make yourself popular by your behaviour, and you do yourself no good. I shall have to take you in hand,' and poor Wang was frogmarched back to class, to be kept under Harry's stern eye, sullenly learning geography.

As Wang left that night – first out of class – Harry looked despairingly after him. 'Whatever will become of him – if he won't go back to the farm, can you imagine what future he has on the streets of Peking? Did you notice him in class, Henry? He hated it – but he got it right! He has a brain, if only the ninny would use it.'

That evening the subject of Wang was debated in the sitting room. Everyone groaned on hearing the name. He was only too well known. Harry threw down the gauntlet. 'I think you give up on him too easily – I'll show you – the only thing I can teach him is carpentry – I'll do that!'

'We've tried that craft training idea before,' came the reply. 'It never works.'

'Then it's our fault for not trying hard enough,' was Harry's response.

Harry made the business into a real challenge. Day after day he

Harry in his College robe.
Studio portrait taken in Salisbury.

Bishop Charles Scott with his staff and Chinese men and boys.
Harry is on the Bishop's left

The rudimentary building at Lung Hua Tien which served
both as school and church.

The church at Tai Whang Chuang, built in a
few weeks by local people

Harry (left) and Charles Robinson
in Chinese clothes.

Harry itinerating, with his donkey Faithful.

Harry's house at Yung Ching.

Harry's grave at Hsin-Min Chuang.

sought Wang out and took him aside at school to teach him carpentry. It cost him personally in wood, and tools of all sorts, but Wang began to respond. Harry then badgered the staff for little orders for Wang to make shelves, tables, anything simple. The mission slowly filled with half-wanted articles. Poor Frank Norris, caught on a visit up from the villages, became the proud possessor of a table he called a 'curiosity'. 'We had all thought the experiment had tried and failed,' he reminded them all, 'but then we were not Norman!' Eventually Wang was good enough, and was finally taken to a carpenter in the city to be apprenticed.

'He's taken him on,' called Harry on his return.

'So who's paying for it?' they all replied.

'I am.' There was no response to that.

Sometime later, Harry visited the master carpenter and pronounced him inferior. Wang was removed and sent – at Harry's expense – to Chefoo, to one of the best carpenters in North China, Tong Hing. There he remained for three years, and became a master craftsman, eventually passing on his skills to other Christian boys, and earning a good wage into the bargain. Harry gave, and had not counted the cost, little knowing that Wang would enter his life again later, and help him no less than he had been helped.

Above all, Harry loved teaching and working with the youngsters, and although he was responsible for all the work with the Chinese in Peking by this time, his heart was in the boys' school. Nevertheless, whenever he was called on to visit outlying stations, or to travel south to Yung Ching to help Frank Norris, he went with a good heart. Being concerned, as he was, for the schoolboys, he was appalled one day to hear, when working in one of the villages, that one of the boys had met with an accident and was dangerously ill back in Peking. As hastily as he could, he packed his bags, and rushed to the family of the boy, living in one of the nearby villages, and he urged the father to return to Peking with him then and there to collect the boy. The poor man had already buried his eldest son, and Fu Tien was his only remaining child. Harry's secret fear was that the child might have died before they reached him. The best hope was to be able to return him to his family for his last days.

By the time Harry and the distraught father reached Peking, Harry knew the malaise he himself had felt for weeks was developing seriously, the heat and limited sanitation continued to destroy the toughest of constitutions. He gingerly lowered himself from the cart, the world spinning round him, while sounds floated in and out of his ears in a disjointed way, and clammy sweat poured off him. 'This way' – he pointed to the front door, where the boy's father was welcomed by no less a person than Frank. He was no stranger, for he had been a schoolboy in the Peking school himself years earlier and had recently been confirmed, to everyone's joy. Once the man had been settled, Frank returned to Harry, who had sat, without so much as removing his jacket, in an armchair, his head propped on his arm.

'You look dreadful,' Frank said, concerned at the sight of Harry.

'I feel it. Whatever I have is getting worse. I've not been right for weeks really, but the journey back has finished me!'

'Bed for you,' the order came decisively.

'No, Frank.' Harry was weary to the point of exhaustion. 'I must go to the American hospital to see how the boy is.'

'Now that's plain ridiculous. You don't look as if you could get there. Anyway they won't thank you for bringing whatever you've got to sick people. The boy is beyond help, Harry – he has had his leg amputated above the knee, and is so weak, he hasn't many days to live. We've been every day to see him, all that can be done, has been.' Frank put his arms on Harry's shoulders and half-lifted him. 'Come on, no "buts", we can't have a second invalid.'

Harry turned to Frank shakily. 'How did it happen, Frank? He was so fit when I left.'

'It's too stupid. He fell off a wall and cracked his leg. Infection set in, and I expect gangrene. By the time his parents brought him to the hospital, it was too far gone.'

'Poor lad,' said Harry, and fainted.

By the next morning Harry felt a great deal better. The world had stopped its crazy motion, and he thought his temperature was down. Leaving his bed, though, was a major task, which he admitted was asking too much. The Chinese doctor recommended prolonged rest and a stay at Chefoo for the summer. Harry, with all his strength, resisted the idea as unnecessary and impractical. Weakly he fought off attempts to organize a convalescence. Geoffrey and Frank pleaded with him, to no avail. Just to prove the point, Harry began to get up for short periods and potter about the mission house. 'Almost back to my old self,' he said with a pale smile after a few days, but he convinced no one but himself.

They had given up trying to change his mind, when a few days later, Harry suddenly announced, 'You're right. Chefoo is a sensible option. As soon as I'm fit, I shall go there for a few weeks, it's just what I need.'

'I give up.' Geoffrey flung his arms in the air. 'You're talking sense at last. When we suggested it, it was a crazy idea, now it's obvious. Honestly. At least we can arrange things now. I'll get the cart organized to take you to the station, one day next week, when you feel well enough. Thank goodness you've come to your senses!'

Privately Geoffrey was puzzled. Why on earth had Harry changed his mind so radically? He had become quite preoccupied with the idea of Chefoo, and seemed to be sending the servant lad out on errands to buy things for the journey at the least whim. Perhaps his illness had unhinged him, he was behaving very oddly!

On the Tuesday morning Harry was due to leave for Chefoo, Geoffrey watched him prepare for his journey, saying goodbye to everyone, with a special word for Fu Tien's father. The door chime rang out, and Harry was at once on his feet and at the door.

'There's no need to go that fast,' Geoffrey called.

'It's for me, someone for me,' Harry replied over his shoulder.

'What on earth is he up to now?' Frank and Geoffrey looked at each other, perplexed.

A few minutes later Harry returned, still weak and therefore staggering under the weight of what he was carrying. There in his arms, smiling broadly, was the little one-legged boy, fresh from the hospital.

'Baggage ready for the station!' Harry was exultant as he carefully placed Fu Tien on the sofa near his father.

'What on earth are you doing now? How did he get here? What's all this about?'

Harry beamed an even wider smile than usual. 'I just decided that if I had to leave Peking the lad could come wi' me. We both need the air of Chefoo, and his father is agreeable – so there we are!' and he ruffled the boy's hair. 'You ready then, lad?'

No one replied. Frank raised his eyes and hands to heaven and Geoffrey smiled and shook his head. Minutes later the little group trooped to the cart, Harry carrying the boy, his father, Norris with the baggage, and the whole mission staff. After much packing and last minute organizing, the cart trundled off to the station, with the two invalids happily wedged in by their cases, and Frank Norris, who was travelling as far as Tientsin.

Norris was the only one of the three who was really up to the journey. For eight long miles they jogged along until they reached the station, aiming for the 11 a.m. train. 11 o'clock came, and noon, without luck. They decided to trundle off to where the goods train would pass, but with no greater fortune. Being at the goods station, they missed the 11 a.m. train, when it finally passed through the passenger station at 4 p.m.!

Utterly dejected and tired, all three took the cart a further mile, where they stayed overnight at a little wayside inn. At 4 a.m. on the Wednesday they finally caught the Tientsin train, arduous enough for anyone, but for two sick people, it was a nightmarish journey. Fu Tien, though, was remarkably bright. He had never seen a train before, and sat smiling and asking questions for most of the journey.

At Tientsin, Harry and Fu Tien separated from Norris, and travelled by steamer to Chefoo, and stayed at the mission house with Miles Greenwood, where they passed many happy weeks. As Harry grew stronger he fashioned the boy a pair of crutches and taught him to use them. Both recovered fully, Harry eventually returning a healthy lad to his relieved parents. He simply had no conception of the word 'cannot'.

Life was not always like that. Many a time Harry had to admit depression, if not defeat. He had cause to write to Mr Welsh. 'Alas, our hopes were never realized to the extent we had expected. Our neighbours did not respond to our invitations.

There was no hostile feeling but people generally avoided open intercourse with us. Consequently our work has fallen flat.' But it never lasted long. Soon something positive happened, which encouraged them all to work again. They learned to notice and respond to the smallest signs of interest.

The spring of 1895 saw two changes in the mission house in Peking. The Bishop, ever eager for more staff, had continued the bombardment of SPG headquarters in London, and the result was a new recruit. Roland Allen, trained and ready for full duties, turned up in Peking that spring. Harry, seeing the opportunity, requested the chance to spread his wings and travel further than Yung Ching and Chefoo for the first time in three years. Logic dictated that an extra man in Peking would allow an old hand to be released. Having eased Henry Mathews into life in the city, Harry was keen to try something new. Charles Scott approved the journey in March, as soon as he judged the Japanese danger to have abated, and Harry set off south on the 350 mile journey to the southernmost station at Tai-an, where Francis Sprent was in charge, and where Bill Pigrum still toiled away.

The journey south, he thought, as he plodded along on the donkey, was rather different from his journey up just a few years previously. For a start, the warm spring weather was an improvement. He knew the language, he was a fully-trained priest, and he was in command of the situation at last. He was quite excited at the prospect of Tai-an, a large city, considered holy by the Chinese, as it nestled at the base of the holy Tai Shan mountain. Pilgrims visited in hundreds, and the missionaries lost no opportunity in addressing the crowds.

The first person Harry saw when he approached the mission house was his old friend Bill Pigrum. 'Bill! Good to see you. You've not changed a bit! How are you, how's the Chinese going?'

Bill smiled, for he was genuinely pleased to see Harry, but he was ashamed that his studies had not gone any better recently than they had in Peking.

'I'm so glad you've come. Cheer me up if you can. Francis tries hard with me,' he admitted, 'but I'm a useless student, I don't think I will ever get the hang of it. I think the Bishop's disappointed in me. I certainly am. He only considers me worth £20 a quarter still, which shows you.'

Harry nodded sadly. There was little he could say, as he knew Bill had still not been priested and had heard of his problems. It also occurred to him that he himself received £30 a quarter, and even before he was ordained had been given £25.

'It's a slow business, I know.' He put his arm on Bill's shoulder. 'I'm sure you're improving. Let's hear what Francis says,' and they entered the mission.

What Francis said, privately, only reinforced Bill's misgivings about himself. He was willing and earnest, but not gifted enough for the examinations he had to sit. 'He might manage in an English speaking country – eventually – but I've done all I can, and I have had to admit defeat. It's a shame, he is so dejected and feels such a failure.'

Harry determined to take Bill's mind off his troubles, and listened while Bill related the history of the station during the evenings. Charles Scott and Miles Greenwood had set up the mission over twenty years earlier, and Harry immediately remembered his Bishop telling him the story of those early days. In the weeks which followed, Harry joined Francis and Bill in their travels round the villages, especially the area of Ping Yin, about fifty miles west, which had been worked hard by Francis. In the southern province, people travelled by wheelbarrow, with two men to guide it – one at the front, the other behind. The padded, but unsprung vehicle was remarkably comfortable, and they could easily travel thirty miles in a day. Only too eagerly Harry rolled up his sleeves to help in their new dispensary. He soon discovered that work in country areas was immensely rewarding, far nearer his preference than the city of Peking. He got to know whole families, and responded to the needs of the community much more naturally, as he travelled from village to village. The people were poor, the area low lying and unhealthy, full of mosquitoes, the problems of disease and hunger ever present – but was that so much worse than a shipwreck off the Dorset coast, or a bad corn harvest?

Slowly, but with increasing certainty, Harry knew he wanted to leave Peking and serve in a station in a country area. Every time he helped officiate at a service in a little hut, or even in the open air, he saw in his mind a little village station that would be his to run one day.

Francis was keen to let Bill and Harry have some time together. They were both still relatively young, and he hoped Harry could console and guide poor Bill. He packed them off for a couple of days to climb the holy mountain Tai Shan. They went with no particular provisions, other than some basic foodstuffs, hoping to shelter where they could in the warm nights. They visited the shrine of Confucius, where he was said to have been buried, and climbed to the top of the mountain, an arduous journey of some seven hours, despite the steps placed into the steep hillside. At the top they stayed for two nights, hiring a small room. Harry took the opportunity to write home to his brothers, and related their adventure.

'I stayed up there two days, but one night we were compelled to turn out of our small room that we hired, because the owner of the house came! It was night, and as there were no other rooms, it was not pleasant to turn out. We had to sleep on a very wet and dirty floor of an idol temple. We had no plates, knives or forks to eat our food with, but still we enjoyed it.'

The letter was meant for Josiah and George, by now fourteen and fifteen, and in the world themselves. In the busyness of the last three years, Harry admitted to Bill that he had sometimes almost forgotten home. 'I think of China as more home than anywhere. Young Jo, for example, he was only nine or ten when I last saw him, and scarcely at school when I left home. They will have changed out of all recognition – and so will I. I've grown away from them so much, I'm almost nervous of my first furlough, you know.'

'I wish I could say I thought of China as home.' Bill was disconsolate, 'I don't think I fit in here – more to the point, I don't think God wants me here. I have asked about transfer – perhaps to South Africa. I just hope I will fit in there better.'

Harry looked at him deeply. 'There will still be language problems there, Bill. Why not try an English speaking colony – Canada or Australia. I've heard there is great work to be done there.'

Bill shrugged his shoulders miserably. 'We'll see,' he said.

That evening Harry's conscience attacked him once again, and he decided to use some time to write to his little brother, Jo. If he did not keep up the contact, they would all be strangers to him in a few years time.

'Dear Brother, You wrote to me some time ago, so now I write this short note to you. You will see from the above address (Tai-an) that I am not in Peking. I have been here about six weeks. The journey down here was very bad. I stopped at a few places on the way down, but I was nearly three weeks on the road. There are about ten Englishmen down here. Three weeks ago I went to another of our mission places called Ping Yin. I stayed there a week … Down here it is very hot, 108° degrees in the shade. We feel almost roasted sometimes. I shall be going back to Peking in about 4–5 weeks time, so write to me there.'

He stopped, and began to think about Portland, the first time he had done so in months. He heard the gulls, smelt the ozone on the air and felt the solid Portland stone, reflecting whitely in the sunlight. It was all half a world away, and Ma and Pa so distant. He continued. 'How are things getting on at home and elsewhere? Some time must pass away before I see the old place again. You must be grown up quite tall by this time. I hope that Willie and Albert are taking care of themselves and behaving as they ought.

I shall tell you some things about my journey later on. It all but killed me to travel here. You get jolted to pieces. I might send some photos by and by, if I can get any.'

The letter was rather losing the way. He had very little to talk about to a boy he hadn't seen for years. He had much more in common with the boys in the school in Peking. How wonderful it would be to open up a school in a country area like this. Imagine the vast numbers who had never heard of Christianity, who could be contacted! His thoughts gave him an idea and he scribbled:

'I want you to buy two books for me, and send them out as soon as you can – a good geography, and an arithmetic book. To get the books you should go to Weymouth, and ask the best bookseller to get them for you.

(1) Arithmetic book – *Smith's Arithmetic*. It is a large book of

112

about 200 pages, price 2/6–5/–. It has answers to all the sums, from simple addition, decimals etc.

(2) Geography book – Ask for the latest and best book containing not English geography only, but geography about all the world. There is one by a man – Canon Bevan – and called *The Students Manual of Modern Geography*, price 7/6d. There is another by a man, John Richardson, price 2/6d, either of these will do, but only one of them. I shall send some money soon, and then you can take out what you have spent. Be sure, get good books. Send books per book post.'

He read the letter – yes, that would do. It was clear. Who better to ask than a boy who had just left school himself, rather than his parents, whose memories of school days were sketchy, and who probably had never used such books. The boys in Peking would make good use of them, once his quarterly stipend came through and he could post money to England.

Harry smiled as he imagined Jo – he still thought of him as about ten – talking man to man with the bookseller about books 'for my brother in China'. He would feel so important carrying a whole sovereign to Weymouth, playing his part in Harry's work on the other side of the world. He could also imagine the books being parcelled up on the kitchen table, together with useful bits and pieces, small gifts and letters, all to be sent to London for shipment.

Finally, Harry's happy stay in Tai-an had to come to an end, and he packed his bags for the gruelling journey northwards. 'At least there's one thing,' he confessed to Francis, 'the roads are better kept and wider than in the north, and some are lit, but it's still all so slow. Tientsin has a railway. This journey is tedious in the extreme.'

Francis agreed. 'I only make the journey when I have to, but it's mighty lonely down here. I don't think I shall have Bill much longer either.'

'What's to become of him?'

'I think Charles has arranged for him to go to Perth next year, if he can get him accepted. At least he can concentrate on his studies without the problems of language. Let's hope that does the trick.'

It did. The next year Bill resigned from China and travelled to

Australia, where he was priested and worked successfully for many years.

Harry said farewell to his two friends, knowing that he was not likely to see Bill again. He took letters from Francis to Bishop Scott, and the other staff, and set off again on the long journey north. The time gave him ample opportunity to think. He was now even more sure that he wanted to work in an outstation, away from Peking. He knew he would revel in the responsibilities of directing church life, preaching, teaching and living at close quarters with the Chinese. He was sure he was ready. The only question was – would the Bishop agree, and where would he decide to send him?

4

In Yung Ching

By the end of his travels back to Peking, Harry had a very clear idea of what he wanted to do next. Unfortunately, the Bishop was in no position to comply with his wishes.

'Do you realize what's been happening since you've been gone? We have all been worried to death about you.'

Harry was puzzled. Nothing special or out of the way seemed to have occurred.

'The Chinese,' Charles explained, 'especially round the area where you were, have been causing dreadful trouble with the authorities, ever since the problems with Japan came to a head. They hate foreigners of any description, and Shantung of course, is full of them. They say the area is 'swarming with missionaries, soldiers and businessmen' and I dare say they are right.'

'Not where I was.' Harry was vehement.

'Nevertheless, in the towns it seems to be the case. They put us all in one pot and accuse us of taking over the country. They've murdered two German missionaries.'

'Murdered! Good heavens, I hadn't realized.'

The Bishop nodded. 'The local people accused them of interfering with the courts set up to try Chinese Christians. I expect they were only trying to save the dear faithful people, but the locals hate the Chinese converts even more than they despise us. Thank God you're back safely anyway. I just hope Pigrum and Sprent have the sense to lie low a bit.'

Harry could see what was coming, 'I suppose that means you feel we should stay close to Peking, and not venture out? I had hopes of talking to you about village work – there's so much work to be done in those hamlets and small towns. That's where the need is – Peking has hundreds of staff in all the missions!'

'Not now, Harry.' The Bishop was firm. 'I've even pulled Frank Norris back from Yung Ching, which is only fifty miles away. It's not safe. I let him go down for short periods, but only when it looks calm. No, for the time being you stay here.'

The silence said more than any eloquent speech.

Charles looked across at Harry, who eventually returned a smile of resignation. Charles recognized that Harry meant a lot to him, he hated to see him disappointed, or held back from what he would undoubtedly be able and competent to do.

'If you want a challenge …' Harry looked up. The bait had been taken, interest already sparkled in his eyes. 'I've been looking around for some time for a typeface for the old printing press we were given, and I have got some secondhand Chinese typeface – I'll need you to look it over, with your knowledge of printing. It is expensive, but would be invaluable.'

'How much is it?'

'£33–8–6d, or your stipend till the Autumn!'

'Well, if you think I can remember the printing techniques from four years ago, I'll try. But I'm no engineer. I hope it's in working order!'

Inevitably, it wasn't – quite. But with a bit of work, stripping it down and reassembling parts, oiling it and cajoling it, the thing worked. In an outhouse behind the school, Harry was to be found most days, covered in grease, and later, once the machine had been tried out, ink.

Roland Allen, who by now had been installed as the legation chaplain, could scarcely come to terms with the sight of a brother priest, filthy and inkstained, wandering round the mission house.

'For goodness sake don't show yourself at the legation looking like that, or we'll all be turned out! How are you going to take the communion with ink in your nails and halfway up your arms! Ugh.' He shuddered and jumped back as Harry advanced on him with black paws outstretched.

'This is good honest dirt,' he laughed. 'You wait – you'll be pleased I took the trouble,' and he wagged a blackened finger at him.

A few days later, after much cranking and heaving of the

manually operated beast, he achieved a reasonable copy of a single sheet. It was passed round with great solemnity, and Harry was well complimented. But as with any success, it bred on itself. Orders for tracts came in from everyone, and he was busy every spare hour he had, setting type or cranking the handle, as one by one, the sheets were pressed on to the inked typeface.

But Harry and Charles Scott had another project in mind, one which they didn't reveal to the others. Shortly, often by candle light in the evenings, Harry assembled the type for a Prayer Book, and produced the first ever version of it in Chinese.

'There you are,' he announced. 'As long as they can read, they can follow the services in their own tongue, and not have to memorize it all. You can throw away the hand copied sheets you use now. Once these are bound, we can use hundreds all over the province – in Chefoo and Tientsin, in Yung Ching whenever Frank goes, and we can even send them down to Tai-an.'

Unfortunately, Harry was quite right – hundreds were ordered, and he could see his versatility becoming a handicap. He hadn't, surely, come all this way to be a printer, and shackled to Peking as well! He saw everyone else seemingly moving on, while he made no progress. Roland had not been there more than a few months, and had a legation chaplaincy. Two new lady workers arrived, one a nurse, and were both coping with an outbreak of cholera in the city. Henry Mathews, now fully fledged, had taken over Henry Brown's work while he was on furlough. Francis Sprent and Geoffrey Iliff in the south sent back reports of success. Meanwhile – Harry looked at the printing press – it felt as if he was getting nowhere. He sighed, and bent to his task, determined not to complain.

As usual, things happened when they were least expected. Just as Harry was deep into the production of carol sheets for Christmas, the Bishop, on his way to Chefoo for the winter, announced: 'It looks as if neither of us will be in Peking for Christmas.'

'Neither of us?' Harry regarded the pile of printing to be done with trepidation.

'Well, things have calmed down a bit, and the British Minister seems happier for us to travel about now. It doesn't mean that things are absolutely safe – there are always bands of ruffians who will antagonize foreigners, but it seems reasonably secure. How do you fancy a trip down to Yung Ching for a few weeks to minister to them over Christmas? I want a candid report on the work that needs doing, I don't want Frank Norris' work to come to nothing, now he's stationed at Tientsin.'

'I'm already there.' Harry was delighted. It would mean extra work on the press before he went, but now it was operating, others could work it easily in his absence. 'When do I go?'

'Perhaps a week or so before Christmas? You had better take a lad with you, and plan an itinerary. Frank left me a list of villages and maps when he went to Tientsin recently, so you can decide which places to visit. The Christian villagers will also organize things for you, I imagine, they usually have things well planned.'

The organizing of the trip took longer than Harry had anticipated. Instructions had to be left for others to operate 'the contraption'. Teaching in the school had to be spread among the others, and Nurse Sands had to take on some dispensary work. Most importantly, Harry was given money to purchase a donkey, and he spent ages inspecting a line of them in the market, before selecting a large-eared dark grey animal, which he christened Faithful. He filled Faithful's side panniers with thick clothes, tracts and Prayer Books, and with a trusted boy from the mission house proudly astride the animal, led them through the streets, and out on to the open road, for the fifty mile trip south.

It was a strange Christmas, staying in the homes of local people, sleeping on floors, or to his great embarrassment, being given the best bed near the stove, relegating his hosts to the floor. He travelled with Faithful to village after village, quietly visiting homes, and celebrating the eucharist, with the lad as acolyte. Word got about, and when he arrived, numbers had gathered in one house. He counted heads, and was amazed to realize the numbers there were. They had also travelled long distances to be there – they hadn't seen a priest for months, some for a year, since they had last seen Frank Norris.

In one village, a group of potential confirmees came forward, and he taught them as best he could in the time he had available, promising to arrange the ceremony for late January, if he could.

118

In Yung Ching town itself, there was a little church, and there Harry conducted services on Christmas Day. It was a joyous occasion, the lack of the trappings of festivity didn't matter to him a bit. 'It was the happiest Christmas I have ever spent,' he said afterwards. 'Why? Because our little church was packed full, and the services had a Christmas ring about them.'

On his return, only too soon, to Peking, Harry set about his plans for work in the villages, estimating the areas of strength and weakness, calculating cost and setting objectives. His first aim, predictably, was to revitalize the school which Norris had built for the local boys. After that he hoped to organize a regular trip to the outlying villages. He had been shaken to realize that so many of them had not had benefit of communion for so long.

When Scott returned to Peking at the end of January, to accompany Harry back to Yung Ching for the confirmation, he was bombarded with Harry's ideas. 'I know, I know,' was all he could say. 'I do realize, you know, what needs to be done. I have already written to the SPG highlighting the needs of Yung Ching. Particularly I've asked for two men to be sent there.'

Harry was surprised. 'Two?'

'Well, you say yourself there is need for both a teacher and an itinerating priest – the work could really spread. Until I get permission, would you go alone and set things up?'

There was no need for a second bidding, and before long Harry was established next to the church at Yung Ching. The donkey slept in a makeshift lean-to alongside. Harry became inordinately proud of Faithful, brushing her down and tweaking her ears, as he talked to her about his hopes. She had a speed second to none, according to Harry, sure feet on the stony roads, and a dependable temperament. The relationship between the two grew, until Faithful could sense when her master needed her to go quietly down the dark alleys at night to a secret meeting, or when – tired at the end of a day – he longed to be home. When he finally took off her bridle, cloth saddle and stirrups, she knew that the pair of them could look forward to food and the satisfaction of a job well done, for she also played her part in the promotion of the gospel.

Day after day, Harry put Faithful in the lean- to and returned to the little two-roomed home bequeathed to him by Frank Norris.

119

He lit the stove, his only source of heat, and removed his ankle-length habit, balaclava style headgear, and padded shoes, and set about feeding himself, and preparing for the next journey.

It was a lonely life, but slowly, the local Christians began to call, and he made genuine friends with them. Often he gained a welcome to a home through the children, who wanted to attend the school. The main trouble was that so many people lived so far from Yung Ching town, the children had to walk miles. To make matters worse, whenever the farms were busy, the children were kept at home to help. Nor, he soon discovered, was every local person keen on the new Christian priest. He was taunted, and he knew the Christian Chinese were badly treated if it was known that they fraternized with the third-class devil!

He realized he had to take great care with his work, in order not to antagonize or frighten anybody. He timed himself and Faithful, so that he would reach villages in the evening, just after dark. As he reached the gate of each village, he dismounted, there to be met by a local Christian as arranged. He was led, with the donkey, to where the converts were gathered, usually a private home. By this stage, he had acquired not only Chinese dress, but a false black pigtail, so at night he was taken for a Chinese with no difficulty. Quickly and quietly, Faithful would be hitched outside, and the men slipped into the back entrance of the house.

Once inside, the routine continued. By candlelight, Harry changed into his surplice, then set up his portable altar on a table. Having introduced himself, he gazed into the bright eyes of another new set of Chinese faces, and set about instructing them in Christian beliefs. They were always extremely keen, the teaching went on for hours, frequently until midnight. At that point, they would all break for a few hours rest, Harry on the hard brick bed – the place of honour – with the others round him. By 3 a.m., they rose for the main service, and Harry, again dressed in the surplice, would celebrate holy communion. Before daybreak, his guide prepared him to leave, loading his bedding on the donkey, and again disguised as a Chinese, he led the donkey out through the village gates, to return to Yung Ching, or carry on to another village.

Often he would be away from his base for days or even weeks,

120

nightly slipping into villages to meet yet more new converts. He was constantly amazed at the numbers, and reassured that his work was necessary. Itinerating took its toll. Lack of sleep, and constant travel were exhausting. The need to take care, and protect the Chinese from their own people, was constant. The heat, the cold, the damp conditions, were only added inconveniences. Above all it was hard to be on show, the upright, confident man of God, with an answer for everyone's troubles, and none of his own. He rarely saw another European, and missed the language and culture of his homeland. By his little house, in front of the cloistered verandah, he grew roses, surrounding the bed with a low wall. 'Perhaps,' he thought, 'it might look like a little bit of England,' at those moments when he knew that his faith in what he was doing was being put to the test.

From time to time he would travel back to Peking, for contact with his own people, and for a rest from the strain of the work. Life in Yung Ching seemed light years away, once back in the mission house.

'You have it easy here,' he reminded Roland Allen, as they sat over the fire in the sitting room. 'I have a boy who comes in to cook sometimes, but apart from that, I do for myself. Basics only – no carpets – no home organized for me. Not a rickshaw in sight, and only Faithful to talk to half the time.'

'It's what you argued for, I seem to remember.'

'Oh – don't misunderstand me – I wouldn't change it for the world. The people there are so interested, and there is such potential. You know, there are 400 villages round Yung Ching, and I've only visited a fraction of them in what, a year now almost.'

'Very different from Peking,' Roland acknowledged. 'One day, I must try to get down to visit. I expect you could do with an extra pair of hands.'

'I certainly could. The Bishop mentioned that before I left, but nothing came of it. Still, as long as I can keep coming up to Peking, I can manage.'

Roland thought, then said meaningfully: 'We do have a new man due out from England any day now. I know Scott said he had arranged something, you could always sound him out to see what his plans are for him. Hopefully you'll meet the chap before you return. I think the Bishop said he was another from Warminster, so that should please you!'

Harry's eyes brightened. 'Interesting! Perhaps that's my assistant at last. Let's hope he's out of the mould of Henry Brown, and not poor old Pigrum! I think I might venture along to see the Bishop, as you say. Slip it into the conversation. Do you know the new chap's name?'

'Robinson, I think.'

'Thanks,' and with that Harry was down the corridor like a bullet, changing to a careless saunter as he reached Frances and Charles Scott's sitting room, where he knew he would find the Bishop at work over his reports to London.

'May I come in, Sir?'

'Harry, come in. Pull up a chair. Enjoying your break back in Peking?'

'Definitely,' replied Harry. 'Things change so fast, the faces in the school are different in a few months. Either that, or I've forgotten some. I get the Peking children confused with the Yung Ching ones.'

'There's a lot of work to do there. I've read your reports – you're doing well. I'm pleased with the way the area is improving. On that score I have some news for you. We've a new man coming tomorrow.'

'Really?' Harry suppressed his eagerness. This was it, for good or ill.

'Young chap from St Boniface. Already been deaconed, and – you will be relieved to hear – a year into his Chinese studies, and passed with credit. We learned our lesson. The colleges are testing their language skills before students are sent out now! Anyway, he'll have to start off in Peking, learning the ropes, but if he seems suitable, could you use an assistant at Yung Ching?'

'I could use a dozen, but one will do for now!' Harry was ecstatic. 'You say he's due tomorrow? So I shall meet him. We can have a look at him and see what he has to offer. That's great news!'

The Bishop smiled. 'Thought you'd be pleased. We mustn't overtax the poor chap, don't overstretch him. I know you too well.

He'll be half-dead from exhaustion within the year if you have your way. My brother John was quite impressed with him. The lad's from Leeds, so he has known of him for some time. Got a good sensible head on him, by all accounts. Anyway – I'll leave you to take him round town a bit – get to know him before you go back.'

Harry was delighted. 'I've got him,' he announced to Roland minutes later.

'Got who?'

'The new man. He's to come to Yung Ching with me after he's settled in. What we won't be able to do, with two of us! We can really get the school going full time, and attend more to the villages.' The plans were underway immediately. Harry just prayed that Robinson would be mature and sensible enough to get his teeth into the work straight away.

In the event he was more than that. The two liked each other from the first meeting. Charles Robinson was only a little younger than Harry, as full of enthusiasm, with a fresh, eager, almost handsome face, and an easy smile. They walked together, talking of the Mission House in Warminster, exchanging memories. The blossom was out in the gardens of Peking, and it was a relaxed and happy introduction for the pair of them.

'I think we have a lot in common, you and I,' said Harry, having assumed the role of senior as naturally as Charles acted the student. 'We've neither of us had an academic background, nor a gentrified home. We've even both been to the same college, and within five years of each other. I think we will work together well. Now tell me – how is the old place – is the pavilion still in use?'

'The pavilion – yes, we used it twice a week, regularly.' Charles was a fast, eager talker, looking straight back into Harry's eyes with confidence. 'We played other colleges last season, and won all but two games. Anyway, the pavilion comes in handy – it was made by an ex-student, you know.'

'I know.' Harry smiled. 'It was me.'

'You! You made that?' Charles closed his mouth, having realized it had dropped open.

'I was superintendent of the joinery workshop, and they cornered me, and asked me to do it, that's all. Anyway, I'm sure you have talents too. What did you get talked into?'

'Well,' Charles admitted, 'I was the college organist, actually.'

'Excellent,' cried Harry. 'I need someone to build up the music in the services at Yung Ching. This is going to be a fine team we'll make!'

The more Harry thought about it, the luckier he was. They were to be thrown together whether they worked well as a pair, or not. Chance, or God – he preferred to believe the latter – dictated that they were to understand each other well, men of similar backgrounds and age. Until Charles was priested, his stipend would be a mere £17-10-0 a quarter, but no matter. They arranged to meet again in the summer, when the Bishop insisted he 'catch all his men' for a conference. Charles was due, finally, to transfer to Yung Ching in the autumn.

Harry worked on happily during the summer, preparing, as far as he was able, for a less solitary life. He feared he might have become selfish, living alone as he had, for so long. He turned out the little bungalow, to make way for a second occupant, purchasing more furniture, and consolidated his own belongings into less space. He even went so far as to procure a rickety piano for the church, to honour the advent of someone competent to use it!

Charles was delighted with the whole arrangement. The little house seemed to amuse him – it was a bit like a dolls' house, Harry admitted, with its little fretted wall containing Harry's neat rose garden, the arched and columned portico, and shuttered windows. Even more amazing were his lessons in coping with the dress – they decided to order two of everything, so consequently went round like two peas from the same pod, in long skirts, thick soled shoes or slippers, and long sleeved jackets with frogging closures. The only problem was Faithful, who seemed not to appreciate having two masters, so they bought a second beast for Charles.

Day by day, Charles became more accepted into the Chinese community, understanding their ways and their language. 'Whatever they speak,' he said, 'it's not the brand of Mandarin I was taught in England. They must have a regional accent.'

'And you haven't?' Harry raised an eyebrow 'Your Yorkshire dialect baffled me to start with.'

'Well, so did yours!' and they laughed. They talked well into the Chinese nights, as Harry prepared Charles for his ordination, and were all too easily sidetracked into matters of their future work together.

'You know,' said Harry stretching his legs in front of the stove, 'I feel strongly that we need to set up a dispensary down here. Have you seen the condition of some of the people – lung problems because of the damp, all sorts of water-born diseases, and the wretched opium smoking has taken hold too. If we advertised a medical service, we would get crowds. All I need is to get some basic supplies from Peking, and we could start.'

'I haven't any medical knowledge.'

'So what?' Harry replied. 'I can always train you. Dressings and medicines aren't that difficult to master. Now surgery is another matter, we all fumble in the dark with that, but if the choice is nothing, you do the best with what you have.'

'I didn't realize you did operations.' Charles was shocked. 'What do you do for anaesthetics?'

'Whatever you can get – often nothing. We could set up a simple wooden table for operations and examinations, even offer a service to the villages.'

And so it came into being. The Chinese formed orderly English queues at first in the open, later in a hut the two built for the purpose. Few were turned away – those who 'grew the poppy' were asked to destroy it before returning, but everyone else received help in their turn, even if the tropical diseases were unknown to the medical staff. What was known locally as 'Jesus opium' was another matter. Any 'foreign devil' was accused of dealing in it, and thereby ruining people's lives. Harry and Charles had no medicine for this. The only method was will-power and practical care. Harry developed quite a technique, and managed by strong tactics to wean some people off the wretched poppy. He began to get a name for it, and new addicts, or their families, came regularly. Knowing that behind every addict was a whole family in trouble, they both did their best, but the problem was always larger than their available time. Harry watched time and again, as children went hungry or uneducated, mothers wrestled to feed and clothe a family on next to nothing, and addicts lay about in a stupor, out of control and slipping towards

125

death. As there was no known cure, most addicts died an ignominious death, but those whom Harry sat with during the agonizing days and weeks of withdrawal, quickly gave him the praise. This man had magical powers!

He wrote back to his parents, to try to give them some insight into the problem.

'I've opened a dispensary in a very quiet sort of way for the benefit of these sick people. There is no need to go into details – a rumour got about that there was a "foreigner" who could heal ulcers and abcesses of the worst kind, in a very wonderful way (and without cost, too!) so they come in great numbers. Such sights I never saw before, and though the numbers and cases of the patients cause me to despair of ever getting through so much, yet I enjoy it. In the absence of anaesthetics, surgery in its simplest form cannot be performed without some amount of pain. Occasionally the screeching of children, crying of women, and groaning, and what is more, the fainting of men, are almost unbearable.'

Very quickly it became apparent that Harry and Charles needed help. They encouraged local Christians, and established regular routines of help from two lay workers. English staff from Peking came down on a regular basis, both to help and to bring fresh provisions, books and drugs, for little was obtainable locally. One of the newer lady workers came on a number of occasions, and stayed with a nearby family. It was good to have some female company for once, they had become only too monastic, and reminded each other of the niceties of social life.

Harry admitted, 'I'm afraid we behave like savages, snatch meals, eat as we go, and rarely tidy up. What the boy doesn't do remains undone, Jessie.'

Jessie, a trained deaconess, knew of the strains of overwork. 'You should make some time for quiet each day, you men. You tear about the country – you especially Harry – you're on that poor donkey or teaching in the school most of the time. If not that, you're playing football or cricket with the boys or listening to the hundred and one wants or difficulties which are always being poured into your ears – and you never allow that you are tired.'

'I know.' Harry was well aware of the need for both of them to pace themselves. 'But how do you say "no" to them? Last night it was almost midnight and someone came for me – how can they be turned away? Simply, Jessie, I love it. I wouldn't be doing anything else but be here for these dear people – nor would Charles. I'm just grateful we both have strong constitutions and good health.'

'You must come up to Peking for a break sometime, it would do you good, and we miss you too. Anyway, the printing press is bad tempered at present, so we need you.'

Harry shrugged. 'You can cope for now. I'll try to come sometime, but just now it's too busy. Charles, help me out, I'm being got at.'

Charles smiled. 'You won't change him,' he told Jessie. 'Nor me. We've got a new project afoot.' He looked at Harry. 'Can I tell her?'

'Go on, the Bishop has agreed, so it's as good as out.'

'Well.' Charles settled, rather proud to be the bearer of important news. 'We – well Harry mainly – we've been concerned that there's little to draw this whole area together – hundreds of villages you see. Add to that the fact that very few of the children in the isolated hamlets can even read or write – what do you have? A new school. The little one we have now only has eighteen scholars, either because they can't get to it, or because they can't afford to let the children off the farms – they work from such an early age to help the family out. The original school closed in 1882, and the best boys were taken to Peking. Frank Norris tried to re-open a school a few years back, but it was very small.'

'But,' Harry held up a finger, 'every single one of our boys is baptized. Now, a larger school, think how many new Christians there would be – and their families, if we keep in touch with them.'

'It's all very commendable.' Jessie picked her words carefully. 'But why should they attend a new school rather than the other?'

'Ah!' Harry was getting into top gear by now, sitting forward in his chair. 'I've tried for ages to get them to come – but there were always as many excuses as pupils – they were needed at home, it was too wet, they could not walk, as their feet were frozen, it was too far, and so on. But they have the makings of educated men, able to learn a trade or even enter the Ministry themselves. There are six or seven I could name from round here who went to school in Peking and on to greater things – a deacon, and three medical students. What an honour it would be to the area, to have even more.'

'So?'

'So we felt our present boys, for their perseverance amidst many difficulties, are deserving of something better than a day school. Look – all the year round they commence school shortly after sunrise, and with the exception of short intervals for food and recreation, morning and noon, they work on until after sunset, then, having read evensong, they go home. So – we offer them a boarding school.'

'A boarding school? What, here?'

'It's obvious – the boys can stay at school during the week, concentrate on their studies without having the tiring journey home. Up to thirty or forty could be accommodated.'

Charles was agog. 'Isn't it brilliant? I can't wait.'

'Just where is the money to come from?' Jessie was practical and down to earth, if not sceptical.

'I'm coming to that.' Harry took a deep breath. 'I've costed it out – each family will be asked to pay 1s 4d a year to defray the expense – a pitifully small amount, but it's a lot to them. The real cost is about £4 a year, and the Bishop is hopeful that the SPG will sponsor it.'

Jessie frowned 'Whew! I hope you're right. They are scarcely known for their generosity, Harry. You'll be lucky to get it – you're asking for about £150.'

'Well, we're starting with four boys. Charles and I are helping out from our stipends to begin with. You see – it will work.'

It was true, they did start, but the SPG never came forward with the money, and the boarding side of the school never came to fruition. There were never more than four boarders. Nevertheless the school flourished, and Harry had to be contented with a growing number of day pupils.

One of the villages, Lung Hua Tien, was developing fast. Not to be put off by the lack of a boarding school, Harry and Charles opened a second day school there that summer. The pupils were mainly non-Christian, but eager to learn. The little school, carefully planned, doubled as a church, and was simple in the extreme. It had to be, for Charles and Harry, with help from a few skilled Chinese, painstakingly assembled it brick by brick. One door, one window and a flat roof – it had only the basics. From a stick propped against the wall hung a large Chinese bell, shaped like an inverted tulip, acquired from no one quite knew where. Its sound was capable of raising the heartbeat of any latecomer in seconds.

Within eighteen months there were fifteen regular pupils – and five – Harry reminded everyone – were baptized. It was a matter of time, he was sure, before he salvaged the other ten.

Whenever he returned to Peking, on a flying visit for some reason or other, Harry badgered for books, for medicines, but above all for money.

'Just £10, and I could do so much. I don't mind having less in my stipend, we need it so badly to forward the work.'

The Bishop was only too aware of the needs, as he tried to reassure Harry. 'I know your needs,' he said, 'but they are spreading their funds worldwide from London, and they're all worthy causes. I daren't ask any more about money just at present. Last time I tried to argue that stipends were insufficient – I asked for a single man in full orders with two years' experience to command 800 US dollars, rising to 1000 dollars after five years. It's what others get. That's reasonable, isn't it?'

'I don't know, I don't think about salaries.'

'Well, I have to. I suggested $1200 after first furlough, when you all seem to return to me with wives. And what happened – I got a reply revising the stipends – downwards. $600 for a qualified man. It's incredible. And you think you'll get money for your school. It's hopeless, Harry.'

Sadly, Harry had to acknowledge that on this occasion, he was beaten. But the work could not fall apart for need of such paltry sums, he was convinced.

The work was painstakingly carried on, day in and day out. Harry did the majority of the itinerating, as with his priestly status, he could conduct all the services. Sometimes Charles accompanied him, but most of the time he continued to go alone, leaving Charles with the school to run in Yung Ching, doing his best with his daily improving command of Chinese. Progress was usually measured in terms of numbers – attenders at services, baptisms, confirmations, and so on. The pace was so slow, and the scale so small that only the most strong-willed could maintain hope. Neither became disheartened – not a man or woman in the whole North China Mission appears to have lost their vocation – except, perhaps the bibulous Thompson. The most likely reason for ending service in China was death or ill-health. Harry and Charles were fortunate in this respect, and carried on without a break. On the contrary, the two fit and eager young men threw themselves into planning, Harry measuring progress in years, Charles on a more daily basis. The number of baptisms continued to rise, and local Christians were reported to be popular in the villages – not the case in every area.

Harry sent reports to Peking regularly, as well as the reports required by the SPG in London. 'I can only say we have 270 Christians to show for some 26 years work here,' he complained wearily one evening. 'It's a pitiful result. I expect we saw 270 in the Minster at Warminster regularly.'

'You can't measure success by heads in church alone.' Charles had a wise old head for his young age. 'Think of the impression we must make among the heathen too. And you say yourself, – we've only had a handful fallen away.'

Harry nodded. 'You're right. I'm just a bit tired. Christianity has made faster progress in China than any other movement. I often think – we could have held out temporal advantages – we would have grown rapidly. A meal costing about ½d, would win a great many with whom we come in contact; the chance of a position as teacher would buy the literary men, naturally when there is a chance of gaining a livelihood, no matter how poor, many would try to get it, not caring one bit about religion. No, better not to offer inducements.' He thought about the local assistant teacher taken on and recently sacked as being un-suitable. 'How do you distinguish a true convert from a "rice Christian", Charles?'

'In time you can.' Charles' innate simple wisdom showed itself yet again. 'By their fruits, and so on.'

'You're right. Dear God, I'm glad you're here, Charles. You keep me sane!' Harry smiled at his student, who by now was clearly becoming a partner.

Christmas of 1897 was a time of true celebration for the two in Yung Ching. It was their first Christmas together, and Harry's third in the area. Together on their donkeys they visited village after village in the weeks of the festive time, in a seemingly endless round of services and meetings. Harry had managed to obtain a magic lantern when on a visit to Peking, and proudly unveiled it to Charles.

'It's by way of a Christmas present for everyone,' he said.

Charles was well pleased. 'We had those back home in Leeds,' he observed. 'The children loved them, and the parents almost admitted so, too. I wonder what they'll make of it here!'

In fact, the little box went down extremely well, rather too well in fact. Dozens of people flocked to see it, adults and children, it made no difference. Order had to be maintained with a firm hand! Word got about and queues got larger in every village. One evening Harry returned after a long day. Charles met him with, 'You really have done it this time, Harry.'

'Done what?'

'That magic lantern. A message came this morning that the magistrate wants to come and see it. Now, that either means he is as curious as the rest, or he thinks it's subversive, and wants to check up on us. Anyway, he's coming this evening, whether we like it or not.'

'Can't be helped. It's innocent enough, but I can't say I relish the thought of him and his supporters glaring at it. We must find something as an official gift – he will surely bring one. We'll manage. Just pray me through it from the back of the room, Charles.'

That evening, through the darkness came the magistrate, resplendent in his official robes, in a palanquin, with a whole retinue of staff, in grand Chinese style. The Chinese Christians already assembled looked on nervously as official welcomes were made, and special chairs put out with the best view.

At last the show began, the first pictures flickering into view. The silence was electric – would the magistrate approve? He did, and pronounced himself very satisfied. After the main show, Harry addressed the group with a little homily, carols were sung and the blessing said. At the back, Charles prayed silently, and added to it by crossing his fingers. At the end, tea was served, and the magistrate sat with Harry, while Charles tidied up the lantern for its next performance. Finally, with a great flourish and flouncing of robes, official bowing, and correct forms of address, the magistrate left.

'Whew! I'm glad that's over!' said Charles.

Harry looked up from the lantern box.' It's only just begun,' he said softly. 'He wants to come back. I think we've aroused his curiosity. Anyway, in the short term I have the dubious honour of a return visit.'

'What magic does he have to show you then?'

'I have the privilege of inspecting the local prison.'

'What!' Charles laughed. 'You're not serious!'

Sadly he was, for it was no pleasure, even if it was a privilege for a European. A few days later Harry, dressed in his best European clothes, set off for Yung Ching prison. It was well known that, apart from basic rations, prisoners depended on friends and relatives to visit and push food through the bars to them. Pedlars abounded in the area, prepared to sell food to any prisoner who had cash to give them. The area was notorious, and depressing.

On his return Harry shuddered. 'That's one treat I don't want again, Charles. Honestly – the magistrate is so proud of the wretched place. I grant the prisoners look happy and contented, though for the life of me I can't see why. They even ply their trades in there to earn a livelihood. Some have been there years waiting for trials which never come. They just get two basins of bad rice a day. No wonder they carry on their trades, they survive on food they bribe the guards or pedlars for. It's all self help – no justice there at all. I tell you, it wouldn't happen in the prison back home on Portland, that's for sure.'

'It's over now, and no bones broken.' Charles was always cheerful. 'At least the magistrate is more for us than against us, God willing.'

Hopefully, Charles was right, but when, at Easter, the magistrate returned, again with his retinue, to look at the content of the services, it caused consternation. The Chinese Christians were terrified. Had he come to spy on them, to take note of the communicants, to close the church down? Would people end up in prison?

Harry and Charles tried to put their minds at rest, assuring them that the magistrate was coming out of genuine interest, and with no evil intentions. In truth, they had little on which to base their assurances. One thing was certain – if a local bigwig was taking the trouble to attend a major Christian festival, Christianity was being taken seriously. Either the church would be closed down, or allowed to continue. If allowed, the magistrate would have been positively impressed, seeing it as a force for good, or at least, as harmless.

Easter came, and with it, the magistrate. It was a repetition of the Christmas lantern show, with bowing and formal conversations. Harry and Charles remained calm, smiling benignly at their flock, conducting the service as normal. Charles rattled out the hymns on the piano, leading the choir in the Easter anthems. All went off well. There were no repercussions, and the magistrate did not return. They concluded that they had been considered harmless, and with relief in their hearts, went on with their work. Occasionally officials dropped by out of curiosity, but not for sinister reasons. One mandarin struck fear into Charles one day, by gatecrashing a choir practice. 'How charmingly soothing to one's mind,' he noted, and drifted away, leaving Charles and the choir boys quivering internally.

1898 continued its accustomed way. Easter gave way to high summer, and the heat was unbearable. Most Chinese were busy in the fields and even the schools were less full than normal, as boys stayed at home to help. By the autumn, the harvest had raised work levels to fever pitch, and Harry lost no opportunity of setting up special harvest services. Any rural community celebrated harvest seriously, but where people lived on the margins of poverty, it was specially significant. Harvest came late in Northern China, and Harry arranged for harvest services to

133

coincide with All Saints Day, thereby achieving the highest attendance possible at a religious occasion. Ancestor worship, so important to the Chinese, was prominent in the celebration of All Saints, and likely to be most meaningful to the wary unconverted.

'Your first harvest in the country, Charles,' Harry almost announced it. 'Last year you were still in Peking, and still quite green. By this time next year, you will have been priested. So much seems to have happened. I don't know how I did without you. Now, this is the plan I have for harvest – we can make it a bigger event this year, with two of us. We can have two communion services here in Yung Ching. For one thing the church won't hold them all at once, and the people travelling in from the villages will need to have a later service. Add those who come but are not communicants, and we will have the church full both times. Jessie Ransome can come down from Peking, so there will be three of us to officiate, as well as native lay workers.'

In the morning, the day was perfect, as it should be for harvest. The sun shone warmly, and the autumn colours were bright. The team, now three, were up early, preparing for the day. In fact preparations had been going on for days, and Jessie had not been slow to help the parishioners decorate the church.

'It's beautiful, Jessie,' Charles congratulated her. 'Almost like home. That must be a new yellow altar frontal, and the pots of chrysanthemums and grasses are gorgeous. The decorations are splendid. Everyone's worked so hard.'

'Thank you Charles, but I only helped. The women have done it all, and the children have made the baskets of fruit and vegetables.' With that, some of the self-same children, early to church, tugged at her sleeve, wanting her to see their baskets.

Charles busied himself with the music for the day, before both joined Harry in the quiet of the sanctuary, to prepare themselves for the service. Soon the chatter and shuffling alerted them to the numbers arriving, and Harry went to the door to welcome strangers, while Charles played the piano softly.

As they filed in, the congregation were evidently rough, but reverent. Women stood on one side, men on the other, as was the Chinese custom. The men were rugged from hard work in the fields, all sporting huge padded jackets against the chill of the autumn morning. Their hair was tied back in shaggy pigtails, still a novelty to Jessie, however often she saw them. She noticed with pleasure how many women were there, almost all of whom had learned the service, as few could read – girls' schools were rare. The men, if they needed, made use of Harry's printed Prayer Books.

The first communion was followed by the second, for distant villagers, who had been waiting outside from the time they arrived. Again, another tight squeeze, and all were in. The same service, and all was apparently over. But no. Having made the effort, they wanted to stay, and clamoured for Mattins, so at midday Harry started his third service of the day, in the full knowledge that half his congregation must, perforce, be outside. For ninety minutes Charles and Harry conducted a true English Mattins, Charles leading them all in the Old Hundredth, followed by 'Now thank we all our God', and Harry giving a rousing thirty minute sermon. As a performance, it was carried off to perfection, but even to the Chinese, who had never seen England, it had meaning.

It was hard to tell who was more exhausted at the end of it; Harry and Charles, or the congregation. 'That was quite something.' Charles was visibly impressed.

'It's not over yet – we have the food to come,' and Harry was half way across the yard. 'These people have come miles and will be starving. Jessie, can you organize the women and children into the dispensary. Charles – get the men and boys to line up in the waiting room. I'll tell our cooks for the day that we are ready.'

With that Harry was gone, striding off along the road. Charles and Jessie did their best, trying to make themselves heard above the noise. There were inevitably too many males to squeeze into the waiting room, so some remained outside in the warm sun.

After a few minutes, Harry returned with two men and a boy, carrying cauldrons of something which smelt good. When the lids were removed, hungry eyes saw stewed meat, soup, rice and vegetables. God's bounty proven! Most people had brought containers, and produced them in line. Within minutes, it seemed, they were all fed, and there was even some over for seconds. 'If you'd walked or stood since 6 a.m., you would be hungry too!'

Harry commented, when Jessie reproved a lad for returning a third time.

By about 3.30, those who had travelled farthest had to make their farewells, for they had a long walk, hopefully in daylight. Small children were getting fractious, and the thought of the new week concentrated minds. One by one, each family trudged off along the dirt roads or piled into ox carts. Local non-believers looked on, as they had all day, at the strange gathering, and commented, and occasionally jeered.

Undeterred, the local people turned to the problems of cleaning up, and finally, at the end of a very long day, attended a short Evensong, before, exhausted, the English trio finally closed the church door and went home to relax.

'That was quite a day,' said Jessie, with satisfaction.

'You enjoyed it?' Harry handed her a bowl of tea.

'Very much. Somehow the people here have a genuineness, I suppose it's a lack of sophistication, but the political problems of Peking seem miles away. The anti-European feeling is all but missing.'

Harry nodded seriously. 'I'd generally agree. We have some problem, but not much. You can easily love these people. Charles, tea?' He passed Charles a bowl. 'Take this afternoon. You know, after lunch, without anyone knowing, those people – and they're all poorer than we are – made a spontaneous collection – about thirty American dollars. The man has just given it to me – they want it to go to a fund set aside to pay the salary of a native worker. Now that's the true expression of faith. Whatever else do we need, when they do that? I was speechless, I can tell you. You know, I could stay here another thirty years with no trouble, where could one have a better parish?'

There was no answer. They were all agreed on that. The day had gone well. There was every sign that progress was being made. Any amount of work was worth the results that were beginning to be shown.

The following day Jessie left to return to Peking, to her sister Edith, in the girls' school. As she left, she was given letters and wishes for all at Peking, including Christmas greetings sent early. Charles and Harry waved her off and turned to plan for another

Christmas and 1899. As they walked back to their mission house, they discussed the future.

'The railway's going to be the main change, I'll be bound,' Harry explained. 'Apparently a new line will be laid in the spring, through Ch'i Chou, and wherever the railway is, people will be in large numbers. That's the place for a new mission station for certain.'

'What about the water routes?' Charles was also concerned for the advantages which could be gained from the transport system. 'The steamers are going between the treaty ports in increasing numbers, and the Europeans are stationed there as well – even British on the coast at Wei-hai-wei?'

'I'm sure the waterways have been considered Charles.' Harry stopped, and faced Charles, as if wanting, by so doing, to underline his point. 'But look, we have the new railway coming right through our patch now, and although the Chinese hate it, they have been partially funding it, and will use it. Look how the railways changed England – even my own home village was revolutionized by the access it gave to large towns. It's the transport of the future, and will afford us so much opportunity. We can but try.' With that he clapped Charles on the back, and the two entered their house, to clear up and look from harvest towards yet another Christmas at Yung Ching.

'You happy to conduct Evensong tomorrow?' Harry asked, over the clearing up.

Charles looked up. 'Certainly, once school is over.'

'Good. I must get down to the end of year report back to the SPG. It's a thing I hate, but it has to be faced, and if I can get most of it written now, before Christmas, I will only need to add the final touch when I get back from the villages at New Year.'

So Harry forced himself to his desk, and the business of report writing, never his favourite job. He was always happier to be active, rather than sitting over papers, but he knew the outcome of the mission depended on it, so he steeled himself to his task.

He thought back over the year, to the official census which had taken place in the spring, and remembered the problems it had caused. 'It was taken,' he wrote, 'in a very ostentatious way, which scared weak Christians very much, and gave anti-

Christians a good opportunity of showing their dislike in such phrases as "seize the Christians" and "Kill the followers of the foreigner". The missionary and the Christian were charged with changing the good old customs which had been handed down from antiquity, and had sufficed for generations of generations.'

The year had definitely not been without problems. 'I did get more abuse heaped upon me,' he continued, 'which sometimes led to un-missionary like scenes. The (native) Christians likewise have suffered.'

With no protection, and no inclination to carrying weapons, both the missionaries and native Christians had every right to admit fear in the face of blatant opposition. There were too many examples of intimidation and violence to ignore, and Harry had to acknowledge that even some of his lay workers had stayed away in recent months. He wrote: 'There is a great deal of uphill work, owing to the fear of some, and the falling away of others. But though there has been a great decrease in the number of our converts for this year, still there has been a moving forward.'

As he totted up the numbers for the report to London, Harry counted thirty-six new hearers – the lowest level of lay trainees – with only seven progressing to the next stage of catechumen. Only seven adults had been baptized, against fifty-two in 1897. For infant baptism it was little better, fifteen, against forty-nine a year before. He could only count nine confirmees against sixty for 1897. About thirty regulars had fallen away. He sighed, pushed the paper away and ran his hand through his hair. It looked a dismal report on the face of it, and yet he knew there was so much to do, and so many people to reach. He knew that those who had stayed firm were increasing in conviction, and argued that numbers at communion were actually rising. He and Charles just had to stand firm and keep their nerve, and eventually the antipathy would surely pass.

One very real advantage had been the visits from Peking of Dr Marsdon and Deaconess Ransome. They had begun to minister to the women and girls, an element almost impossible for the men to reach, due to the rules of propriety. Harry hoped the increasing number of women communicants would be a calming influence among the congregations. He reported: 'These women, inwardly so earnest, outwardly so changed in their appearance, I was moved to thankfulness. No one who could compare them with non-Christians would say with a clear conscience that missions were a failure.'

As he continued to report, Harry mentioned the recruitment of a Chinese doctor for the dispensary, and also his ideas for new stations along the railway line. Certainly, the latter half of the year had seen fewer anti-European riots. Perhaps the signs were not all bad, he could write a tolerably positive report to London.

Christmas, when it came, was as busy as usual for the pair of them. They could scarcely believe another year had gone, and next year would be the last of the century. The festivities were unlike an English Christmas, and even unlike a Peking one, but it didn't seem to matter. The services were as joyful as they were the world over and the occasional hidden delicacy, produced with a flourish, made the day itself special, though it was busy.

After Christmas, Harry and Faithful left Charles, to visit the villages of the area. 'Four hundred miles at least,' Harry calculated. 'Poor old Faithful, she'll earn her keep in the next two weeks, and she hates the stony ground where the roads aren't made up.'

'Just wait till the railway comes and you can leave Faithful at home. Anyway, next year I'll be priested, and perhaps you can stay at home.' Charles was eagerly planning his post ordination life. 'Ten days or more itinerating between villages is too much, especially at this time of year. You know what the Chinese say, 'Nine nines calculates winter', and we're now in the period of the 81 days. You'll be tired, saddle sore and cold when you return. Next year we can share it more equally.'

Harry smiled. 'Next year there will just be more to do Charles, and the year after. There is just so much to be done, we could use four men easily, then we could build more churches, and have truly local parishes for people to attend. The little rooms at Lung-Hua-Tien and Tai Whang Chuang are simply bursting at the seams. I'm glad in one way, but it can't go on. When I get back, we must submit a request for money to build, Charles. Bend your mind to that while I'm away!'

When Harry returned they did just that, but even the plans

paled into insignificance, against the news Harry brought with him from Tai Whang Chuang: 'You'll never guess who I met there!'

'No – how can I?' Charles was confused.

'Did I ever tell you about the lad Wang, in Peking? Hopeless lad, but in the end we got him trained in carpentry, first in Peking and then in Chefoo.'

'Yes, I think so.' Charles couldn't see where this was all leading. 'So what?'

'So, he's back! His family come from near Tai Whang Chuang, and he has just come back for Christmas, and hopes to settle here permanently. I couldn't believe my eyes when I saw him. Quite adult now – known as Mr Wang, so I had to follow suit, but he will always be a lad to me. You wait!' Harry wagged his finger. 'I'll find work for that young man to do. He's too good a carpenter to overlook. And, Charles ... he's a regular church-goer, and has been spreading the gospel in Chefoo, so will be a big help back here.'

'What have you planned for him?' Charles was resigned to the certain knowledge that Harry's plans were way in advance of his own.

'Well, this is the best part. Wang's father, well the whole family really, have offered us some of their land to build a church on – free.'

'Free.'

'Yes, absolutely. It's ideally situated by the crossroads, you know where I mean, next to the market area? Couldn't be better. Can you imagine the influence of a church there!'

'And all that as a result of you taking young Wang in hand years ago!' Charles shook his head. 'You get some luck Harry, honestly, no one else would get offers of land gratis.'

Suddenly Harry's face darkened. 'No Charles, no. It's not me, no more than it's Wang's father. It's the providence of Almighty God, and his perfect way that produce this sort of thing, not we mere instruments.'

Charles had to acknowledge it, but knew, nevertheless, that Harry's work those years ago had borne fruit. The Wang family had always shown interest, and church meetings were often conducted in their house, so to them it was an obvious extension of the work.

Over the next three months, Harry, Charles, and when he could Mr Wang, sat down to make plans, and Harry continued to pester the Bishop in Peking for extra funds, although he knew the practical problems which had to be overcome in releasing funds.

It was only at Easter, when Harry journeyed out to the villages for the Easter festival, that the practical details were discussed. Charles had stayed in Yung Ching, so Harry alone journeyed out with Faithful, arranging to be at Tai Whang Chuang on Easter Day.

Predictably the building was full to bursting, as if to prove the need. Even the meetings in the Wang's home were well attended. While he was there, Harry conducted services daily, and the people, more eager than he had expected, turned up for eucharist daily. After the Tuesday communion Mr Wang, Harry and the church elders settled to a meeting in the Wang's house. There were differences of opinion as Harry unfolded the scale plan. Some people wanted a window here, others a door there. But things were concluded amicably, and accordingly a final plan and bill of quantities were drawn up. All of a sudden it looked daunting. These materials would have to be bought, skilled men found to do the job. Together they knelt and prayed for God's blessing, guidance and protection for the period of construction, and left confident that everything was in safe hands.

Whether Harry or Wang was the guiding force will never be known, but the next morning – losing no time at all – men appeared, ready to start work. Dressed in working clothes, they appeared at daybreak, when they could well have been employed in the fields. Harry borrowed some rough clothes, and turned his hands to practical work as well, remembering that his greatest achievement to date had been a mere sports pavilion! The measurements were paced out, and marked. Weeds and rubbish were cleared, and men were eager to begin to dig. Local people stopped and watched them, commenting to each other and shouting words (mainly of encouragement!) to the dirty hot brigade of workmen.

However much Harry wanted to stay, he knew he had to return

to Yung Ching, and eventually, having tidied himself up, he packed his belongings and loaded the donkey, promising to return in three weeks. As he clopped back along the road, he wondered just what changes he would see by then. He would dearly love to have stayed, but the other villages, not to mention Charles, had need of him.

On his return he was met by Wang, who was in a perfect dither of excitement, as he pulled Harry's baggage off Faithful's back, and urged him to make haste. 'You won't believe it!' he said. 'You can see just where it will be already.'

Without a chance to change or eat, Harry was propelled to the site, where it seemed, the local Christians had assembled for him. The smiles couldn't have been broader, and he could see they were proud of their achievement. 'This is wonderful,' he said, spreading his hands out in front. 'All this in three weeks. You have truly worked a miracle by God's grace.' The area of scrub was now totally clear, with not a weed on it, all rubbish was gone, and instead the boundaries of the building were obvious, and the foundations ready to be laid. He knew these, in the main, were no professional builders, they were farmers, shopkeepers, artisans and cooks, with other jobs to do.

'How did you manage it?' he asked Wang later.

Wang shrugged. 'We came early in the mornings, and in the evenings after work – slowly we accomplish much. Now we wait for bricks!'

Sadly, as so often happens, everyone waited and waited for the bricks – for a full fortnight. Harry could not help them on that visit – no-one could do anything but wait. When the bricks finally arrived, the building slowly began, moving ahead in fits and starts as building projects do. The little grey miracle slowly took shape.

As it developed, it was evident that it was no simple shack, thrown together by a bunch of amateurs. It looked surprisingly like an English church, and caused considerable interest among the inhabitants, who were intensely curious. Harry tried to blend it with other buildings round it, insisting it face north to south as was the Chinese custom. He designed a roof in keeping with Chinese styles, although at 24 feet, its apex was far higher than any other roof in the village. At 64 feet by 20 feet, it was arguably the largest too. The bell turret – so far with no promise of a bell, finished it off. Harry wrote to Frank Norris back in Peking begging for a bell, for how could there possibly be a bell turret with no bell! 'We cannot,' he wrote, 'boast of a church built entirely of native money, but we can truly say that most of the Christians did as much as we could expect, and some even more, for they gave of their money to buy, they lent their beasts of burden to draw the material, and as many as could be spared from farming occupations came and helped as labourers for the masons.'

Harry visited the Wangs again in June, and noticed immediately the strides that had been made. The shell of the building was almost finished. 'What a difference, Wang! You must have been working every evening on it.'

'Yes, almost.' Wang was obviously tired, but absolutely happy. 'You see, we have the steps in up to the sanctuary, and a metal altar rail is coming next week. The doors are ready to hang, and my friend will put glass in the windows.'

He had to shout, for the banging and shouting of men at work, even late in the hot summer evening, was deafening. Harry smelled the smell of wood, and his palms itched to help.

Harry nodded and watched as a man chiselled away at wood for a rood screen, and another less accomplished carpenter attempted simple benches.

'Do you remember those things I got you to make in Peking, Wang? A bit like that,' and Harry nodded at the bench.

'Please, no.' Wang flinched as he remembered the curiosities presented in the mission house.

'How you have come on since then, Wang – and I don't just mean in carpentry. I can't tell you what a joy it is to have you as a Christian co-worker on this project.'

'Not just me – all these.' Wang gesticulated.

'And plenty of interest.' Harry nodded to the faces at the window, passers-by attracted by the goings on. He sidestepped a man at the last minute, who was busily laying a floorboard in the sanctuary, and descended to the comparative safety of the already bricked nave.

'This church will be such a force for Christ here,' he continued.

143

'Could you see it finished in a month, Wang? The Bishop is eager to visit about then, and there seems no advantage in waiting till the autumn to consecrate it.'

And so it was arranged. Wang dashed about with the energy of two men in his attempt to have everything ready for the consecration. The women were persuaded to help with the furnishings, and slowly curtains appeared behind the altar and round the vestry. Kneelers were put in place, and flowers arranged in the chancel. Finally a long curtain was put in place, to screen the inner church from an outer courtyard, where the unbaptized were to sit. Still Wang worried about the lack of a bell, and indeed of an altar, and sent word to Harry in Yung Ching. Ever practical, facing the consecration day ever nearer, Harry and Charles looked at each other, and without a further word, went into the church in Yung Ching and began to heave the altar out of position. Together with a pair of bedroom candlesticks from Portland, a vase, and Sam's little wooden cross, so beloved of Harry, the whole lot was put in a cart and sent off as a matter of urgency.

'Now we are forced to have a new altar at Yung Ching, which is no bad thing!' Harry remarked with some satisfaction, surveying the space. Indeed that summer, Wang and Harry designed and built a new wooden altar. Stained black, its high relief pattern picked out in gilt, it was a handsome replacement. Even Harry's cook helped with the draughting, and together they were justly proud of it. So proud, that they carried on to design a matching reredos, hoping perhaps next year to rebuild Yung Ching.

But 1899 was definitely Tai Whang Chuang's year.

The date for the dedication had been set some weeks before and Bishop Scott journeyed south for the event. Harry had kept all in Peking abreast of developments and the Bishop was eager to see the completed church.

The Bishop looked over the new church with Harry, shaking his head in wonder. 'It really is a remarkable building, erected so quickly, and with such little cost,' he marvelled. 'Now your job is to fill it!'

The service was arranged for 11 a.m. possibly to allow time for the more distant parishes to send members, so that everyone could be represented. By that time of day it was getting hot, making it sticky and uncomfortable in clerical vestments. The church was bound to be packed, so a happy but hot morning would be had by all. Anyone who could be spared travelled from Yung Ching for the occasion. Certainly Charles was there, still in his deacon's robes for the time being. Someone was sent to check the church, and it was full to overflowing, with a small crowd outside too. It was almost 11 a.m. and time for the procession. With due solemnity the acolyte led the way, followed by the Bishop, resplendent in his official robes, followed by Harry and Charles and at least three Chinese readers. As they moved forward, up the nave, their shoes sounding on the brick floor, the readers read from Psalm 122, 'I was glad when they said unto me, "Let us go into the house of the Lord."' The clergy reached their stalls, and prayers were said, hymns were sung, and finally the high point of the service had come.

Harry stood up and publicly requested that the Bishop dedicate the church to St Peter. The Bishop formally assented, and rose to walk up the sanctuary steps to the altar, to the singing of Psalm 24, 'The earth is the Lord's and the fullness thereof ... who shall stand in His holy place? He that hath clean hands, and a pure heart.' Everyone strained to see and hear better, as the Bishop, making the sign of the cross, dedicated the church and prayed for all those who would serve in it, and those to whom they would minister. Mattins was then sung, and the eucharist performed. The Bishop also preached the sermon, exhorting the congregation 'to be bold in confessing Christ before men, as St Peter had been'. He could not have realized how soon his advice would have to be taken, and what sad part in the story this church would play.

Finally it was over. The procession left by the nave door, and the rush of air, even though hot, was welcome as a spring breeze in the stuffy and crowded church. The congregation spilled out, chattering happily after what must have taken a couple of hours. Local non-Christians were fascinated by the goings on, watching, or retreating quickly, having pressed their noses to the windows during the service! Certainly over a hundred non-Christian women were reported to have attended, coming from a number of villages round about. Some men watched as well, making it quite a crowd. The number of people eating lunch in shade, where it could be found, made the dedication quite an event. It took on the appearance of a major day out in the village, and at least encouraged some people to visit the next Sunday to see what went on in the strange tall building that seemed to be so important, situated next door to the Buddhist temple and the market.

Harry knew that the next few weeks would be vital, if more people were to be reached, and finally converted. But the dedication day was not yet over, and after a well-earned lunch, he returned to the church to baptize the first Chinese baby in the new font. Later the Bishop confirmed four school children. Certainly if 'the better the day, the better the deed' had any Victorian truth in it, it was well practised that day!

Finally Harry and Bishop Scott were alone together in the church, at the end of a very long day. The servers and church attendants were clearing up, and there was time to reflect on the building programme as a whole. The Bishop was truly impressed, and he said as much to Harry. He had grown to know Harry well over the last few years, watching him develop from an untested recruit, to an experienced, fully-fledged priest, who had well proved that he could be entrusted with the responsibilities of his own parish. 'You've made a fine job of Yung Ching, Harry,' said Scott. 'It's easy to say that I knew you would, but all this doesn't surprise me, although perhaps it should. It's a fine achievement – but even finer is the obvious commitment and love of your parishioners. They're true Christians, not the "rice Christians" we are always being told about. It's a hard job out here, but you're well up to it – and doing well with young Robinson too, I see. He'll be priested in the autumn without a doubt.'

'Good, it's about time – he's getting restless.'

'There's another reason, Harry.' The Bishop looked at him very straight. 'You've been out here over seven years now, eight shortly. It's about time you went home on furlough. I'd been told you were looking tired, and you are. As soon as Robinson's priested, you're on furlough, my man. No arguments.'

'But …'

'No. That's it Harry. You're no good out here without a break sometime. Believe me, I know. I shall miss you, Harry. I own that I think of you as a son sometimes, but all the more reason, eh!'

'I shall have mixed feelings,' Harry replied. 'I'm more Chinese than English now, but my parents have been asking when I'm to come home. To be honest, I'm half afraid of it, you know, it's a different world.'

'True. They won't understand – they cannot. It's hard going back, but it's essential. One of the problems of being a missionary.' Scott smiled, and clapped Harry on the back. 'Come on, we must settle the finances of this place before I return to Peking.'

The financial situation was, for once, better than usual. The cost had been estimated at £260, but with rigid financial control exerted by Wang and Harry, added to gifts donated in kind, the money needed was merely half of that, to the Bishop's delight.

'I suppose you want this for another project now.' He was resigned to what was coming.

'Well, that would be nice,' came the simple reply.

During the autumn, Harry mentally adjusted himself to the idea of furlough, perhaps the following spring, after the cold weather had abated.

Charles was formally priested in Peking in October, with Harry in support. It was good to be able to send Charles off at last to the villages, and concentrate once more on the little school, with its minute boarding element. Harry wondered how Charles would feel, to be left alone in the mission house, but he need not have worried – Charles was transformed firstly by his new professional status, and secondly by the news that his fiancée of three years standing was to join him in China, for the Bishop had given his permission for them to marry, now he was fully trained. Tentatively he was making wedding plans. It was a lonely time for Harry, knowing that he would leave the mission house to return to single quarters after furlough, or perhaps to a totally new posting. He and Charles remained each with his individual hopes for the future. Both would be denied them, in ways which neither could possibly have guessed.

Intermission:

Hatred of the Foreigners

The story of Harry and Charles and the other workers of the North China Mission could have continued in the same vein for the years to come, amid setbacks, some successes, tales of increasing numbers, and new departures in their ministry. The small scale of their successes was never a cause for disquiet or anger for the Chinese authorities, one small church more or less scarcely bothered them. Sometimes the work of the missionaries – especially in medicine and education – was even encouraged, as it provided an entrée into Western civilization, so necessary in a world increasingly dependent on trade and international relationships.

But few had bargained for the depth of feeling among the ordinary working people. At best the Westerners – particularly the merchants – were tolerated, at worst foreign powers were hated. The missionaries were unwittingly caught up in the politics of the day, and the responsibility for the subjugation of China by external powers was laid at their door, every bit as much as at that of the political and merchant classes.

By 1899 there were – and had been for some years – signs that dissidents were banding together to resist Western influence. Curbing the Europeans was not enough, they wanted them out – the third-class devils from over the seas. Secret societies were formed, and plots were hatched to repulse any European, regardless of who they were, or what their reason for being in China. Certainly in Chihli and Shantung provinces to the east and south of the mission, such societies had been mushrooming throughout the 1890s. There would be an outburst of activity, then a period of quiet, but it was an undercurrent that would not entirely be silenced, even when it was apparently contained. One group in particular, the Tong Haks, operated as anti-Western bandits, driven to patriotic action after two successive bad harvests, but they were soon overtaken and subsumed within the stronger and faster growing Boxer movement.

The Boxers, whose full Chinese title meant 'fists of righteous harmony', which hopefully was more easily translated to the Chinese than to us, began to spread in numbers rapidly in Shantung province throughout 1898. Any dissident movement relied in part on hard times for a catalyst to activate opposition. The two poor harvests were heaven sent for them. People were needy, hungry and anxious. The bad harvest was the last straw, on top of defeat in war and high levels of unemployment. The traditional handicrafts had been superseded by the Western manufactured imports which flooded the market, seemingly without check.

The sight of a Boxer, let alone a mob of them, was awe-inspiring. They travelled around in bands, apparently with little control. They were mainly young and from the rural areas. On the whole they were male, but surprisingly for the time there were also some girls – called 'red lanterns' – who acted in a support role. As so often with activist groups, they invented for them-selves a uniform, so that the public would immediately know with whom they were dealing. In their case they wore red wrist ribbons and head scarves, for red was a lucky colour in China. In addition they sported yellow sashes and neck talismans. Per-versely, in their red headscarves, the idiograph for happiness was often stamped, although very rarely did they seem to bring happiness with them. Most of the Boxers were of peasant class, so lived often hand-to-mouth. They had little by way of financial help to support their activities. In modern terms they bring to mind chapters of Hells Angels or National Front mobs, or even Ninja turtles complete with head bands and swords! They were, to be serious, far more deadly, partly because their beliefs degenerated into blind prejudice, and partly because the Empress saw fit to be ambivalent towards their anti-Western militancy.

The beliefs of the Boxers, such as they were, may seem laugh-able to us nowadays, but they were sincerely held then, and had to be dealt with. They claimed to have fantastic powers, to be possessed by the spirits of heroic men of the past, and to be supported by an army of spirit soldiers. All this was seen as evidence of their righteousness; if the spirits supported them against Westerners, they must be right, for after all, the spirits of ancestors were revered and obeyed. As the Boxers travelled around, village children were often enticed to serve in the little army, following the older boys and girls, chanting choruses and hearing of their magical feats. The Boxers were often capable of whipping themselves up into hysterical frenzies, claiming supernatural powers. In village squares they would gather together crowds of spectators, and claim to be able to cut themselves without bleeding, to be able to fly, or be unaffected by bullets which would simply pass through them. They performed feats in front of the villagers. A millstone would be lifted by a thread, a spear driven through a brick. To gasps of amazement, the spear would be retrieved intact. In such a way, they promised, their followers would be unaffected by the weapons of the foreigners, for heaven was angry with the foreigners and all their works, and would protect their adversaries. The Boxers were 'charged with purging China of this venom'. Religion was as much a part of the venom, as were trade and land hunger.

Exactly what the truth was behind the Boxers' bizarre activities was hard to fathom. To an extent the forces of will-power, hysteria and trance would have achieved much of it, but it is also possible that an element of trickery was used by some to seduce a gullible audience. Whatever the truth, it worked. Increasing numbers were swayed towards the movement, and some joined the gangs, although numbers were never huge. It was almost impossible to disagree with a group which firmly planted the guilt for hardship on outsiders who obviously did have a lot to do with their predicament. The problem was that logic gave way to fanaticism. The fires of hatred were fuelled with stories of the abominable activities and evil intent of Westerners.

The Boxers lost no time in whipping up stories about the Europeans, who used strange Western machines, spoke and wrote oddly, dressed differently, and taught that the Chinese gods were powerless. It was not long, therefore, before the Westerners were accused, for example, of extracting the hearts and eyes of the dead to turn them into medicaments. In accepting Western medicine, one could be receiving elements of an ancestor – a total sacrilege! Even worse, children in the orphanages run by the missionaries were supposedly killed and their entrails used to assist magical transmutation of lead into silver. Local people were scandalized. It must be true, whatever could be the reason for lying?

Western engineers fared little better. However innocent their activities apparently were, they were perceived to be at least as evil. Recently railway track had been successfully laid through to Peking, bringing yet more Europeans and their manufactured goods on to the scene. The iron road with its thundering trains was swiftly accused of being a monster capable of disturbing the Chinese terrestrial dragon. The telegraph system, painstakingly installed, unfortunately rusted in winter, and the slow dripping of red oxidized water from the wires was interpreted as the blood of the spirits of the air, which had been angered by the 'iron snake'. So it went on. Almost nothing that Westerners did was free from accidental or intentional misrepresentation. Even in drought, the Boxers pleaded with villagers to throw away well water, which they believed to have been poisoned by native Christians, subversively acting within their own villages on behalf of the foreigners.

In those areas in which Boxer fever was rife (and the line moved daily northward towards Peking), the battle for the trust of the Chinese was well and truly on. The people mainly dealing with the problem were the local Chinese officials – who were ambivalent to say the least – and the missionaries, who formed the bulk of the European presence in country areas. As early as the autumn of 1898 one riot involving a thousand Boxers resulted in the death of two Christians and the burning of a chapel. News spread fast of the atrocity, and the missionaries grew increasingly alert for signs of Boxer activity.

Clearly something had to be done. The Boxers' trump card was the Dowager Empress. She hovered between ordering the Imperial Guard to arrest the Boxers and tacitly encouraging anti-Western insurrection, by doing nothing. She did set up a militia in the areas of most trouble, but never let them press for total subjugation of the young hoodlums. To make things worse, the recently appointed Governor of Shantung silently approved of Boxer activities, and did nothing, as he hated the foreigners as much as they themselves did. On balance the Empress decided that the Boxers were better venting their considerable anger on the foreigners than on her – so she wavered.

Had it not been so evil, the final straw might have been divinely sent. The weather deteriorated throughout the whole of 1899. What was excellent weather for the building of Harry's church was disastrous for the crops. By August the ground was bone dry to a depth of six feet (Chinese measure). No seeds could successfully be planted for the winter crops, so essential to a society living hand-to-mouth at the best of times. The people were therefore, of necessity, idle, and the devil worked his usual way with idle hands. The missionaries were also only too well aware of the dangers inherent in the situation, and continually prayed for rain, so that the people could return to orderly work in the fields. But the God they trusted in and invoked appeared to have deserted them. Perversely, every time the Boxers attacked, it seemed that a small shower resulted! It did not go unnoticed by anyone. At last the rains did come – except that when they did, they were minimal. Heaven, apparently, was displeased.

The worst of the problem was in Shantung, south from where Harry was, but the word spread fast, and signs were evident that a difficult winter lay ahead, with low supplies, and major, unchecked discontent. It was going to be hard to persuade people that a bountiful God, who loved them, would provide for them. On the contrary, there were few reasons for being attracted to the Christian faith in North China in 1899. It is even more to the credit of the native Christians than the missionaries that the faith was kept alive. Sufficient numbers retained a strong enough belief to survive the rigours of privation, and later, persecution. What was contained in 1899 – just – was seen to spill over into a far greater revolt, and as the Empress continued her half-hearted control of the problem, the mounting evidence of increasing violence both in its scale and in its severity demonstrated that something serious was almost inevitable.

Meanwhile, Harry and the rest of the North China missionaries pressed on almost unchecked. There were certainly instances of tauntings and ugly scenes, but nothing that Harry and Charles could not handle. The Bishop had been warned, back in the days of the Japanese war, to look to the safety of his staff. Peking was certainly as safe as houses – the presence of the Imperial Guard and the Empress, quite apart from the dignified position of the International Embassies, ensured that. Or so they thought. Right up to the end of 1899 there was so little hard evidence that Europeans were in physical danger of their lives, that the potential of the Boxer movement may well have been underestimated. The last three days of 1899 put a stop to all that, for events then brought home to the British, if no one else, that the situation they were in was far more grave than they had bargained for. Within six months even the horror of December 1899 would be obliterated by the vastly more terrible blood bath that was to be reported world wide, and came to be known as the Boxer Rebellion.

5

Danger Draws Near

During 1899, the Europeans in China grew increasingly aware of the existence of the Boxers, especially in the provinces far south of the capital. Disquieting stories percolated through to Peking, and from there to Harry and Charles, of disturbances in the stations three hundred miles south where Henry Brown and a new young deacon, Sidney Brooks, had witnessed Boxer activity. Fifty miles from them Henry Mathews, having left Tientsin, was stationed alone at Ping Yin, the concern of many.

'I wouldn't fancy that!' Charles commented. 'All alone with those crazed ruffians parading round the villages. It's not as if there are any protecting troops.'

Harry nodded. 'Thank God we don't have those problems. I can truthfully report we have scarcely a Boxer here, and travelling around poses no problem. Let's hope that it stays that way.'

That summer the two had other things to take their minds off the Boxers. Firstly came the sad trip to Chefoo, to attend the funeral of Miles Greenwood, who had finally died a quarter of a century after landing in China with Bishop Scott. His sight, memory and general faculties had all failed, and at 62, the climate and life-style had claimed a devoted missionary, who had laboured without pay for years. Mr Wang was particularly distressed at the loss, having lived and worked in Chefoo with Miles, while he was training in carpentry. The Bishop, too, was obviously moved as he conducted the funeral. He had lost an old friend, who shared so many memories of the early work of the mission. Francis Sprent wrote the epitaph, duly sent back to England, with which they all concurred. 'He was humble, gentle, and generous. His sheer goodness had won the Chinese to him.' From his middle thirties Miles had devoted his life to the Chinese,

154

and particularly to the people of Chefoo. His entire estate was left to the SPG, for he had given up England twenty-five years before, and his life and finally his death, were contained in China.

Sadly, Harry and Charles returned to Yung Ching from Chefoo, unaware that the funeral in early September marked the beginning of a descent into disaster for the mission. As far as they were aware, the death was an isolated event, and work had to go on.

'I didn't tell you till now,' Harry said as they bounced along in the unsprung cart, on the road back into Yung Ching.

'I've finally heard that we have a small grant, so we can at last begin serious work along the new railway line between Peking and Hankow. We can really do something positive at the halt at Ch'i Chou, and my first aim is this autumn. They have a medicine fair there each year, and thousands come. It's just the opportunity we need.'

'Are we both going, then?' Charles asked.

'As long as you don't get behind with your preparation for ordination. I suppose so.' Harry smiled. 'I had thought of taking Mr Ch'en from Yung Ching, and a lad from the training school in Peking. Roland Allen says he has a young man who seems ready, and two are always better than one. Yes, why not. We'll go as a foursome and get the thing set up.'

So they went. The district through which they travelled, east of Yung Ching, was a cotton-growing area, and Ch'i Chou was a centre for spinning and weaving. The cloth sellers were every-where, every street corner boasted a brightly covered stall. Charles lingered over these and touched the cloth thoughtfully.

Harry was irritated by his dawdling. 'Come on Charles, we're not here to buy fripperies. You can't possibly want all that pink flouncy stuff!'

'I might.' Charles looked straight back at Harry. 'As soon as I'm priested, I shall be asking for my fiancée to come out to China. I might well be in the market for some of this.'

'Oh – it's definite then?'

'Of course it is – she's not a fiancée for nothing. We plan to marry as soon as I can support her. We're not waiting for my first furlough. If you're anything to go by, it could be years!'

155

They laughed. 'Well, haggle for that stuff later,' Harry replied. We have to go to the Yamen to see the magistrate to get permission to rent somewhere, or we'll be beggars here.'

The Yamen was busy with people requiring the magistrate, but finally they made themselves known, and the four staff rented somewhere quite close by, and installed themselves. Really it was only sufficient for two, but within days Harry and Charles would be returning to Yung Ching, once things were settled. Harry proposed to visit the two Chinese monthly, to conduct services and support them, while they did what they could to attract people from the fair into their rented home. No Boxer activity disturbed them, and work was progressing unaffected by anti-European dissent.

True to his word, Harry visited Ch'i Chou monthly, and brought back good reports. 'Over 600 people have visited the house, Charles,' he said as he tethered Faithful on one return. 'That fair seems to bring in people from all over North China – one or two from Peking even.' He slapped Faithful's flanks. 'I'll be doing without you, my girl, if we get any more railway lines. How have things been Charles? Everything all right?'

'Fine. Almost ready for Peking now, and my ordination. I've also heard that my fiancée has booked her passage, and will arrive in China in the spring. Hopefully she'll come out on the same steamer as Frank Norris, on his return from furlough, which will be nice for her.'

'So we have to plan for an Easter wedding?'

'I hope so,' Charles replied quietly and blushed, suddenly self-conscious, but very, very happy.

Harry was genuinely pleased for Charles, but at the back of his mind was the knowledge that by the spring he himself would be likely to be on furlough, and Charles would have to look after the station single-handed, unless a replacement could be found. His thoughts inevitably turned to Ch'i Chou again.

'They've got their hands full in Ch'i Chou, you know,' he said, as they both lugged the contents of Faithful's panniers into the bungalow. 'They had one chap there, who asked to see me – only wanted the priest. Apparently he was a nice, respectable fellow –

anxious to be a lay trainee.' He dumped the bedding in a corner, and dusted his hands. 'Anyway, you wouldn't believe it – he asked Mr Ch'en what could be done about his "affair". Apparently he was engaged in a lawsuit, his son had been sued for some offence or other, and was condemned to banishment. Of course I told him we couldn't interfere, it wasn't our business, and he would have to see the magistrate.'

'That wouldn't do much good,' said Charles.

'Well, quite, but what could I do? Anyhow, before we knew what had happened, his opponents were at the door to thank us for refusing him help, and wanting to be taught Christianity, if you please. We had an invitation to their village, because they thought we would support their cause. Pretty tricky situation. They couldn't understand that we weren't siding with anyone.'

Charles raised his eyebrows. 'I hope Ch'en can cope.'

'He'll manage.' Harry put away his coat, and helped himself to some tea kept warm on the stove. 'That's better. For all her strengths, Faithful isn't the warmest form of transport.'

'Winter's come early,' Charles agreed.

'The weather's my major concern – not the cold, Charles, but the drought. The hearts of the people are hardening against us because of it. I know some people blame the Empress in Peking, but we foreigners get our share of the blame too. On the way back I saw them repairing the temples, performing religious rites, and idols were being carried through the streets in procession. Usually, apparently, the idols are seated in chairs, Wang says, but this year they have been laid on their back to compel them to look heavenward. They have even been shaken to wake them from their supposed slumbers! And after all of that, the foreigners get blamed. If we don't get rain soon, we will have trouble, you mark my words.'

Charles was quiet. 'I hope you're wrong,' he said at last. 'We have been fortunate, the trouble seems to have been mainly south of here. I think Henry Brown and his trio have had more to contend with. I suppose we just pray for rain.'

'And for them too,' Harry added. 'I gather Henry Mathews has been in Peking for a while, and will be travelling back soon. I only hope it can coincide with our Peking trip for your ordination, and we can hear about it all first hand. He has even offered to take me back there for a week or two, to see the place again. It's four years or more since I was in the region. I wouldn't mind a visit, if you think you could cope.'

'What, as sole priest here at last? Only too pleased.' Charles rubbed his hands gleefully. 'You won't recognize the place by the time you get back!'

'That's just', said Harry contentedly, 'what I had hoped you would say!'

Henry Mathews, in the event, did meet Charles and Harry in late October, for Charles' priesting, and all three travelled south together afterwards, leaving Charles at Yung Ching on the way while Harry carried on with his old student, another 250 miles south to their mission at Tai-an. Travelling along by cart, Harry noticed evidence the further south they went of placards and banners warning people of the evils of the foreigners. About half way, they crossed one of the main railway lines, freshly laid, and still hated. There a band of Boxers were hanging around, and began cursing and threatening them.

'What now?' Harry asked.

'Bluff it out,' said Henry. 'We've dealt with these before. They look ugly, but we've never been in serious trouble.' He ducked as a stone shot past him. 'On second thoughts, we'll go to the local Yamen, for safety, I think.'

Harry was only too pleased to see the magistrate.

'Do we stay here, or what?'

'No,' said Henry, cynically, 'we won't be able to stay here. They don't want to seem to side with us, because they also could incur the Boxer's wrath. But neither do they want to see us come to harm, and find the might of the West descend on them. They're a lilylivered lot – I'll talk to the magistrate. Wait a minute.'

Harry waited and watched the Boxers, who laughed and jeered outside.

Finally Henry returned. 'As usual the magistrate said we have to return to where we came from. I said we would not, so as a compromise he has lent us three carts and two horses. A contingent of soldiers will escort us round this area, and a safer way south. It's the best I could do.'

Eventually, at 2.30 a.m. thirty soldiers turned up, and the group made their way out of the village, round in a wide loop, away from the Boxers, and eventually once again south. It was a long trip, but they arrived safely, to Henry Brown's relief.

'Oh Harry, I've been worried,' he said privately. 'Young Mathews will do anything, but honestly he's fearless. It worries me to death sometimes.'

'He's responsible for himself now,' Harry rejoined. 'He handled it very well, you know. After all, he's stationed by himself at Ping Yin, and that's fifty miles away. He has to be able to handle situations by himself. Anyway, I see you have a new trainee now,' and he nodded towards the figure of a young man earnestly correcting the slate of a Chinese boy in a group.

'Oh, Sidney – just a novice. I think he's the youngest we've got in the mission, just – came out on the same boat as your Charles, I gather. They look so young – twenty-four and not yet priested. £12–10–0 a quarter! It takes me back a bit to remember those days!'

Harry and Henry walked round the compound, hands tucked in their enormous quilted sleeves for warmth. 'He's almost a member of the family,' Henry continued. 'I'm engaged to his sister! Known the family years. I actually wrote one of his references while I was on furlough, and went down to preach to the students at Canterbury, where he trained, so I can say I'm partly responsible for him being here.'

'Quite a family affair!' Harry was not above pulling a leg. 'You're marrying as well are you? With Charles also throwing away a life of peace and independence, it seems to be a disease which is catching.'

'Well worth it,' Henry responded. 'She's coming out for Christmas, so we will be a happy band then. It's going to be a wonderful festival! Wedding in January, God willing, then – who knows.'

Sidney seemed just as happy with the arrangement when Harry quizzed him. 'She'll travel up on the train from Shanghai and we're going to have a splendid time, organizing accommodation, teaching her to use chopsticks, and to speak Chinese. She'll be another member of staff in no time!'

'It seems,' Harry observed, 'as if you are making similar plans to us. My Charles is marrying in the spring, so you and I will be looking elsewhere to lodge! You knew Charles, didn't you?'

Sidney brightened again. 'Yes, we travelled out together. Good chap, Charles. Very different from me, but stout-hearted. I had so little experience of life – I'd done nothing really before I was twenty, except live at home in Kensington. My father paid my fees to 'Burgh', the missionary feeder college, and I went on to St Augustine's College in Canterbury with very little behind me. Father is a painter, you may know him – Jamyn Brooks – not that successful, so it was a financial struggle. Charles always seemed older than me, and has got on faster. He's priested now, so I have some catching up to do!'

'Yes, priested and nearly married, almost solo at Yung Ching. He's done really well,' agreed Harry. 'But Henry is pleased with you too. You'll get there. I know I felt as if I would never be a proper missionary, with my own station, but it comes, Sidney.'

'Yes.' Sidney was silent. It was almost as if he didn't want to be there suddenly.

Harry caught the change in his mood. 'Something wrong, Sidney?'

'No.'

'Yes there is. Come on, let me have it.'

'It's stupid really.' Sidney looked at his boots. 'I've told other people, but they say it's nothing.' Silence followed. 'Do you believe in dreams?'

'Dreams?'

'That dreams foretell the future?'

Harry was perplexed. 'I never think of them like that.'

'Well nor did I – but recently I've been having a dream – a recurring one. Don't laugh.' Sidney looked at Harry, who could tell by his anxious face that he had been seriously upset by it.

'I won't – go on.'

'Well, I dream I'm back at St Augustines. It's not a bad dream – I loved it there – I did tolerably well, made friends – I even played football in the forward line for Canterbury Town while I was at college. Anyway, in the dream, I'm in the crypt under the chapel. It's also laid out as a chapel, and on the walls are the names of all

160

the ex-students who have served and died abroad – a sort of memorial chapel. In my dream, I am looking at the names, and there's a space – blank – reserved for martyrs of the college. As I look at it, letters form, and slowly I see my own name, in red, a martyr. What do you think? Does it have meaning, or am I just being over-imaginative? It's beginning to get me down.'

Harry reassured him. 'Don't worry. The mind plays odd tricks, Sidney. You probably remember the chapel, and when you're tired, your mind races into fantasy. Put your mind on Christmas, eh! You'll be all right. No one gets killed out here.'

The young man relaxed. 'No, it's just me, I suppose. I must square up and get on with the work. Send my regards to Charles for Christmas, will you?'

'That's the spirit,' said Harry. They were the last words he was ever to speak to Sidney.

At the end of November, Harry journeyed back to Yung Ching, leaving Henry Brown and Sidney awaiting Sidney's sister, and fussing about, preparing the house. Stupidly, Harry couldn't get young Sidney out of his mind, and related it all to Charles on his return.

'How odd!' was Charles' reply. 'Always seemed a perfectly balanced fellow to me. On the journey out he learned quite a bit of Chinese from me – seemed able and practical. Let's hope he will be too busy in the next few months to dwell on it, and so forget it.' And that was that.

Over Christmas Charles and Harry were themselves run off their feet as usual. It really seemed no solution to have a second priest, for there were more and more converts requiring communion in the 400 villages. Certainly if Charles had not been priested, Harry could not have coped, but life was still hectic with two of them. They paused just long enough to exchange gifts – Harry and Wang had carved a little low table for Charles for his new home, and Charles had acquired from somewhere some books for Harry. For once, life took on an ordered and almost routine veneer for a few weeks, the lull before the storm.

The storm itself, when it came, arrived in the form of a letter from Peking. It sat in the bungalow all day till Harry returned. By the time Charles arrived, his face was pale and set.

'Charles, come in and sit down.'

'Just a minute, I must just ...'

'Now.'

Charles understood the tone. 'What's the matter?'

'This.' Harry waved the letter. 'The thing's been sitting here all day and we didn't know.' He was obviously angry.

'What?'

'A letter from Peking, from the mission. They've just heard from Ping Yin – Oh God!' Harry stopped. He looked up at Charles. 'It's Sidney, he's been killed.'

Charles stood dumbfounded in the middle of the room. 'Killed. How?'

'I'll piece it together as best I can for you. Sit down. Apparently it was just after Christmas – probably the 27th. Henry Brown, Sidney and his sister were in Tai-an, when they heard there was some Boxer trouble in the villages – round Ping Yin where Henry Mathews was – alone. They felt someone had to go – Tai-an was safe enough, but these villages can be lonely if you are the only European there, believe me. Anyway, the lot fell on Sidney, and he went off with a Chinese lad and a donkey – no protection. As far as they can tell from the lad, who was too shocked to say much for a while, they seemed to manage all right, and slept at the side of the road unmolested. They got to within twelve miles of Ping Yin when it happened.'

'Go on,' Charles whispered.

'It's awful, Charles. They got to Chang Chia Tien on the Saturday, 29 December, ready to go into Ping Yin – ironic isn't it – "City of peaceful obscurity!" About mid-morning they ran into a band of roaming Boxers – slap into them, no chance of escape. Apparently young Sidney was taunted and pulled about – they weren't interested in the boy, who hid. I don't know whether the rest is his account or Henry's, but Sidney was pulled off his donkey, taunted and injured in front of a crowd of people, not one moved a muscle to help. Perhaps they daren't. The village constable even asked the Boxers to take Sidney out of the village to kill him, to absolve him of the responsibility.'

'Good Lord, and no one helped?'

'No,' continued Harry hoarsely. 'He managed to give them the slip, to his credit. He was a good runner, I suppose being a footballer. They couldn't catch him, so returned to their horses and pursued him along the open road. They caught him and killed him. Poor Henry Mathews, only a few miles on, heard nothing till the Tuesday, when the lad turned up with a garbled version of the horror. He went out with a search party – and that was no safe action – and they found Sidney.

'What had they done to him?' Charles almost knew before he asked.

'They had taken their swords and hacked him to pieces, throwing the body into the ditch. They like that. They believe a soul can find no resting place in a dismembered body.'

The two sat in silence a long time.

Eventually Charles said, 'My God, that's evil – his poor parents.'

'His poor parents, his sister, Henry too. Imagine how Henry Mathews felt, safe, as it happens, in Ping Yin.' Harry was angry now, more angry than Charles had ever seen him. He slung the letter on the table and wheeled round. 'Why are we here Charles? No, don't answer, I know. But it is pointless. He had a life's work to give.'

'That's what he gave,' said Charles quietly. Their eyes met. 'He knew it was coming, Harry.'

'I know,' Harry replied, 'that dream of his – Don't think I haven't been haunted by it, too.'

Harry's anger at the outrage echoed within and beyond the missionary community. The local Christians were reported to have 'wept freely, for they loved Mr Brooks with more than ordinary affection, and the thought of his terrible suffering, and of all their own affliction, was more than they could bear'. Henry Brown comforted his fiancée meanwhile, in stunned disbelief, their mutual consolation was each other. Together they travelled along the same grisly road to Ping Yin, now escorted, to Sidney's funeral. The burial took place at Epiphany at the little cemetery at Ping Yin amidst a large local congregation, horrified and embarrassed by the actions of their countrymen. Sidney was placed in a tomb during a short committal service, and his story ended.

Henry Mathews felt dreadful about the whole business. He had remained perfectly safe throughout, the unwitting cause of Sidney's death. Alone, he could only commit his thoughts to paper, writing: 'Sidney was very dear to me, and it was to no small extent due to his wish to be with me in the time of great anxiety, that he laid down his life in martyrdom. I wrote most strongly to Brown to keep him back, but he (Brooks) felt it his duty to come, with this terrible result. What a New Year to him! It was on New Year's Day we heard of his death. He was a bright and happy fellow, very cheerful, and a most lovable companion. He himself is at rest, and I know that he was not unwilling to lay down his life in martyrdom.'

The shock waves following the murder travelled rapidly up to Peking, where the staff in general, and the Bishop in particular, had been stunned. Apart from informing and warning staff such as Harry and Charles in the villages, to avoid travelling alone, there was little that could be done. Danger was everywhere, and there was rarely a promise of armed protection. Instead, the British looked to the diplomatic presence for support. Scott flew to the British legation, and the Minister, Sir Claude McDonald, relating all he knew. McDonald, together with his American counterpart, made official angry representations to the Chinese government. The ambivalent Governor of Shantung province – who at the least had been lax in the problem of the Boxers, if he had not actually supported them – was hastily replaced, but that did not repair the damage. Meanwhile the Bishop had a miserable time of it, writing letters to Sidney Brooks' family, and meeting time and again with Claude McDonald.

Eventually, news came through that the perpetrators had been identified and captured. Such was the depth of feeling, even in the Chinese community, that the case actually came to court in March in the presence of Mr Campbell, the British consul, who acted as assessor. The culprits, in the pervading climate, stood no chance. Having been turned in, they were left in no doubt that there were sufficient Chinese who despised their actions, to provide evidence. Being tried, in effect, by the British, there was little chance of them being acquitted. Revenge (for that is what it was) was swift. Two of the men were executed, another received life imprisonment. A fourth was imprisoned for ten years, and a fifth exiled for two years.

The British authorities, but not, to be fair, the missionaries, were determined to wring the last drop out of the situation. A very large sum of money was extracted from the Chinese in reparation. £1500 was demanded and used to build a Memorial Church at Ping Yin, and a memorial tablet at St Augustine's College. Sidney's dream thereby became reality. His name was painted in red on the wall of the crypt, a martyr's tablet. The headman of the village where Sidney died was told in no uncertain terms to hand over £70, with which a stone pavilion was built at the site of his death. Such an amount was swingeing in a poor community which had little to offer. It was vicious and merciless. Even the cost of Sidney's training and books was calculated and extracted. The outcome (far from putting an end to the disquiet) was an intensification of the hatred felt by the Chinese towards the British in particular. The missionaries themselves had counselled mercy without success.

It was a miserable time for everyone, not least the Bishop. Even in Yung Ching, Harry and Charles talked incessantly of the trial and the rights and wrongs of the case. Only two things served to cheer them that spring. One was the news, in February, of the bittersweet marriage of Henry Brown in Tai-an. Bonded by adversity as well as love, it was scarcely a joyous wedding, but it was a welcome release for everyone, from the gloom of the trial. The other was Charles' continued preparation for his own bride, and Harry's now imminent departure for England, arranged for early summer, hopefully just after the wedding. Perhaps, they thought, they could put the awful winter behind them, and get back to normal.

To most people it was evident that the difficulties experienced in the south were simply moving north. Sightings of young men sporting yellow sashes became more common. Most people knew someone who said he had seen, or heard of such people. A group had apparently descended on a village and set up a startling show with swords, another had ranted to a gullible group at length, about how the missionaries were cooking and eating babies. Harry and Charles kept an ear open, and tried, through the stalwart Christians, to dispel the more ludicrous suggestions, but without success. Even some whom they trusted came to ask if there was truth in the things they had heard from the Boxers. Others just melted away, and were no longer seen at the church. Not all believed the Boxers, certainly, but a number feared the result of being too closely associated with the Christians, and stayed clear.

Nervously, but with admirable resolution, work went on. Arrangements were made to escort women and children to the comparative safety of Chefoo and Shanghai, but not one of the missionaries themselves budged an inch. No one packed up to go home, no one ran for cover to Peking. Perhaps they ought to have gone, but their sense of responsibility to their people kept them at their stations, watching and waiting.

Bishop Scott argued with Harry to go on furlough. 'You need to go home for a while. I said so last autumn. Charles will be quite able to look after the station by himself – after all, you did.'

'Come on,' interposed Roland Allen, at his side, 'it's about time you went on leave. The Bishop's due to go on leave in the summer, so if you go soon, you can be back in the autumn, and the work will almost be covered. Norris is due back any day, with Charles' bride, and you don't want to play gooseberry!'

'I can't,' Harry said, restlessly countering both attacks. 'There are ten boys on my hands just now.'

The Bishop snorted. 'Next year there will be twenty, and the year after thirty, so I don't see much in that argument.'

'I'll see,' was all Harry would say, fearing that at any minute the decision from his superior would descend, and he would go, regardless.

In the event, the decision was made for them all. Harry had just returned from the school one day, where his ten senior boys were coming along well. There had been no sign of Boxers for over a week, and the sun was shining. He and Wang had been making plans for the carving of a dining table as a wedding present for Charles. He hoped at last to be able to get on with it. The rest of the day looked promising.

'I'm back, Charles,' he called, entering the hallway, seeing Charles' jacket slung over a chair.

'Charles?'

There was no answer.

'Charles, are you there?'

Harry stuck his head round the door of the main living room area and saw Charles sitting on a low chair, reading a letter, oblivious to his calls.

'There you are. Can you manage without me? I have private things to attend to, concerning your wedding.'

'Don't bother.' The voice which came from Charles was flat and low – quite unlike him.

'What?' Harry sensed trouble. 'What is it?'

Charles looked up, and his face was drained, white and without expression. 'There isn't going to be a wedding.'

Harry knelt in front of Charles and took his arms. 'What is it?' He shook him gently.

Charles handed him the letter, rose and went over to the window, where he stood, gazing out at nothing.

Harry took his eyes from Charles and picked up the letter. It was from Frank Norris, who had just docked in Shanghai. Couched in the kindest terms possible, he outlined the journey he and Miss Rule, Charles' fiancée, had had, he trying to answer her questions and prepare her for China. During the journey she had been ill, but it had appeared only to be seasickness at first. She did not get over it, but became weaker, and had finally died just before they reached Colombo. She was not taken ashore, but buried at sea, so swift was her decline. Harry let the letter fall and looked up at Charles.

'Oh Charles – What can I say?'

'Nothing. Nothing can be done.' Charles pushed past him and went out, to be alone in the anonymous streets.

Harry sat for a while, thinking. He returned to the letter, to find more bad news still. Frank had collected Miss Rule's belongings, to bring for Charles, perhaps as some comfort. On the onward journey, the boat had hit storms and everything had been lost in shipwreck. Frank was lucky to be alive, and was still shocked.

Nothing was left of Charles' future wife, no memento, no treasure. It seemed the cruellest of fates. The drama which had hit the mission at Christmas had struck again, much nearer home.

The next few days were difficult to say the least. Charles tried to continue as if nothing had happened, and failed. Harry didn't know whether he needed to be left or comforted. Slowly he began to emerge from the shock sufficiently to listen to reason.

'You must go to meet Frank, as soon as he gets to Chefoo, Charles,' Harry pleaded. 'I know you would have been going there under happier circumstances, but you need to talk to Frank and hear it all first hand. You need to get the facts only Frank can provide. The Bishop agrees with me. Go Charles.'

'There's no point.' Charles shrugged. 'There is no funeral, no personal possession, it's as if she never existed. What can Frank do?'

'Nothing, if you put it like that. I don't know how you feel – I've never had a fiancée. But I do know you can't go on as if nothing happened. It did, and you must acknowledge it, even if it is painful. Frank needs to talk too, he's been through more than enough. It would be good for you both.'

So Charles left for Chefoo.

Frank Norris met Charles when he arrived, and they stayed together at the mission, where such a short time before Miles Greenwood had worked and died. Together they walked along the seashore, and sat looking out on the waves, now so calm and delightful, which in angrier mood had nearly claimed Frank's life, and where somewhere, Charles' beloved lay. Frank spoke at last. 'You're taking it well Charles, almost too well. Stoicism isn't always the best way you know.'

'I'm not stoical, anything but,' Charles replied, miserable, yet very contained. 'I am just trying to trust in God's decisions. Whatever he decides is for the best.'

Frank was impressed. For such a young man, Charles showed an amazing maturity and self-control. They walked on, Frank letting Charles talk as he would, about his hopes, his friendship with his fiancée and their blossoming love. Hopefully he would get his sorrow out of his system in whatever way he found easiest. They stopped, and Charles looked out to sea, distantly, the breeze ruffling his hair. He turned to Frank, and what he said chilled Frank despite the warmth of the spring sun.

'After all, it is best as it is. I shall be freer when the trouble comes at Yung Ching. I could not face it with her.'

'What trouble, Charles?'

'The Boxers and their like. They're moving north week by week. Harry and I are hearing daily now of something or other. We've talked about it, we know they'll cause trouble, it's inevitable.'

Frank was alarmed. 'If it's got so bad since I've been away, you must tell the Bishop. Come over to Chefoo, or go up to Peking for a while. You must. For goodness sake. You'll be like sitting targets there.'

'We can't leave Yung Ching. All we would do would be to save our own skins and abandon the local Christians to the Boxers. We're staying, but we know it's not going to be easy. A wife,' Charles looked away, 'would have been an extra burden.'

Frank realized immediately that arguing would be useless. He hoped Charles was just depressed, and Harry would be more positive. He decided to follow up the discussion, and write to Harry. He disliked the thought of Charles alone, when Harry left on furlough.

Charles delivered Frank's letter to Harry on his return. 'Letter from Frank. I expect he will try to convince you to move back to Peking. I think I frightened him with stories of the Boxers,' he told Harry.

'Oh dear.' Harry raised his eyebrows, as he read. 'Well, that's out, for a start.'

'What?'

'Furlough. I shan't be going for a while. Perhaps the summer.'

Charles was consternation personified. 'Why ever not? I'm perfectly able to cope. Refreshed and ready. See?' And he flexed his arm as if in some proof of his fitness.

'Don't be silly, Charles. Would I be able to live with myself if I left you now, just when you need someone around? I'm not much, but I'm the only Englishman you've got!'

Their eyes met, and each knew the other realized that Charles' loss was an excuse for companionship which masked another need. The need for support was well learned from Sidney's exploit. Two missionaries were safer than one, and neither was going to desert the other, while the Boxer threat lasted.

'Perhaps the summer. I might wait and leave with the Bishop. It would be a good journey home, the three of us.' And it was left there.

Meanwhile Bishop Scott himself was having problems travelling around his not inconsiderable diocese. He had asked Harry to come up to Peking to meet a young recruit, introduced to Peking and Chefoo and ready, by Easter, to begin work in the villages.

'Young Robinson met him in Chefoo, and the two will get on famously,' he explained. 'I really don't like the idea of leaving anyone alone in any station at present. Will is the obvious person for Yung Ching or Ping Yin.'

Harry frowned. 'I thought you said his surname was Williams.'

'It is. William Williams, would you believe! Poor chap. I can't think what his parents were thinking of! He's eager enough – sick of the European life in Chefoo, and keen to work with the Chinese more. We'll all travel down together if it suits you, and I can get to the villages and confirm, while travel is still possible.'

'That's not so easy,' Harry replied. 'We'll need an armed escort. There are bands of those wretched Boxers everywhere. The journey up was pretty nasty – one sight of a yellow sash, and suddenly there are dozens of them, all yelling and swearing. It's definitely worse now.'

The Bishop shook his head. 'I don't know what it's coming to, Harry. The troops do nothing to contain it, the only stopping point will be Peking, and of course they won't get into the capital. In fact Sir Claude has insisted on an escort, so its already arranged. It's funny – the legation staff understand the problem, but London – little understanding. Certainly the SPG haven't the remotest idea. Mind you, I for one don't say too much, especially when writing to friends. What's the point?'

Harry nodded. 'Absolutely. I've not said much to my parents and brothers. Perhaps more to the college when I write. What's the point of telling them how bad it is? They would only worry. There is no kindness in knowledge, if they can do nothing to help.

I water down the armed escorts, contingency plans for retreat, the constant rumours. I think we all do.'

'Do you ever think of the worst?' the Bishop asked, but couldn't meet Harry's eye, and looked past him.

'Of course,' was the quiet reply, 'just as you do.'

He felt a hand on his shoulder. 'Harry, I know the strains. I wish you had gone on furlough. I must admit, I can't wait for us to go in the summer, but I feel guilty myself.'

It was the last week of April, and the trip down to Yung Ching threatened to be a difficult one. Scott had hoped that it would be a welcome relief from the constant demands of the court case, letter and report writing, and the Easter festival, but the appearance of the soldiers with flashing swords, outside the station, quickly dispelled any such naivety. Harry, William and the Bishop sheepishly squeezed into the carts, and they made their way through the streets, stared at by all and sundry, as they clopped along, with a group of mounted soldiers behind, like some malevolent retinue.

'There's only one advantage in this,' he grumbled. 'At least we have come a hundred miles by railway this time, so this dreadful parade is shorter than it would have been. When Peking is eventually linked to Canton we will fly between stations. He's no idea, has he, Harry?' and he nodded towards William.

'It used to take two days, William,' Harry explained. 'Now we can make it in a matter of hours. When we get a new line to Tai-an and Shantung, the Bishop will be able to travel his whole diocese without a foot on the ground!'

'Sooner than you think, I hope,' said the Bishop. 'Someone has provided £200 a year as an endowment towards setting up a second bishopric in Shanghai. That will mean less travel like this, and closer ties to the staff.'

'Anything to do with Miles?' Harry could well imagine that Miles had helped his old friend by a clause in his will. But the Bishop only shrugged and kept his own counsel.

From Yung Ching, once settled, Charles, Harry, William and the Bishop travelled to Ch'i Chou to see Mr Ch'en, and to Lung Hua Tien on the following Sunday for a confirmation. Wherever they went, they were under armed escort, and forays of Boxers

171

were driven off, as they waited, while some of the soldiers galloped into the crowd, swords at the ready, shouting and cursing.

'I'm not too sure about the soldiers,' Charles declared under his breath, 'they seem to have drunk a fair bit.'

'I'm not too sure about paying for it,' Harry whispered back. 'We've kept them in food and wine for a week now, and most of the money is gone.'

Eventually, once the Bishop and William had left to travel to Ping Yin, with the rest of the money and the mounted soldiers for dubious company, Harry set about cheering the local Christians, and encouraging church attendance. Charles was still readjusting to his prospects as a single man, and was fending off both official and personal letters regularly. He agonized over the official one from the SPG, to which he knew he had to make a reply. 'It was exceedingly kind and thoughtful of you to send me such a sympathetic and cheering letter,' he wrote. 'Your prayers and those of many more friends for me at this time have been abundantly answered, for God has given me such a measure of consolation, as has never been my lot to experience before. It is indeed worthwhile going through such a great trouble, to be so greatly comforted. The news, as you may imagine, was a shock to me, but from the first, the fact that God has taken her to himself, seemed to me rather a matter for joy than sorrow. God, as you say, did not create this love in our hearts merely to destroy it: and therefore I am quite content to wait, with patience, until the time when we can enjoy the fullness of this and all other affection, in the presence of Him whom we love more dearly than even our best loved here; because in Him only, the heart finds its truest happiness and full satisfaction.'

He sighed and put his pen down. He hoped that sounded as he meant it to sound. No point in saying more, the thing was over. He continued his letter with a watered-down version of the situation in the country, referring to the Bishop's 'interesting' journey. He chose not to make too much of the event, as in recent days there had, in truth, been less evidence of the Boxers, and Harry was planning to travel up to Tientsin by boat.

As the summer wore on, the missionaries still prayed for rain.

172

April gave way to May, and the temperature rose. As Charles put it to the SPG, 'They (the Boxers) have apparently now left the immediate area of Yung Ching, and we hope they will – in the future – allow us to live in peace. We are heartily wishing rain would come, otherwise there will be no harvest this year. The ground is in most parts dry to a depth of four feet. No doubt if the people had plenty of work to do in the fields, we should hear a good deal less of the Boxers.' He was also particularly concerned, as Harry was by now half-way to Tientsin, and he was worried, in his way, for both of them.

In early May, therefore, the SPG had conflicting messages, more forthright and alarming from the Bishop, much more bland from the missionaries. There was still hope that the unrest was containable, at least so it was felt until June, when Boxer activity reached such a scale that it merited world attention.

Charles was relieved, later in May, to see Harry back safely, and they exchanged news.

'How has it gone, then?' Harry wanted to know immediately he returned, before he even got inside.

'Fewer in the school and definitely fewer in church. Wang says the same and Ch'en's numbers are way down. The people are simply being intimidated, Harry,' Charles replied. 'Anyway, how was your journey?'

'Tientsin's a haven of peace by comparison. Like Peking, there are too many Europeans and troops for there ever to be trouble *there*.' Harry took off his jacket. 'Oh the heat here! At least Tientsin's nearer the coast and breezy. What would I do for a good cloudburst! It's still dry as a bone out there. People have given up on the crops, they're just coming to nothing. Should be so high by now,' and he indicated the height. 'They're just sitting around, and listening to those wretched young thugs, with their vile message. Dozens of them along the route – more here than further north. By the way, I went to see the consul in Tientsin.'

'Did you, by George, that was brave,' said Charles.

'Someone has to do something. I begged him to get the British Minister, Claude McDonald, to send troops down to get the Boxers out of here. If I'm going on furlough, it won't be with that lot snapping round the compound with you alone inside.'

'The Imperial Guard won't come down for me!' Charles exploded. 'What did he say?'

'He seemed to understand, actually. I think he really will organize a detachment to come down in a few weeks. Meanwhile, we must pray things don't get worse.'

Eventually the consul got through to Peking, and Sir Claude did organize the guard to go to Yung Ching. Harry and Charles were not to know that they were coming, or exactly when. They both continued their work quietly, as they watched and waited. If they had only had eyes to see, they could have seen the clouds darkening and multiplying, building into the storm that was to break at the end of May.

6

Massacres and Martyrdom

During April and May, the concern that was so obvious in the villages began to spread north, to affect even the staff in Peking. Roland Allen read Harry's report with anxiety, becoming more concerned for his safety in the light of the increasing attacks from Boxers. Their influence was being felt even in the streets of Peking, where, outside the diplomatic district, it became less safe for a European to be seen. Roland made it his business to transmit Harry's reports to the legation, whenever he had cause to be there on chapel duties.

One day in the middle of May, he found himself conversing with a particularly pleasant member of the diplomatic staff, who often attended services.

'Have you heard the latest?' he asked Roland.

'No, what?'

'Sir Claude has just telegraphed to the Prime Minister that he has confirmed a report that sixty-one Chinese converts have been massacred just ninety miles from Peking.'

'Sixty-one!' Roland's mind raced, and his heart thumped, as he thought of the missionaries in the villages. 'That's terrible. It was converts, you say? At least they've stopped short of killing our people. They wouldn't ever go that far, surely.'

'Don't be too certain,' his friend replied. 'We've protested to the Yamen, but to no obvious purpose. Apparently the Belgian legation has reported that a group of their people have been rescued from a village where they were almost trapped. Shortly after, the Boxers got there and burned their homes to the ground.'

Roland sighed and shook his head. 'I'm dreadfully afraid it's getting out of hand. We've got men in villages south of here with no protection. At least the engineers and merchants can arm themselves. We must live by our wits and our faith.'

The civil servant nodded. 'If it's any help, all the ambassadors have pressed their home governments to do something. We're only too well aware of our nationals in danger. The Chinese can't or won't do anything! Apparently troops have been promised – some hundreds – German, Austrian and American. Trouble is, our chaps are tied up in South Africa at present, with the Boers, but we may get a vessel up from Hong Kong.'

Roland mused on these worrying developments as he walked back to the mission house. He was lost in thought, considering that if there was talk of troops, the whole business must be escalating. He did not hear a call behind him. The man called again, and touched Roland's arm.

'Mr Allen. You are lost in thought, I see.'

Roland wheeled round. 'Monseigneur Favier, do forgive me!' The Catholic Bishop smiled and offered his hand. 'I am sorry – I startled you.'

'To be honest,' Roland admitted, 'I have just heard from our legation that troops have been requested to put down the Boxers in the provinces. We must get women and children up here soon, to safety.'

'I'm not so sure.' Favier shook his head. 'I have just reported what my men have told me – there is a known Boxer intention to enter Peking at a given signal. Women would be better off in Tientsin or Shanghai, you know.'

'Enter Peking?' Roland knew that his face had gone pale. His mouth felt dry, and fear crept into his bones. 'Surely not here. The Imperial troops would keep them out.'

Favier looked back at him, his eyebrows raised. He said nothing.

'Are you serious? Women and children have been coming into Peking recently. We haven't any special supplies of food. We could be isolated here, once the city gates are closed.' What had seemed to be the advantage of being in the capital was fast becoming a potential hazard to Roland's mind.

'We'll see,' was all Favier said, but his face said so much more. Roland began to wonder whether the missionaries in the villages might actually be better placed after all.

Harry and Charles, in Yung Ching, would not have agreed with him. They knew, with growing certainty, that life was getting more precarious. They began to take precautions by travelling together or with a native assistant for company. Both were relieved, at the end of the day, to return to the bungalow and lock the door. The temperature, in more ways than one, was rising. May was fast disappearing, and rain was still needed. Neither the winter crops, nor the spring ones had taken hold, and yet another poor harvest was forecast.

'Never mind idle, the poor souls are hungry,' said Charles, one evening, as he watched a group of Chinese, including some who had attended the church and fallen away. 'See them? The man on the right even asked about baptism last year, now he's wearing a yellow sash. He spat at me this morning!'

'Can you blame them?' Harry stood at the window as well. I've heard of two Christian families who have had their homes looted, and one chap in a village up the road had his house burned. They're accusing us of everything, Charles. I don't blame them for keeping their distance from us.' He laughed cynically. 'We're blamed even for the locusts which have been bothering everyone. Eaten what little crop there is! I don't quite know how we're to blame, but we are.'

Charles nodded. 'I caught a man trying to eat the locusts yesterday. I doubt it was worth the trouble, but it's all he could find.'

'That reminds me,' said Harry. 'I must ask young Peter what there is for our dinner,' and Harry looked across to the servant boy busy in the cooking area.

'Not much. Potatoes, or if you prefer, potatoes,' laughed Charles.

Harry groaned. 'Again! The only advantage now, I can see, is that Williams has gone to Chefoo, which leaves more potatoes for the two of us and the servant boy. Lucky Williams! I expect he's dining off fish and fruit by now. Thank goodness he got there safely. The line between Tientsin and Peking is under threat by the Boxers I gather, and no one can get through at all at present.'

Charles nodded. 'But that's just another example. Can you

177

blame them? Just like here – the carters and boatmen have been put out of business by the railway. Of course they hate it. We – the Europeans I mean – are half to blame for our own situation. The rest is blind hatred, but it's understandable – like the chap out there,' and he pointed to the Chinese with the yellow sash.

Harry rubbed his face with his hands. The strain was telling, and his face was taut and tired. 'I don't know Charles. Where will it end? We've spent years working with these people, and in a few short months, it's all falling to bits. I don't mind for us, but for the local converts to be treated like traitors, it's terrible. We're the last people who can help them, but I can't leave them, and I suspect neither can you.'

Charles shook his head sadly. 'Just go on as if nothing is amiss. It's the only course. Control of fear is a skill only perfected by experience.'

Harry reflected that not for the first time, Charles had displayed maturity beyond his years, which made him an equal partner, and not a junior to be protected. They both knew that the situation was deteriorating, that a missionary to the Boxers was a prime catch, that no missionary had any defence, except the Bishop, who merited diplomatic status. There were too many missionaries to be protected, even had there been the will to protect them. They were on their own.

The two of them plodded on for the rest of May, as the temperature rose, the locusts ate busily and the bands of Boxers roamed Yung Ching, taunting and vandalizing as they went. Neither Charles nor Harry admitted fear, there was no need. Occasionally there was a bit of meat to be had on the market, but more than once the traders, being watched by a Boxer group, refused to serve them. Often when they got home, they found the bungalow daubed, and the roses had long been uprooted outside.

By the end of the month Harry had had enough. Fewer and fewer Chinese attended the school and the church, and there was now no question of travelling to other villages. They were all but prisoners in the bungalow, with an occasional sortie for food.

'I can't take any more of this Charles,' he admitted. 'The letter to the consul in Tientsin seems not to have brought any result. We need some support down here for the Christians. Their lives are at risk.'

'What else can we do?'

'Well, I can't swear it would do any good, but when I was in Tientsin once I met the correspondent of the *Standard* newspaper. If I could get word to him, we could get some publicity. The trouble is, no one knows what's going on down here. Peking and Tientsin are safe as houses, and assume we are the same. If I can get a letter published, and there's a good chance of it, people will become more aware of the position we are in.'

Charles grimaced. 'It's worth a try, I suppose. I've got some paper left somewhere. Try, at least.'

By the light of a candle, taken from the stock intended for the church, Harry wrote as best he could. 'May 31st ... places are being burned down, and Christians thrown into the fire, according to reports. We have hundreds of Boxers around us at close quarters, and may be attacked at any moment. But I believe that the magistrate is trying to persuade them not to come here. Times are perilous, and one's life is not free from general danger. I do not know much of the state of the country outside this district, but I have reason to believe it is very bad. Several Boxers have been wounded or killed whilst practising their arts, and evilly-minded people, friends of these wounded people, are spreading scandalous reports about us, saying that we are the cause of the death of these Boxers etc. These reports are quite enough to incite the people to strife. It may be interesting to know, the Boxers offer their swords in sacrifice, before beginning a row. The Roman Catholics are suffering heavily. I am hoping we may get off without much loss, but it is almost too much to hope. Whilst I am writing, swarms of people are prowling about our compound, to see what we are doing to defend ourselves. Of course, we are doing nothing.

Believe me, yours very faithfully

H. V. Norman'

Harry looked across at Charles, to gain his comments on the letter. Charles though, in the dim light and comparative peace, had dozed, and Harry decided there would be little advantage in waking him.

He called to the servant boy who accompanied them so often. 'Peter,' he whispered, 'I want you to go back to your people in your village now. You are not to stay with us any longer.'

'No, Mr Norman, I stay.' Peter was horrified. He had been with Harry and Charles for over a year. Quietly he began to cry.

Harry put an arm round him. 'Peter. You can do me a service. This letter is very important, it must get to Tientsin. Some grown up person must take it – but it must be a Christian. You must find someone. Perhaps Mr Wang, or another who attends the church. Can you do that?'

Peter looked at his feet miserably. 'I will never leave you, never,' he cried.

'Hush!' Harry put his finger on Peter's lips, and looked over at Charles, who didn't stir. 'Don't wake Mr Robinson. You are a good boy Peter. We will never forget you, but this is important. You can help us. It is quieter now, and dark. Off you go.' He put Peter's coat round him, and propelled him to the door. All was pitch dark, and fewer Boxers were about. Silently he opened the door, and pressed the letter into Peter's hand. 'Keep the letter in your inside pocket, Peter. Go straight away now. It's urgent!' and he pushed Peter, unwilling, into the compound, watched, then just as silently closed the door. 'God speed,' he whispered.

The minimal noise was enough, and Charles woke. 'Have I been asleep?'

'Yes.'

Charles looked up at Harry. 'What is it? Where's Peter?'

'Gone.'

'Where?'

'I've sent him back to his people, Charles. It's not safe with us now. At least he will be all right. I watched him run off down the lane opposite. No one saw him, and he has my letter for the *Standard*, which may get through.'

There was no answer. Both knew Peter had to go, for his own safety, and their conscience sake. Equally they knew that the letter would probably get no further than the gates of Yung Ching. A dismal silence fell over them, and neither spoke for a long time, each alone with his thoughts.

The letter, once outside the compound, acquired divine wings.

Peter handed it over to a trusted Christian, and the letter then proceeded by foot and mule, across country, endangering its bearer, but it reached the offices of the *Standard* in Tientsin at the same time as the report that Bishop Scott had arrived in Tientsin from Ping Yin that same day. In his hurry to advise the legation, the correspondent reported that Harry had written also from Ping Yin, which he most certainly had not. What were to be Harry's last words to the world arrived courtesy of young Peter. Shortly after, the Bishop himself was brought Harry's letter by a local American Wesleyan Minister, and began to fear the worst.

Unknown to anyone in Yung Ching, help would eventually come from Tientsin. The day before Harry wrote to the *Standard*, the official at the Yamen in Yung Ching finally informed Peking that his town was out of his control. Knowing of the existence of two British missionaries, and undoubtedly badgered by Roland Allen, the viceroy in Tientsin was informed, and obtained permission for a representative group of ten soldiers to be despatched to find Harry and Charles, and to escort them back to the comparative safety of the capital. The soldiers left Tientsin. If only Harry and Charles could hold on those few hours more.

That night, leading into 1 June, was the longest either of them could remember. Despite the heat they closed the shutters, save for a slit, through which they could look out on to the compound and the road beyond.

'Do you think it's quieter now?' Harry strained his ears. 'They seem to have moved off.'

'Seem to have. Perhaps we can relax till morning.'

Harry shook his head. 'No. One of us should stay on watch, I think. At least we could get some advance warning if anything happens. You lie down a while, I'll watch.'

'Later.'

They sat in silence in the dark.

'Harry.'

'Yes?'

'Looking back. Your training, the life you left, would you still have done it?'

'Yes.'

'So would I.'

181

Another silence followed, this time broken by Harry. 'Do you want to write any letters – to your family?'

'No – the only person I want to write to is no longer there – letters won't get through, anyhow.'

Suddenly a thud broke the calm. Someone outside was banging on the shutter. Shouts broke the night quiet, filthy, obscene suggestions. Then the banging was at the back of the bungalow, and chanting began. Both men stood up in readiness.

'Behind the door,' whispered Harry.

There they stayed while the jeering and crashing continued, for an endless age. Then more shouting could be heard further off down the street, which seemed to distract the mob, and they went off, as suddenly as they had come. Charles inched his way to the crack in the shutter and looked out.

'Torches down the street, moving away. We're safe.'

They both breathed again, and sat down at the table.

'At least in daylight you can see what's coming,' Charles observed. 'This night time vigil bothers me.'

Harry disagreed. 'I don't know, at least we stand an equal chance in the dark.'

Sometime that night either may have slept, but if so, it was the sort of twilight sleep which was of little benefit. As the first daylight appeared, both were awake and quite calm. Quite naturally they said the morning Offices and prayed together. Strangely, neither admitted nor felt fear, at that stage. Each derived mutual strength from the other. They ate what they still had left in the bungalow, and sat it out. From their position behind the shutters they saw people they knew so well walking past, but with the fear of the Boxers, none stopped.

About mid-morning a group of Boxers swaggered down the street, armed and shouting. Once again they stopped outside the bungalow and roamed around, rattling the door and shutters.

'That's it,' said Harry. 'They mean business this time. We must destroy the baptismal registers. Whatever happens, the local Christians mustn't be put at risk. So together they tore up as much of it as they could find, and burnt it in the candle flame. The opportunity to do something practical seemed to galvanize both of them, and they put aside their lethargy and tiredness from the night before, looking as they might on the possibilities for the day.

'I think they've got a new idea out there,' Harry said, from the peephole on the world outside. 'Some of them have gone off – I suspect for support or weapons. There are just a few out at the front now. Charles, this is our last chance. When they come back, I hate to think what will be in their hearts. I'm game to make a run for it, if you are.'

'Certainly, but where? We can't compromise the Christians.'

'The only possible place is the Yamen. Once there, surely, they must give us sanctuary from the mob. The way I see it', Harry continued, 'is to get out now – there are only a few there, and later there will be no chance. Are you ready?'

They stood behind the door, and together said the Lord's Prayer in whispers. Then slowly Harry unbolted the door, and they stood blinking in the summer sunlight. The half-dozen Boxers were stunned, never thinking that two missionaries would try simply to walk out unarmed. Harry and Charles slowly moved forward together. As they got closer to the Boxers, a rumpus suddenly started up on the other side of the street, and shouts were heard. They couldn't at first understand what was happening, and the Boxers, in confusion, tried to watch both them and the mayhem behind them.

'Keep walking,' whispered Harry between clenched teeth. 'I think one of our friends is starting alternative entertainment.'

Sure enough, a couple of local Christians had started a fake quarrel, and were acting it out for all they were worth. Harry and Charles counted their lives in footsteps, inching their way closer to the Yamen. The last hundred yards they took at a dash. For frantic seconds they battered on the door, which finally yielded. They were in, and safe.

Once inside, it was hard to judge who was the more surprised, Harry and Charles panting and catching their breath, or the magistrate, confused by the disruption in the hallway.

'I'm so sorry to burst in on you like this,' Harry gasped. 'We were all but under attack at the bungalow, and have had to run here for shelter. As British citizens, you must allow us to stay, and secure us safe passage away from Yung Ching.'

The magistrate said nothing, but continued to stare at them in amazement. After a few seconds he regained control of himself and replied, 'But you cannot stay here. I do not have soldiers here, you must go,' and he wafted his hand, signalling departure. He did not care where, he simply wanted them gone, for the longer they stayed, the longer the Boxers would make his life difficult.

'But we must stay here, you have a duty,' Charles exploded in righteous indignation.

Harry held him back. 'He won't, Charles.' He turned to the magistrate. 'I realize you have no forces to protect us, but surely troops will be coming soon from Peking or Tientsin? It is the honourable course of action to behave within the law of decency. You know us, we have not caused trouble. We will go as soon as we can, but we need to stay here a short while.'

The magistrate wavered, caught between the need to save his own skin, and the wish to appear honourable. Perhaps the Boxers would respect him for once, and let him pass the wretched pair over to the Imperial soldiers, and there would be an end to the problem. He was inclined to let them stay, so he provided them with somewhere to sit and relax, as far as possible. Just when Harry and Charles began to feel they had escaped the worst, a howl went up from the mob outside.

'What now?' Charles groaned.

'There seem to be more of them,' Harry replied.

A member of the Yamen staff was sent to find out what was going on, and the rest waited inside. Within minutes he returned, reporting that the mob had by no means lost interest in getting their hands on the missionaries. He whispered to the magistrate, who twitched visibly, and rapidly lost his self-control again.

'You must go, now, now,' he ordered, fussing around them and shooing them. 'If you do not, the Boxers have threatened to pull the Yamen down. You are too much of a liability. Off you go. I cannot have you here.'

Harry stood his ground and put a restraining hand up. The magistrate, who had not been restrained by anyone for years, looked up and stopped his tirade in mid-sentence.

'Let me try them first,' Harry asked. 'I have always talked to these people. I know quite a lot of them by name. They are local people. I'm sure we can arrange something. Just give me a few moments.'

He guided the quivering magistrate to a chair, and turned to the front door. Charles was too quick for him, and barred his way. 'Harry, have you any idea what they're like? You haven't a chance.'

'Have you a better idea?'

With that, Harry unbolted the door and stepped out.

Some of the howling stopped, and the front line of Boxers watched, some amused, others uncertain. Then a few set up new barracking. Harry put up his hand, which did have some effect. 'Brothers. Why are you behaving like this? We have done nothing to harm you. We have tended you when ill, shared our food with you, taught your children.' He caught the eye of a few he knew, some ex-schoolboys. 'Stop this now.' His voice was full of pity rather than anger. 'You are hurting yourselves.'

To disprove the point, a stone hit him on the side of the face, drawing blood. 'Friends,' he went on, 'the God I serve does not permit violence. We are peace loving.' He indicated Charles, by now standing at his side.

'Get out, you devils, go back across the sea where you belong!' the cry went up. 'You take everything and leave us nothing,' said another. 'Whore lovers,' cried a third. Swords were heard clashing in readiness, and more stones hit Charles and the windows of the Yamen. Harry turned to Charles and he shook his head 'No go. Get back,' and they both retreated inside again.

They looked a sorry sight. Both now had slight cuts and grazes from the stones, and were feeling, if not looking, like cornered animals. The staff just stared at them, and the magistrate sat, as he had been placed, terrified and shaking. He was obviously going to be little further help.

Harry turned to Charles. 'There's only one thing for it. We can't stay here, we'll have to get out at the back as fast as possible.' He turned to the magistrate. 'Thank you for your – hospitality,' and bowed slightly. Then he propelled Charles quickly down the corridor, to the rear of the building, and comparative quiet.

'This is madness, Harry,' Charles complained. 'Our chances of survival are almost nil. We are cornered and outnumbered.'

Harry appreciated logic when he saw it, but nevertheless knew they had to go. 'Are you coming, or not? To stay here means capture. Out there we have some chance. We know the area, and if we can go north, we can get back to Peking. Take courage! Now look, if we can get across the courtyard and over the wall, we can make for the Confucian temple. All right? You first. Go!' and he pushed Charles forward.

Charles ran across the empty courtyard and jumped up at the wall, scrabbling for a hold on the top. He straddled the wall, and lent down to haul up Harry, who was shorter than him by some inches. Finally the two were over, and stood in no man's land. An occasional passer-by looked at them askance, but no Boxer appeared.

'Ready?' Harry had caught his breath back, and dusted himself off. 'Brisk walk to the temple?' Together they travelled on, feeling very obvious and vulnerable, circling the carts and chickens in their way. With blessed relief they got to the temple without mishap, and made for the door.

'It's locked! Charles, it's locked!' Harry rattled the door, and banged on it. 'Let us in, for the love of God, help us!' There was no reply.

'They knew we were coming.' Charles was resigned. 'They had no intention of providing sanctuary. We're on our own.'

'I'm afraid we are,' Harry agreed.

He looked over his shoulder, to check for Boxers, and was appalled to see a man point to them and shout. 'We've been given away, Charles. Run for it.'

Again they were off at full tilt, down the narrow alleys, looking back, dodging, planning as they ran. Neither was prepared to compromise local Christians whom they knew in the area. They both knew their only hope was the city gate, and the vast expanse of open country beyond. At last the north gate was within sight, the same gate that Faithful had taken so many times with Harry. A fresh group of Boxers had posted themselves close by and hearing running feet, were alerted. It was at this point that

Charles' foot slipped and he stumbled. Soon he was up, but he had lost precious seconds.

Harry, aware that Charles was no longer with him, turned back. 'Charles!' he shouted desperately.

At the same time, Boxers came from everywhere, shouting and threatening. Harry had no option but to duck between a cart and a wall and watch, as two Boxers caught Charles and pinned him back down on the ground. Ropes were attached to his arms and legs, as the Boxers trussed their victim. Finally he was yanked to his feet and hobbled along, surrounded by a gang of chanting young men, down an alley and away from Harry's view.

All was suddenly quiet, and Harry was left, stunned and shaking, to face whatever there was, on his own. Gingerly he stood up and looked around. All the Boxers had gone from the gate, following the parade of Charles. Harry took the shafts of the cart and trundled it along, head down, singleminded, until he reached the gate. There he left the cart, and walked clear of the town, and into open country. He was not going to go undetected for long, an obvious European. Perhaps he could make it to the village of Woo-Kir-Ying. There he knew people reasonably well, the villagers, shopkeepers and carters. It would be a good first base. He hated leaving Charles, but what else could he do?

The village was not far, and Harry was used to walking fast. The sun was by now hot, but he scarcely noticed it for once, except for his dry mouth and perspiring forehead.

Suddenly, he heard crunching stones. Someone was walking behind him, keeping close. He looked round. 'Peter! What are you doing here? Go back to Yung Ching.'

'No. I not leave you, Mr Norman.' Peter was resolute.

'Go back!' Harry pushed Peter roughly. Surely he would be deterred, but he stuck like glue, and the two carried on silently together. As they entered the village, Harry heard the sound of horses hooves behind him, and looked back. There in the sunlight was the tell-tale gleam of yellow and red. There were about twenty of them, and obviously on the lookout for him. With heart thumping he dashed into the nearest place of safety, the local shop, Chance's at the crossroads. Inside were all manner of goods for sale for cash, as opposed to barter. He pulled Peter in, and looked round for the owner, whom he knew slightly.

'Can you look after Peter for me? The Boxers out there want me, not him.'

Within minutes the Boxers were outside, horses tethered, waiting and laughing. A local Mandarin, a man of high standing, was ordered by the Boxers to tell Harry to come out.

'Please,' the Mandarin pleaded. 'You must meet them.'

So once again Harry stood on the steps of a place of potential safety, to argue his way out. This time however, the Boxers were more practical, they wanted the money from Chance's shop.

'I haven't got money to bargain with,' Harry explained.

'Then borrow it,' they insisted.

Harry turned to the shop owner, who shook his head. 'You have nothing with you, no silver. Why should I lend you cash?'

'Please. The mission will repay you. It's my life I'm buying. Look, if nothing else, do it for the friendship of the Christian people round here.'

The shopkeeper knew what he meant, remembering the care given his wife when she was ill. The Christian women had kept his family together for him. He went to the money box and counted out 1200 cash on strings.

'Bless you.' Harry took the money gratefully. 'And, please, get Peter back to Yung Ching for me.'

At this point Peter clung to him, and Harry forcibly prised him off. 'Peter, you will do me a favour by putting my mind at rest if you go home. Did you give my letter to a grown up?' Peter nodded. Harry breathed a sigh of relief. 'Good lad.'

He placed Peter close to the shopkeeper, and signed for him to stay there. Then he turned with the cash, and went out to bargain again.

'Here's 1200 cash,' he argued. 'You get me safely into Woo-Kir- Ying and you can have it.' The Boxers mumbled among themselves.

'Yes, and don't forget,' said the shopkeeper, 'that's my cash you've got, so keep that man safe. You kill him, and I have no way of getting the money back.' More mumbling and discussion, while Harry waited, defenceless.

188

Finally they agreed, snatched the money and Harry, and set off for Woo-Kir-Ying, to the accompaniment of the plentiful shouts and sobs of Peter, held fast by the miserable shopkeeper at Chance's.

The deal struck at the crossroads was not worth the breath used. A few yards further on the Boxers taunted Harry and took his shoes and jacket. They argued over who should have what, trying to judge the relative value of a shoe against cash. They dug around his capacious pockets and found odd trinkets – a hand-kerchief, a Prayer Book, and not least, his ammonite, always deep in his pocket, a memory of his childhood on the beaches. His heart sank as he heard them argue over it. Was it an amulet? Could it call up spirits? No amount of explaining would make any difference. Having taken all his possessions, they were left with their last trophy, the man himself. Passively he let them tie his hands, and he was proudly shown off to passers by like a captive bear. He realized that he was being led right back to Yung Ching. As they neared the town they stopped, and extracted another length of rope, which they wound into a noose. This they put round his neck like a halter, and yanked him along, coughing and gasping.

Harry looked around the town he had left only a few hours earlier. Faces he knew stared back at him. Behind shutters he could feel the gaze of frightened onlookers. In vain he searched for Charles to right and left. Surely, they were likely to be held together? He asked, begged to know where he was. 'Mr Robin-son, where is he? You should have us together.'

The Boxers laughed. 'You want Robinson?' and they led him to a back yard. Harry hobbled over to the heap that he recognized as Charles.

'Charles, are you all right?' But there was no reply. Charles stared back from unseeing eyes, where flies already crawled. His throat had been cut so deeply that his head was all but severed. His arms and legs were hacked about.

Harry almost passed out, but kept himself in control. He knew he cried out, but had no idea what he said. A terrible anger welled up in him, and he rounded on his aggressors. A swift tug of the rope checked his voice, and he struggled for air. Another yank, and he was forced to follow them, away from the dreadful scene, and on down the street.

There was now no doubt, the Boxers would stop at nothing. It was only too likely that he would die. His only hope was in the letter Peter had passed on, and salvation by soldiers. If only even a rumour of the military could spread, it might be enough.

For the next thirty hours Harry waited, praying in the moments he had to himself. He was questioned continually about the local Christians. Who were they? Where did they live? Did they try to keep people away from the temples? With difficulty he kept silence. Finally, as he knew it would, the whip came, and he was flogged, and flogged. Once or twice he lost consciousness. At one point he came round and was first aware only of searing pain. Slowly, as he opened his eyes he saw red, dancing red lights, which slowly merged into focus. They were flames. All too quickly he realized where they were. His beloved church, with the new reredos and altar, carefully carved with Wang, was going up in smoke. Eventually the flames spread to the bungalow, and his home, where he and Charles had been so recently.

'Now your devil church is gone! Soon you go too!' the cry went up, to cheers.

By daylight on Saturday 2 June, all that was left of his church buildings were smouldering ruins. In a strange way, though, Harry was no longer frightened. He had seen the worst and was ready for it. He crouched as best he could on the stony roadway, and considered his fate. His tired mind played tricks with him, and he heard a jumble of his mother, Mr Welsh, Bishop Scott, Mr Fairbairn, all talking in snatches. He smelt the sea and woodshavings, recited snatches of the Creed and stray parts of hymns. He felt himself jolted into the present by the rope, and realized they were on their way again. Where this time? God only knew. His back was agony, his feet bleeding, and his mouth dry as dust.

Harry's last journey took only a few minutes. He was led along at the end of the rope to the edge of the town. There, under a convenient tree, the rope was attached to a branch, and Harry was hung. That day, the 'benevolence, not far from divine' which Harry had seen in the Chinese on his arrival in the country, was not evident. A few hours later, probably on the Monday, the gallop of hooves marked the arrival in Yung Ching of the Viceroy's emissary and ten soldiers.

The Boxers, appreciating discretion for once, made themselves scarce, their work accomplished. It was left to the soldiers to cut Harry's body down, and collect the mutilated remains of Charles. Him they buried in Yung Ching, Harry, at the edge of town, near where he died, at Shin-Min-Chuang. There was little else to be done, and the soldiers themselves were only too eager to get back to Tientsin, as the reported numbers of Boxers in the area was estimated to be over 2000. Without the men they had come to save, they cautiously returned by a different route. Along the way, the freshly butchered bodies of eight native Catholics underlined the need for safety. They hastened back to the gates of Tientsin. It was Whitsun, when the Holy Spirit, the comforter, is traditionally accepted by Christians.

The Sunday was, as usual, a busy time for the Peking mission. Apart from services at the legation chapel and at the Chinese church, they were making preparations to receive back their two missionaries under armed escort. Roland was relieved at the thought of having Charles and Harry safe in Peking, and at last being able to telegraph the Bishop in Tientsin that all was well. By the time the main services were over at the legation, Roland was ready to rush back to greet his friends. He was stopped in his tracks by one of the administrative officers. 'You're wanted, chaplain.'

'Wanted, by whom?'

'Sir Claude's office, he asked for you as soon as the service was over.'

'Ah' Roland raised an acknowledging finger. 'I know. There's news of our men,' and grinning broadly, strode off to the Minister's office. As he got there he saw three or four men talking quietly outside the door. They saw him and silence fell like a stone. 'Good evening,' he said breezily, 'I have an appointment, I understand.'

One man stepped forward. 'Chaplain,' he said, and put a steadying hand on Roland's shoulder.

Roland was confused, and frowned at him. 'What?' he asked.

191

The man seemed to reconsider. 'Never mind. You'd better go in.'

The door was opened, and Roland was ushered in to see the Minister, a tall, mustachioed middle-aged man, with the cares of the world on his shoulders. They shook hands, and Sir Claude Mcdonald signalled Roland to sit.

'I'm afraid, Allen, I have some very grave news.' Roland looked up at him, towering now, stern, with his hands clasped behind his back. He began to pace the floor, and Roland felt each pace drum out, 'Harry, Charles, Harry, Charles.'

'Your two young men in Yung Ching,' he continued. 'We have had an unconfirmed report from a Chinese who has escaped from Yung Ching, that Mr Norman and Mr Robinson were captured. It's still unconfirmed, but it looks bad. I am so sorry. Norman appears to have been captured, and may still be alive – only maybe, but Robinson is dead.'

'Dead?' Roland first felt disbelief, then slowly horror fill his heart. 'They can't be. Oh dear God, no.' He looked away.

Sir Claude continued solemnly. 'The reports vary. The man came in pretty shaken. He says there were 2000 Boxers in the area, but it might have been closer to 200. We shouldn't have left your men there unprotected for so long, and a group of soldiers has been detailed to go down to assess the situation. I thought we had seen the worst with Brooks, but I may have misjudged the business. Those darned Boxers will stop at nothing. They have even infiltrated into Peking. Your friends were sitting targets. I have already telegraphed to your Bishop in Tientsin, and to the consul, and Mr Cockburn has gone to the Yamen now.'

There was little more to say, just then. Roland made his miserable way back to the mission and broke the news. He hoped that the other missionaries, further south, were safe. He also hoped that staff with him in Peking would remain unmolested, and issued warnings to everyone to be on their guard.

The promised telegrams from Peking sped their way along the telegraph wires which the Boxers claimed dripped the blood of the spirits of the air. Aided by the technology of the twentieth century, the messages from Sir Claude and the Bishop reached London on Monday evening, the 4th. They were handed in to the Foreign Office, then in Piccadilly, between 6 and 7 p.m. on a warm summer's evening, as carriages trotted by, taking businessmen home, and early travellers to theatres and restaurants. The first message was concise: 'Bishop Scott writes from Tientsin – Norman and Robinson killed. Others safe.' It was deemed to be a proper matter for the SPG, and duly sent by messenger to Mr Thornton, who had been expecting unpleasant news, but nothing as bad as this.

No sooner was the Bishop's note received, than a longer report from Claude McDonald reached the Marquis of Salisbury at the Foreign Office.

'June 10 1900. On the evening of Sunday, June 30, a Chinese workman from Yung Ching, a town about 40 miles south of Peking, brought the news that a party of some 100 Boxers had entered the town early on the morning of June 1, had attacked the English Church Mission there, had murdered Mr Robinson ... and had carried off Mr Norman, in captivity, to a neighbour-ing village... On the following day (Monday June 4) ... I called by appointment at the Tsungli Yamen, in order to try to impress on the Chinese Government the gravity of the Yung Ching tragedy, but I found the tone of the Ministers present so indifferent and helpless – one of the four present fell fast asleep while Mr Cockburn was interpreting what I said – that I left abruptly after appointing an interview with Prince Ch'ing for the next day.'

Sir Claude did all he could. Having established from both eyewitnesses and the viceroy's emissary that both Charles and Harry had perished, he telegraphed to the Admiral, in some distress, begging for 75 more men, for, he said, 'the British missions would soon be abandoned if they could not be guarded, and each deserted compound would be in danger of an attack, which might lead to a general conflagration'.

The Bishop, in Tientsin, was only too well aware of the escalating problem, as he observed troops collecting to be sent up to Peking. Warships waited in the bay, and he knew something was building up. But his concern was primarily for his men, and with sorrow he wrote back to England. 'Norman was a most earnest and experienced missionary of 8 years standing, simply and entirely devoted to his calling, and singularly qualified for it in many respects. His death is an immense loss to us, and fills us with with deep sorrow, as the loss of a loved and honoured fellow worker … He was a man of singular purity and aim, single minded devotion, great capacity for work, and a great variety of gifts.'

Meanwhile, it had been a wonderful weekend on the Dorset island of Portland. The new Wesleyan Chapel had been opened on Whit Monday, and preparations had gone on all weekend. Although not members, the Normans, and five hundred others had watched the ceremony and attended a public tea afterwards, little realizing as they strolled home down the hill, that the fatal telegram was being delivered in London. The following morning Jo gathered himself for a week's work, and departed for the railway station with the cart. With the family grown up, life had taken on a far more ordered, peaceful air. As he trundled up the road, Jo contemplated that things were looking up. Thankfully young William, who had joined the Navy, seemed to have escaped the trouble in South Africa, Harry was soon due home, and even the youngest was now earning.

'Ere, Jo!' an urgent shout brought him back to reality. It was a neighbour, running towards him and waving.

'Morning, Bert.'

'Jo, you'd best get on home fast I reckon. Summats up.'

'What d'ye mean?'

'Telegraph boy has just been to your door, and your Missus looked queer. Go on, I'll hold the horse.'

Jo was down from the cart in an instant and ran for all he was worth up the steep slope. 'Dear God,' he prayed, 'Don't let it be Will. Don't say the *Terrible* has sunk.'

As he hurtled in the back door, out of breath and with heart racing, Margaret looked very still, standing in the kitchen. ''Tis Harry,' she said. 'He's dead.'

The two sat for a long while together at the kitchen table, trying to read more facts into the few words in the black-edged telegram. Jo went next door to break the news to Margaret's sister and husband. He returned half-eagerly to care for Margaret, and half-unwillingly, not wanting to face it.

'All the time, Marg,' he said thickly, 'I was feared 'twas Will, as he was at war. I never thought of Harry. He never harmed anyone. Those damned Boxers, they'll pay for it!'

'No swearing will bring him back, Jo.' Margaret was practical and realistic. 'We'd heard in papers that there were ruffians running wild in China. We just didn't know how bad 'twas. Harry never said much in his letters.' They fell silent again. Margaret had brought down all her letters from Harry, and the photographs he had sent. 'He'd changed so much. I'd given to wondering what he would be like when he came home on furlough. He'd not be the same boy we lost, Jo.'

'Don't make it, easier,' Jo mumbled.

Together they continued, unable to vent their grief through a funeral or even the presence of personal effects. The word shot round the village like wildfire. By evening everyone knew of the Normans' loss. The vicar called, and hot on his heels, the man from the Dorset County Chronicle. By the weekly edition on Thursday, there were no fewer than three separate articles mentioning Harry and Charles. Jo bought the paper as soon as it arrived at the station, and Margaret cut out the relevant columns. However stoical she was, her stomach turned at the word 'murdered' in cold print. She bit her lip, she never wept, she continued the mechanical necessities of life.

The news, inevitably, was also transmitted to Warminster as it was to Portland. That day, the 5th, was the feast of St Boniface. It could not have been more poignant. The whole college was assembled, the Bishop of Salisbury was due to preach. He was concerned to mention the missionaries without frightening the young trainees, and losing potential future staff for missions abroad. 'No student,' he reminded them, 'has previously died in such circumstances. We do not, of course, feel happy when we think of the terrible sufferings which the missionaries endured ... but that two of your own brothers, well-known to many of these present (here he looked at the staff) whose hands you have constantly clasped ... should have given up their lives, with perfect readiness, for the faith of Christ, is a cause of unfeigned joy, and we cannot help feeling ourselves the better and nobler for it.'

The faces stared back at him, and he could feel the thoughts of the young men, most of whom did not remember Charles, let alone Harry. The staff, he was aware, knew the pair of them much better.

'Norman,' he continued, 'was the son of a resident of Portland. You all know what kind of men the Portlanders are – a strong and hard race of men, powerful for good, and powerful for evil. This young man was powerful for good. Wherever he went, he made an impression. He was, I believe, like a son to Bishop Scott. Therefore you will see the sort of material there is in this diocese, as through your hearts there has gone a throb of satisfaction and content, when you think of the bravery of these young men, so a similar feeling will be experienced deeply by the people of Portland.'

A few heads nodded in agreement. He continued: 'Everybody who knows Bishop Scott and Mrs Scott, and his dear friend (Frank) Norris, who had gone out to join them, knows what devoted people they are. They are not ordinary people, but persons whom anyone might be proud to call friends.'

In the back of his mind the Bishop was warily considering the possible future for any of the staff in China. The Bishop concluded his sermon and descended to the group of staff and major visitors. One hand he shook especially warmly. 'This must be a bad time for you,' he said. Directly into his eyes looked the sad eyes of Francis Sprent, home on furlough, feeling miserable and guilty.

The Bishop clutched Francis' arm. 'Do you feel up to speaking? I know, as an ex-student, you were expecting to preach, but with all this ... The press are here in force too, making life difficult as usual.'

'Yes, I'm fine' Francis managed a wan smile. He drew a deep breath and ascended the rostrum. 'I am certain,' he pronounced, his voice all but cracking, 'that Norman and Robinson's deaths have cast a halo over the college. It is a matter for rejoicing rather than sadness ... Hundreds of priests of different nationalities have laid down their lives (here he looked across at the press) –

never reported by the press. There is no cause to be especially surprised on this occasion. The reason you have heard so much about the present trouble is that the British Ambassador and his lady are in danger. That is why all England is up in arms, and the people are full of it!'

Harry and Charles had, in their deaths, become minor celebrities, mentioned in the national as well as provincial press. Bishops, Archbishops and Ministers mentioned their names, and their deaths were bargaining points in Embassies and courtrooms around the world.

The young men of Warminster were undeterred. Neither Harry nor Charles were unique. Many more young men and latterly women were equally prepared, if need be, to sacrifice themselves. Even Francis' graphic descriptions did not put them off.

'Let me tell you,' he continued to the attentive audience, 'Chinese converts are often cruelly treated by their countrymen. One of the tortures is to put them in a cage where they can stand on tiptoe on a couple of bricks on the floor, with their heads through a hole in the top. Whenever missionaries went by, they could encourage them – but if they were absent, friends and relatives were always ready to come round and call them names, and tell them that the British were all swept off into the sea.' The audience murmured, and they shuffled in their seats.

The high point of the proceedings was supposed to be an address by Archbishop Temple, who almost broke down as he spoke of the two murdered men. So much for a joyous patronal festival.

Intermission:
The International Force Regains Control

Throughout June the situation deteriorated in North China. The smells, flies and burning heat made life almost intolerable. In Peking, Roland and Frank, aided by three lady workers, tried to keep the school, the hospital, and the services going as best they could. Around them refugees poured in, rail lines into the city were destroyed, and stocks of basic foodstuffs dwindled. Those who could were advised to leave, but few did. The Chinese Christians had nowhere to go. The Europeans had the legations at least, and commandeered adjacent palaces as they could.

Extraordinary things happened in Peking that summer. At one point an American pastor arrived at the city gate with thirty Chinese and two Americans, who had simply walked from Boxer territory. On another day the Japanese Chancellor marched through the city to see if he could see the troops coming. Hours later his heart was deposited at the legation – a present from the Boxers. The 500 Europeans huddled in the legation district and determined to fight to the end. The 3000 Chinese Christians were not so lucky. They had little protection and even less food.

During the siege Frank and Roland continued to minister to the physical and spiritual needs of both communities. Between the howls of the Boxers and the crash of 'Old Betsy', the ancient cannon hauled into use within the city walls, they risked their lives taking medicines and food to those in need, dodging the kerosene arrows which flew around them, and keeping an eye out for the exit holes from Boxer tunnels, cunningly disguised by brushwood. Frank Norris by so doing won himself a commendation at the end of the siege.

The troops so desperately needed by Sir Claude McDonald, and so eagerly awaited, failed to arrive. Daily people strained their eyes and ears, but no one came. Stories grew of people eating donkey, rat, and even tree bark, and silently smallpox began to spread through the city. Unknown to the besieged, a meagre group of some 2,200 troops of seven nations had set off from the coast in a convoy of five trains, but became bogged down after just fifteen miles; and sat, impotent in the face of the Boxers. It was not until early August, a full seven weeks after the start of the siege, that the second expeditionary force, with a far more realistic muster of 24,000 troops, left Tientsin, their first task being to relieve the first expeditionary force.

One morning, someone in Peking heard gunfire. Relief was coming! When it did arrive, freedom was sweet. But it was too late for many Chinese, and too late for the mission, the school and the dispensary. All had been utterly destroyed. Looting was rife – soldiers and even missionaries were said to have collected trophies; but at last the siege of Peking was over.

The Bishop in Tientsin was assumed to have been safer, but it was not so. He himself had a tale to tell, almost under siege in the mission with his wife, Geoffrey (by now with a wife and small child) and another Dorset clergyman, Henry Moule and his wife, and lastly a schoolmistress and seven little pupils. The Scotts had had to delay their journey home at the end of June, and could only watch the ships in the bay from their captivity.

One night, when the situation became desperate, all fifteen made a daring journey across the rubble of the streets of Tientsin to the safety of the town hall, crawling and scrambling the 500 yards as silently as they could. Once in the town hall they and the other nationalities waited for rescue from the expeditionary force sweeping towards Peking. It was the men of HMS *Algerina* who landed the marines who first breached the walls. Within days the Boxers were in retreat, and the Bishop's party staggered out to see the ransacked buildings which had been their homes.

The party were bundled on to a lighter, commandeered by the troops, and were taken up to the Taku forts and safety by a Chinese who Mrs Moule, horrified, had to admit was a heathen! Once there, they stayed for a short while on HMS *Algerina* in relative ease. Most were shipped out to Japan and eventually to Britain, but Charles and Frances returned to Tientsin as soon as they were allowed. They had concerns and responsibilities for their staff. Not long after they heard that the Browns and Henry Mathews were safe in Ping Yin. The fate of those in Peking was another, darker matter. They were entirely in the hands of the soldiers and sailors.

7

William

During June and July the coast of northern China began to bristle with vessels of the international relief force. Among them, coming late on the scene, was HMS *Terrible*, distinctive with her four funnels and searchlight. Her men, in truth, did not consider themselves so much battle-hardened as battle-weary. They had set sail from Tilbury the previous September and had undergone exercises in Simons Bay for most of the autumn. By November, *Terrible* had docked in Durban harbour, landing brigades for Ladysmith, supporting the troop activities. By the spring they had travelled on to Mauritius, Colombo and Singapore, and were ready to go home. But the Captain, Percy Scott, RN, had other orders. 'We sail for North China in a few days,' he announced, 'to relieve those British men and women evilly held in Peking.' It was going to be a long trip.

Standing on deck in formation, the crew listened to their captain, then the senior officers, as they addressed them as usual. Inwardly most groaned, but one young stoker admitted to looking forward to the trip.

'Yer daft!' his mates called. 'We're in for another go like before, but this time it'll be worse.'

'P'raps,' the stoker replied, as he descended to his underground world yet again, to check that all was well for their journey. The ship was taking receipt of as much coal as possible – it would have to last for a long while. The piles of dusty black nuggets heaped up. It was cramped, dirty work. The dust got everywhere, and everyone coughed, blinked and shovelled by turns. When the engines started it was noisy and hot as well, no place to be in scalding summer temperatures, and in a hostile sea. The stoker, William, worked his shifts and rested as best he could, dealing with the ingrained black grime with carbolic and a scrubbing brush. 'You all be brown from the sun,' he jested. 'I be black from coal dust. I'll never be white again.'

Finally they had set sail through the Yellow Sea for North China, and eventually the coast at the entrance to the Peiho river, near the Taku Forts, could be seen. William hung over the rail with his mates one evening, gazing at the strange country. 'You can see the fires there,' one friend pointed. 'See, there's houses ablaze.'

'That's 'cos some of the ships have landed men already who are bombarding the town,' William replied. 'I can't wait to get inland.'

'You're mad. Stay on board long as you can, until you're detailed.'

William shook his head. ''Tis different for me. You see, I have a brother in all that somewhere. I need to find out what's happened to 'en.'

'You've never! Go on, not there!'

William replied very quietly, 'I have, truly I have. He is a missionary, been in China years, since I was a lad. I just remember him leaving, when I was a nipper of eight. He's got his own place, and does school-mastering and doctoring besides.' The more William explained, the more credible it seemed. His brother, Harry, sounded quite a character to them all, and William was determined to find out where he was, and check that he was safe. That evening, as they slid nearer to the Peiho river, and cast anchor, the siege of Peking began. It was 21 June.

A few days later, ten officers and 200 fusiliers and engineers were disembarked, closely followed by guns and boxes of ammunition. William watched as the famous 12-pounder gun was established on the river bank, and directed at Tientsin. Hour after hour it pounded away. 'Don't cheer too loud,' William pulled their legs. 'Once 'tis clear out there, we'll be next in, and fighting our way to Tientsin.'

William was quite right. At the beginning of July, marines left the ship in sizeable numbers under Captain Mullins and overran settlements north of the Peiho, despite being under constant Boxer fire. A few days later, on the 11th, *Terrible* knocked out a pagoda used as a Boxer lookout, which had bothered them for days. A great roar of cheering went up. That evening the men heard the reports of the day. There were apparently up to 20,000 Boxers on land, ranged against 12,000 allies of eight nations, which included some 1,420 British. It was obviously hard. That day casualties had been light, 11 wounded and only one dead from the ship. To add to success, Lieutenant Drummond and acting gunner Wright were to be mentioned in despatches. Just two days more, and the battle for Tientsin would be joined in earnest.

William's work was not done, even though the vessel was anchored. He was called upon to transport sick and injured, and to help at the makeshift hospital which had been set up. He watched as the dead sailor was lowered from the ship, and buried on Chinese soil. He hoped that the trouble here was the worst of it. Surely, the little villages inland where Harry must be, had no such trouble. Back home any disturbances seemed to be in towns, where city folk complained! But then he thought of the Tolpuddle Martyrs, and his heart sank. Perhaps when all this was over, he could get permission to go to see his brother, or might at least get to Peking where Harry's friends were. He had the address, knew it from years of practice. He fell to remembering all the strange things Harry had written about. How he longed to see them for himself. How surprised Harry would be to see him!

In the meantime, the miserable business of securing Tientsin was paramount. Stoker or not, William was expected to take weapons and fight his way through with the Marines. He was camped near Tientsin, and had spent some days there, marching into the city to check out deserted buildings for Boxers, clear up and help the desperate inhabitants. The place was a shambles, the British residences were empty, the railway station destroyed, and fires burned everywhere. How on earth could he find his brother from this chaotic start?

That evening, in camp, he asked to see one of the officers. 'Yes, Norman?'

'Sir. Please, I want to know if you can help me to find out about my brother. I don't know who to ask.'

'Oh.' his commanding officer relaxed. 'So *you're* the man I've heard has a relative out here? He's a missionary, is he not?'

'Yessir.'

'Give me his name and details, and I will endeavour to reach the consul, although they are in a pitiful state and may have no way of knowing his whereabouts.'

'Harry Norman, Sir. The Reverend Harry Vine Norman. He'll be 32 going on 33 now Sir, and is stationed south of Peking at a place called Yung Ching, I'm told.'

'Right.' The officer wrote it down. 'I'll do my best, Norman.'

'Thank 'ee Sir,' William replied, and was dismissed.

That night he curled up in the camp, in the makeshift accommodation, and felt a warm glow as he was sure now that he would soon hear of Harry. The consul would be bound to know his brother, he thought. It would only be days before he could get a letter through. After all, mail was coming from home already. He slipped into a warm and happy sleep for the first time in weeks, despite the blasting and crashing round him.

The next thing he knew, he was being shaken awake. 'Ere, Norman, letter come for ye.' In his dazed half sleep he imagined it to be a letter from Harry, till he saw the stamps and familiar handwriting which signified a letter from his mother in Portland. Rubbing his eyes, he blearily opened the letter and read it, then read it again. He couldn't believe it. It was impossible. A while later, he scarcely knew how long, he stumbled over to his commanding officer, and asked for a few words. He also requested a sheet of paper and a pen, as he needed to write home. The only paper to hand was a sheet from an exercise book, the only implement, a small stub of pencil. These he shoved in his pocket, as he blindly went on sentry duty till evening. In the comparative quiet later, he hunched himself miserably and set to write:

'25th July. Dear Mother.

Just a few lines in answer to your very sad letter about poor Harry. I have been trying to find out whether anyone knows him in Tientsin ... some gentleman told me this morning that there are about 40 missing, but they didn't know whether they are killed or not yet, but I hope he is not. I will try and see more about it, and

203

will do all I can. I was asleep in the camp when the letter came this morning. I have not known what to do all the day. I am on sentry go now while (writing) this letter, we don't get five minutes to ourselves. We had very hard fighting here ... I gave my number up last week, when we took Tientsin, it was very hard fighting, and we lost a lot of men – not many belonging to the *Terrible* – but we all gave it up for a bad job. They were falling down by dozens around, trying to take Tientsin city. We took it after about 32 hours fighting. We bombarded the place down. All the city was on fire. We are going to make an attack on Peking about 10th of next month. I don't think that will be so hard, as we shall (have) more troops up there.

I will do all I can to find out about Harry. I dare say I shall see the place, and someone that knows him, before it is over. You need not trouble about me, as I think I shall crawl through it now, as we (have) got through the worst of it, but I can't help thinking of Harry. Yet the Boxers are a bad lot. We have been with the Chinese soldiers as well, – they all turn together. We have got a lot of prisoners but if any get in my hands they won't get made prisoners – they will get the lead!

So dear Mother, when you write to the ship, I shall get it just as quickly. I will write and let you know if I get any news from anyone out here. You will have to excuse my writing. So good-bye at present.'

The eagerly opened letter from his mother had told him what his commander and the consul could not. He simply went on in the hope that the news was false, but knew it was not. Some men were due back on board HMS *Terrible*, but William begged to be allowed to stay near the city, in camp, and return to find out more. Every day he asked any European he could find, if they knew a Reverend Harry Norman. Every day he drew a blank.

The enquiries of his commanding officer bore more fruit. He approached the consulate direct, who put him in touch with Bishop Scott. 'Good Lord,' said Scott, on hearing the news. 'Frances, listen to this. It is a note left for me at the consulate by an officer from HMS *Terrible*. It's almost unbelievable, but there is apparently a stoker on board by the name of Norman – Harry's younger brother. By Jove! That must be fate taking a hand!'

Frances stood dumbfounded. 'Surely not. It's too much of a coincidence.'

'It says so here. Parents from Portland in Dorset, brother a missionary with the North China Mission. Poor lad, what a time he must be having!'

'Well, he must come over. Charles, ask his superior if he can have leave to call on us. It's the least we can do, for his brother's sake.'

So it was that William, feeling red raw with scrubbing, and polished until he shone, nervously stood outside the temporary home of the Scotts in Tientsin. He had never met a bishop before and could only assume he wouldn't go far wrong if he treated him like the captain. Eventually he was ushered into a spartan but peaceful drawing room, which might have been a thousand miles from camp. Immediately he was warmly welcomed.

'Mr Norman, how good to meet you. So like your brother. Isn't he Frances?'

William blushed, but felt proud at the thought.

'May I introduce my wife, Frances? My dear, this is William, Harry's brother.'

'Pleased to meet you Sir, Ma'am. Thank you for inviting me. 'Tis good to meet someone who knows about poor Harry. I've been searching days, to no avail.'

They sat and talked, Charles carefully relaying the details of Harry's death, without making it too painful. The ill-at-ease young man in his uniform reminded Charles so much of Harry some nine years before, when he had first come out, with every hope for the future, and his soft Dorset accent. This chap was made of similar material, determined, practical and positive. He liked him very much. Charles made sure he gave William every consolation he could. 'It's a miracle you are here. Of all the possibilities, and here you are now. I am sure God intended you to see the land your brother loved so well. He was well loved in return, and respected. You must try not to think ill of the Chinese, William. Most are good people, even the non-believers. It's only a small minority who have caused the trouble. I have written to

your mother, of course. As soon as this is all over, we will see
about a proper, fitting memorial for Harry. He was a brave, good
Christian man, and he did not die in vain, you must believe that.'

William looked down and felt a pricking behind his eyes for the
first time in the whole awful affair. The Bishop touched his arm.
'Come now. Be stout-hearted. Harry would be proud of you after
all you have done.'

William looked back at him and smiled bravely. 'Yessir, I feel
he's near me, here in China. 'Tis strange.'

'No it's not. I'm sure he is,' and the Bishop invited William to
pray for a moment. That calmed him a lot, and when he left, he
had a fresh strength to carry on, if it had to be, to Peking, and all
the danger and turmoil he would endure before he sailed for
home.

As William returned to camp that evening, he saw a ship in the
bay for the first time. She had been there a week, but with the
duties of the day, he had not noticed her before. He squinted
in the half light, and just made out the name – SS *Ballaarat*.
Commandeered as a troop ship, she was still a fine vessel,
faithfully plying her way to China, so long after she had brought
Harry there, years before.

Finally the war ended, and slowly life returned to normal. Most
missionaries returned home on furlough, but in Peking Roland
and Frank continued, in loaned accommodation, without a
church. By the autumn of 1901 the Bishop had returned to Peking
from England and Roland was at last due to take furlough.

As Roland prepared to go, Frank and Charles sat over a late
meal, discussing what had to be done. Frank started earnestly.
'There's the question of compensation to deal with. The legation
wants to know the value of the mission and its contents, and of
Yung Ching. No one has been down there yet. We have been
advised it has not been safe. I think the mission house is gone, or
at least part of it, and the church. I suppose that is all quantifiable,
but they want a sum put on the heads of Harry and Charles.'

'That's preposterous!'

'I know. But it's the way it is being done. Do you remember we
had the same situation when poor Sidney Brooks was killed?'

Charles shook his head. 'It's a wicked idea. The characters of the men preclude any idea of self-seeking, or desire to be vindictive towards the Chinese. Perhaps we can submit a charge against the cost of their training and possibly something towards rebuilding, but that's as far as I can go.'

The haggling had gone on all summer. How much did the schoolroom cost, the printing press, the price of a priest's training? They became fed up with it all, and longed to get on with their pastoral work. That, sadly was limited. Fewer Christian Chinese associated themselves with the temporary mission, and there was little time or money for the children to attend a school. Frank and Charles shared legation duties, but the rest of their work was a pale shadow of its former self.

Just over a year after the deaths at Yung Ching, when their minds turned to the year before, and memories of their friends, they had a bittersweet message. Frank told the Bishop that permission had been granted for someone to visit their property in Yung Ching, to assess the damage. The fifty mile journey was deemed safe at last.

Frank, with a few Chinese converts for company and protection, had made his way south. All looked peaceful, as if nothing had happened. He remembered when he had been in charge of the station before Harry, and could scarcely believe that those same people had watched two missionaries murdered. The first call he made in Yung Ching was to the mission, which Frank found to be in a better state than he had expected. Charred and ransacked, it had been partly boarded up and made safe, and was almost habitable. The church was gone, rubble was all that was left. He went next to the Yamen, on a duty call. The same fearful magistrate was still in charge.

'I have come for information about Mr Norman and Mr Robinson. Do you know where they are laid?'

The magistrate nodded. 'Mr Robinson is buried here in Yung Ching, Mr Norman just outside the town. It was seen to. A catechist also died, a Chinese fellow named Ma-Te-Lu, we buried him also. I am sorry; your men did us no harm.'

Frank bit his tongue as he thought of his friends' last hours. 'I want permission to exhume the bodies, to bury them together, with the rites of the Christian church.'

The magistrate assented. 'I have some things for you, please, come;' and he led Frank into an adjacent room. There on the table was a box, which the magistrate's assistant opened. 'These are some possessions which we saved, which you may wish to have.' In the box were two pale blue silk cassocks, obviously belonging to Harry and Charles, saved from the house. There was also a small wooden cross, given to Harry by Sam, when he left Abbotsbury. At the bottom of the box was one last article – a length of stained rope. Frank checked himself, and looked at the magistrate. Their eyes met and the magistrate nodded silently.

Frank could do nothing but thank the magistrate and take the box back to what was left of Harry's bungalow. He sat there for a long time, thinking of his own time in the town, and wondering about Harry and Charles' last days there. Even though the Chinese he had brought with him were round about, he felt very isolated. The thoughts of the work of the next day scarcely improved matters, as he prepared his sermon for the service.

The next morning he and his companions started the day by celebrating Mattins. Local Christians brought them breakfast. A few he remembered from the old days.

The exhumations were a grisly business. The first was of Ma-te-lu, a man he remembered as a lad at the school in Peking. They put his remains in a coffin and took it to a shed prepared for the purpose just outside the north-east wall of the town. Later they collected Charles' body and brought it there too. The clouds darkened, and they took cover in the shed as thunder, lightning and hail suddenly and dramatically transformed the place. Just when they were to set off for the funeral. No one would turn up, and the occasion would have to be postponed.

'Sir.' One of the Chinese Frank had brought pulled at his sleeve 'It has stopped raining now, we must begin.'

'Yes. I suppose so,' Frank replied, and dusted himself off as he stood up. He went out to look at the sky from the doors of the shed. 'Good Heavens. Have you seen this?' What had met Frank's eyes was not only a clearing sky and a beautiful sunset, but what he estimated to be between five and six hundred people.

'All here for the funeral?' he said in wonder.

'Yes.'

So at 6 p.m. Frank read the first part of the funeral service, and addressed the people. Then the whole crowd, led by Frank, and a group of Christians carrying the coffins, walked into the country, to the spot where Harry was buried. Two graves had been dug next to where Harry lay, and first Charles and then Ma-te-lu were laid to rest beside him, under the very tree where Harry had been hung.

Here Frank addressed the crowd. 'The sky now seems typical of the glory which we trust awaits them at the close of their day, after their short, sharp storm of suffering has passed ...' The service finished with the Nunc Dimittis and some special prayers, and the crowd walked back to Yung Ching in the dusk.

Shortly after, Frank returned to Peking and related it all to the Bishop. 'I'm glad you gave them proper burial,' Charles said. 'I hated to think of them just left there. And a young Peking catechist too, I hadn't realized. I thought of you there. It was the anniversary, you know, of the day Miles and I left for China all those years ago.' He sighed. 'I hope they can be at peace now, Frank. Thank you for doing that. It can't have been easy.'

'I'm glad I went back. I had felt my heart grow cold to Yung Ching, when I heard what had happened. But it renewed my faith in them. So many Chinese turned out from all the villages. The Wangs were all there, young Peter Tson too. There is work to be done there. It just proves how much Charles and Harry had achieved, that those hundreds came.'

Charles was serious. 'Now I have to write to tell their families about it, which won't be easy. Can you give me any more details?'

'I can do better than that – I have had some photographs taken of the graves, which can be developed. Tell them the graves are in a large piece of ground given to the church, and each grave will be enclosed in open brickwork, with a white plinth and a cross. The people are planting flowers there, and they want to make the graves as beautiful and fine as they possibly can.'

'Good. It will be a help to know that the graves of their sons are cared for and venerated,' Charles agreed.

As he promised, he wrote to the families. Margaret received her letter, one of many, with the photograph and Harry's personal effects.

'Oh, Jo,' she said. 'To think this is all that's left of our dear boy', and she stroked the silk cassock. When they reached the bottom of the box, and brought out the noose, they had no words left for it.

'They didn't ought to have sent that back, Marg,' Jo said bitterly. 'That's no help to have now.' But Margaret kept the noose carefully in a drawer, for there was no chance in her mind that she would throw it away. Macabre it may have been, but the contents of the box were all she had left of her son, and she would cling to them ferociously for many years. Only once would she break down. One day, a kindly intentioned friend suggested she wash the rope, to remove the bloodstains. It was too much to bear.

Meanwhile, in Yung Ching, the graves continued to be whitewashed, and the garden round them to be tended. The three were at peace, under the tree, symbolically outside the city wall. Whether they remain there is doubtful, considering subsequent events in China. As far as Harry and Charles were concerned, their story ended there, but the work of the mission went on, and they would have been glad that their contribution was to be built on in future years.

Postscript:

The Mission Continues

The insurrection which was the Boxer rebellion changed for all time the lives of many people in China and their families back home. The mission buildings could be re-established; relationships were another matter. Hatred of Europeans and missionaries lay deep in Chinese hearts. For some people the scars were permanent. No one could bring back Harry, Charles or Sidney. No one could bring back the Bishop's beloved Frances, who, after all she had suffered, died of dysentery some days out from China on their journey home to England.

With so much to look back on with sadness, it was with great joy that the faithful staff in Peking heard that the magistrate in Yung Ching, who had done so little for Harry and Charles, had finally been ordered to give the native Christians compensation for the deaths of the priests and for the destruction of property. In addition, a local wealthy Chinese had been accused of hindering Imperial troops and had suffered confiscation of his land. This land was handed over for the building of a Christian village. Thirty or forty families were selected and they set about building the houses. The little village of Hsin-Min-Chuang had its own church in use by the time Roland Allen became its next resident missionary in 1903. There was sufficient money left over to support a new catechist to replace Ma-te-lu. The staunchest Christians had set about forming themselves into committees to visit the waverers. They appointed native churchwardens and teachers for the school, and were hoping to set up a catechists' training school and to engage a Christian doctor.

And what of the past? Harry's home and church had gone, but the people were determined, and the church was rebuilt, dedicated suitably to St Stephen and all Martyrs. Wang continued ever faithful and diligent. When last seen he was busy, especially

211

on market days, ranging round the market area, ever trying to induce people to attend services and meetings.

It was no nine-day wonder. By 1918 the village boasted a group of dedicated young men, St Timothy's Guild. At their second reunion in 1920 they visited outlying areas, just as Harry and Charles had done twenty years before. Now, however, the groups were larger – over two thousand people were contacted during lunch breaks in the fields, throughout the reunion week. How pleased the missionaries would have been to see work on such a scale, conducted by the Chinese workers themselves!

Outside the Yung Ching area the work developed just as rapidly. A bequest of £10,000 quietly given by a brother bishop enabled Charles Scott to set up a separate see in Shanghai, over which he put Geoffrey Iliff as its first bishop. Meanwhile he set about designing and supervising the building of a cathedral in Peking. One item Harry would have recognized. The font of the old church, looted in the siege, turned up in a Peking market and was reinstated in the cathedral to continue its work.

By 1908 the workers had grown in numbers. Charles returned from furlough with five new missionaries, of whom three were related to him – the fifth generation of missionary Scotts! Five years later the staff numbered a staggering 55, including doctors, nurses, catechists and lay workers, of whom 22 were Chinese. The lessons of the 1890s had been well learned.

Life was not always easy, even years after the rebellion. There were occasional instances of capture, and one further death of a missionary at the hands of drunken soldiers, anxious to steal the cart he was travelling in. But the worst was over, and the work continued until the Second World War, when most missionaries were encouraged to return home. A few chose to stay in China, and were interned until the end of the war. Any remaining flicker of activity was snuffed out with the coming to power of the communists in 1949.

The heyday of the North China Mission was probably in the 1920s, when the numbers were greatest and the dangers fewest. In 1924 they celebrated their Golden Jubilee in some style. By this stage Geoffrey Iliff had retired to England, and he led the celebrations at home, at which the Reverend Mr Wilkinson was formally acknowledged to have been the founder of the mission, and Charles' brother John its first secretary. In China itself Charles looked on. By now he was 76 and had handed over his bishopric after 33 years to Frank Norris. He had lived, and would die, in China, a dedicated man, fortunate in seeing his aims accomplished and experiencing the mercy of a quiet death. On the day of the Golden Jubilee he had many opportunities to remember his old friends and all they had been through together – Miles, Henry Brereton, Dr Nevins, and later all those other young men and women. As Bishop Norris spoke of all of them, Charles heard him say, 'Harry – Harry Norman – showed us for a few short years what it was to be a missionary.' Charles smiled and nodded. 'After all', he thought to himself, 'what more could one ever ask?'

Bibliography

Published works

Anon., *Under Blackdown: the story of Portesham 1868–1968*, 1968.

Bettey, J.H., *The Island and Royal Manor of Portland*, David & Charles 1970

Cameron, Nigel, *Barbarians and Mandarins*, OUP 1989

Conway, *All the World's Fighting Ships 1860–1905*, Conway Maritime Press 1979

Cooper, T., *Pictorial History of Abbotsbury*, printed by Cox & Sharland, Southampton 1884

Dalison, R.W.H., *A Dorset Captain in the Army of Christ*, W. & E. Frost, Bridport 1906

Dorset County Chronicle, 1900, Dorchester Reference Library

Fleming, Peter, *The Siege of Peking*, OUP 1971

Forsyth, R.C., *The China Martyrs of 1900*, Religious Tract Society 1904

Hahn, Emily, *China only Yesterday*, Weidenfeld & Nicolson 1963

Howell, D., *An Old Postcard Album of Warminster*, Wylye Valley Publications 1985

Jacques, H., *Portesham Parish Church Guide*, nd

Kelly's *Directory of Dorsetshire*, 1885

Keown-Boyd, Henry, *The Fists of Righteous Harmony*, Leo Cooper 1991

Laird-Clowes, Sir W., *The Royal Navy: A History*, Sampson Low Marston & Co. 1903

Land of Sinim Magazine, 1893, 1895, 1896, 1898, 1900, 1901, 1921, 1924, 1927 (includes letters from Roland Allen, Sidney Brooks, H.V. Norman, Charles Robinson, Bishop Scott), USPG, Bodleian

Bibliography

Missionary Conference in Shanghai, 1877, Records, CMS

Moule, W. S., *Abbotsbury: The Church, Abbey and Other Points of Interest*, published by the Churchwardens 1955

O'Connor, Richard, *The Boxer Rebellion*, Robert Hale 1974

Pascoe, C. F., *Two Hundred Years of SPG: 1701–1900*, SPG 1901

Price, E. J., *China Journal: 1889–1990*, Collier Books 1989

Prideaux, S. P. T., *The Story of St Boniface Missionary College*, Council of the College, Warminster 1948

Schirokauer, Conrad, *A Brief History of Chinese Civilization*, Harcourt Brace 1991

St Boniface College Magazine, Spring 1912, WCRO

The Mission Field Magazine, 1939 (contains article by Frank Sprent), USPG

Thompson, H. P., *Into All Lands: The History of the SPG*, SPCK 1951

Warner, Marina, *The Dragon Empress: Life and Times of Tz'u-hsi*, Vintage 1972

Women's Institute, *Portesham, a peep into the past*, Portesham WI 1984

Manuscripts

(a) *Records*

Censuses of 1861, 1871, 1881 for Portesham, Abbotsbury and Portland (DCRO)

HMS *Terrible*, Ship's log, 1900 (Public Record Office)

McDonald, Sir Claude, Report, (Foreign Office Reports, 1900, F/O.17/1413)

Marriage Registers, 1860s (Portesham Parish Church)

Nautical Reports, P. & O. 1891 (National Maritime Museum)

Portesham Parish Registers, 1868 (DCRO)

Record of Shipwrecks, 1870s and 1880s (Portland Museum)

Salisbury General Infirmary, Records 1890–91 (WCRO)

Salisbury General Infirmary, General Management Committee Minutes, 21.3.1891 (WCRO)

SS *Ballaarat*, File P. & O. 65/48 (National Maritime Museum)

(b) *Other*

Allen, Roland, 'Some causes which led to the siege of the foreign legations at Peking', 1900 (USPG, Bodleian)
   'The Anglican Mission in Yung Ching', 1903 (USPG, Bodleian)
   Letter to SPG (USPG, Bodleian)
Brereton, William, Letters to SPG, 1890, 1893 (USPG, Bodleian)
Brown, Henry, Letter to SPG (USPG, Bodleian)
McDonald, Sir Claude, Telegrams to Marquis of Salisbury and SPG, 1900 (USPG, Bodleian)
Matthews, Henry, Letters to SPG, 1900 (USPG, Bodleian)
Norman, H.V., Application and References, 1891 (USPG)
   Career reference sheet, NO.4587 (USPG)
   Letter to Warminster (USPG, Bodleian)
   Letters to family (Norman Family)
Norris, Frank, Letters to SPG, 1893, 1986, 1897, 1898, 1900 (USPG, Bodleian)
Pigrum, W., Letter to SPG (USPG, Bodleian)
Portland Parish Schools, 1857 (Portland Museum)
Scott, Bishop C., Reports to SPG, 1891–1900 (USPG, Bodleian)
Sprent, Francis, Report for students at St Boniface College (WCRO)
St Boniface College, Speeches at Patronal Festival, 1900 (WCRO, 1673/24)
Tson, Peter, Report of Norman's capture and death, 1900 (St Nicholas Church Abbotsbury)
USPG, Letters, 1891 (USPG)

Abbreviations

Bodleian	Bodleian Library, University of Oxford
CMS	Church Missionary Society
DCRO	Dorset County Record Office, Dorchester
SPG	Society for the Propagation of the Gospel
USPG	United Society for the Propagation of the Gospel
WCRO	Wiltshire County Record Office, Devizes